Architectural Practice

Architectural Practice

J J Scott, FRIBA, FBIM

Butterworths
London Boston Durban Singapore Sydney Toronto Wellington

First published 1985

British Library Cataloguing in Publication Data

Scott, J. J.
Architectural practice.
1. Architectural practice–Great Britain
–Management
I. Title
720'.68 NA1996

ISBN 0-408-01400-8

Library of Congress Cataloging in Publication Data

Scott, J. J. (John James), 1921-
Architectural practice.

Bibliography: p.
Includes index.
1. Building laws–Great Britain. 2. Architects–
Legal status, laws, etc. Great Britain. I. Title.
KD1140.S38 1984 343.41'07869 84-17028
ISBN 0-408-01400-8 344.1037869

Photoset by Butterworths Litho Preparation Department
Printed and bound in England by Page Bros Ltd.,
Norwich, Norfolk

Contents

Preface

This book is intended primarily for those preparing for the RIBA Final Examination, the format of which is under review at the time of writing. This book is based upon the present syllabuses for the Part 3, Subject G Examination.

Architectural practice in the United Kingdom is varied, not merely the broad division between the private and public sectors, but also variations in office size, structure, work loads, etc. It follows, therefore, that the experience of candidates for the Examination is also varied, being further complicated by the differences in building legislation between one area and another which make a comprehensive knowledge difficult to achieve.

The introduction of new Building Regulations in 1985 is proposed, which will also affect the present Inner London building control system, which together with the proposed demise of the Greater London Council, will have a profound effect upon the long-established District Surveyors' authority and supervision of works. Presumably, as exists at the present time outside the Inner London boroughs of the Greater London Council, building regulation control and enforcement will pass to the local authorities, and some 'phasing-out' period for the existing system will ensue, but this is conjecture.

No one book can attempt to cover all the material of the Subject G syllabuses, and there will be areas where readers will not find information on a particular subject or point of practice. Furthermore, the book is intended to supplement courses in the subject and provide information for further study.

J.J.S.

Introduction

In 1962 the Royal Institute of British Architects (RIBA) published a report titled *The Architect and His Office* which was based upon a survey of architectural practices in the United Kingdom. Its chief concern was the alleged criticism that many Architects were unable to manage properly not only their own affairs but, due to a lack of proper management training, also those of their clients.

The report caused the RIBA to look closely at management and professional practice education and training of architectural students, in some cases non-existent, relying upon 'intuitive' rather than 'conscious' management techniques and procedures, and to provide direction and guidance for the future study of the subject in recognized schools of architecture.

Also in 1962 Mrs Elizabeth Layton, then Under-Secretary for Education at the RIBA, wrote a book *The Practical Training of Architects*; Appendix 5 of that book quotes interesting comments on the subject from the leading full-time architectural schools at that time.

In 1965 the RIBA set up a Management Advisory Group who, in 1966, produced a document titled *Current Concepts of Management Training in Architectural Education*, the purpose of which was stated to be

(a) To define the role of management in architectural education,
(b) To outline the field of management studies and indicate the scope of the subject,
(c) To outline possible methods of implementation,
(d) To indicate further fields of research and study,
(e) To list sources of reference.

Quoting from the RIBA *Handbook of Architectural Practice and Management*, it defined 'management' as 'the creation of conditions to bring about the optimum use of all resources available in an undertaking, in men, methods, and materials'.

The document also distinguished between 'management' and 'professional practice', and stated 'the subject as a whole must not be confused with one of its familiar components, professional practice, which is largely concerned with legislative and ethical matters'. (a) and (b) above were seen as being the central theme of management studies.

The original report was reviewed in 1972, but very few schools of architecture had adopted the original suggestions; indeed, to this day, attitudes in schools towards management and professional practice studies varies. Some regard the subject as vocational and non-academic, even a hindrance to the development of creational ability, whilst others see it as an inherent part of the overall education of the Architect.

In post-war years most schools gradually introduced some form of professional practice study, together with supportive periods of experience in offices, using the RIBA *Practical Training Record* (the former RIBA *Practical Training Log Book PT1*) for recording experience gained by the student, or using where appropriate, for the more experienced student, the Certificate of Exemption from Keeping a Log Book.

The original *Practical Training Index* contained lists of offices on a regional basis, who at the time, were willing to participate in the training of architectural students, as opposed to merely employing them, and it was a large list. Since the recession of the late nineteen seventies and up to the present time, the list has been reduced to a mere handful of offices, even with assistance from a limited number of government-sponsored grants through the RIBA Training Services Agency which pay to employers a proportion of the salary for six months of the requisite 'year out' of training.

Though the situation is still very difficult for Practical Training Advisers in the schools, they are now well established in recognized schools where their duties include the curriculum of study for management and professional practice, organization of the G1, G2 and G3 Examinations, arranging for the presentation of case studies, office visiting, checking Practical Training Records, etc. Their overall supervision is monitored by the RIBA Practical Training Co-ordinator, who each year organizes a conference of Practical Training Advisers, and invites students and other interested parties to attend and take part in the discussions. There is also an RIBA Standing Committee whose task is to monitor and review as required the procedure for the Final Examination in Architecture, part 3, Subject G, and through the Education and Professional Development Department of the RIBA keep the Council informed. There is also an annual meeting of the RIBA Part 3 Examiners, and the Review Board.

In 1976 the RIBA produced the present *Guide to Good Practice at Part 3 Examinations in Professional Practice and Experience held at Recognized Schools of Architecture*. This document included the broad syllabuses for the four subject headings, and also a guide for the Case Study. It also attempted to attain parity among recognized schools or architecture in terms of the Part 3, Subject G, Examination; the RIBA Visiting Board (with ARCUK representation) on a quinquenial basis, being the monitoring body for the two parties concerned with the examination.

This book is concerned with the syllabuses for the G2, and G3 Examinations, but in part may also be helpful for those sitting the G1 Examination.

The four broad divisions of the areas of study previously mentioned are

(1) Legislation and architecture,
(2) The profession and the industry,
(3) Management and administration,
(4) Project management.

Some 20 years on from the publication of the RIBA report, the discussions, not to say misgivings, about the Architect's competence in controlling and managing effectively is still being voiced, and the Institute's attitude to 'freedom of choice' for recognized schools, as expressed in the Guidance Notes, has perceptively hardened.

No system of education and examination is ever perfect, but seven years of study and training should culminate in a level of competence in all aspects of architecture, of which management and professional practice are integral parts of the 'whole'.

There is little sense in designing a magnificent edifice for your client if in the process you both end up in the Bankruptcy Court!

1

A synopsis of the United Kingdom legal system

1.1.1 Historical outline

The law of England has developed over a thousand years, and some of its early rulings are still in force today. The legal system established by the Romans all but disappeared with their own departure, although derivations of Roman law still survive in many countries today. Because Scottish law, unlike that of the remainder of Great Britain, identifies with Roman law to some extent, its legal system and structure are therefore different. After the Treaty of Union in 1707 the Scottish law and courts system were preserved, but appeals from the Scottish Court of Sessions (civil court) are permitted to the House of Lords without the necessity of leave to appeal, and there has been a Scottish Law Lord since 1876.

Modern English law emanates from Anglo-Saxon times, and before the Norman conquest in 1066, courts in various parts of the country applied both written law and the law of custom. Changes were gradual after the Normal Conquest, the early Norman Kings using existing courts, but with the assistance of the Curia Regis (King's Court) they gradually replaced these with their own judges to hear cases locally, offering better trial methods and procedures, and with the development of the common law courts, eventually all courts came under royal control.

King Henry II (1154–1189) instituted 'circuits' presided over by Judges who, over the course of time, selected the best of local customary laws and applied them to the whole of England; from this is derived the 'common law of England'. In his reign there emerged the Court of the Exchequer, whose principal concern was tax matters, and the Court of Common Pleas.

Many law reforms were made in the reign of Edward I (1272–1307) and another important court was instituted, namely the Court of King's Bench which accompanied the King on his travels, and this was the only court to have criminal jurisdiction.

In the Middle Ages justice, in certain circumstances, was difficult, if not impossible, to obtain, e.g. trusts were not recognized by the courts. A plaintiff bringing an action was obliged to choose a writ from a Register of Writs, and if the wrong writ was chosen then the action would fail, and if the action was not covered by a writ the Court of Common Law would not help the plaintiff. This was not satisfactory since justice was not 'seen to be done', and the plaintiffs turned for help to the King as being the Fountain of Justice. The King referred these pleas to the Lord High Chancellor as 'Keeper of the King's Conscience', and as applications for help increased, there emerged in the fifteenth century the Court of Chancery from which developed the 'law of equity' as opposed to 'common law', 'equity' placing parties on the same footing and considering justice, natural law, fairness, law of conscience, or equality.

The Office of Lord Chancellor had been held mostly by Bishops, but after the Reformation it came to be filled by professional lawers, of whom Sir Thomas More was the first. The laws of equity became almost as inflexible as those of common law. For centuries two sets of courts had existed, the common law administered in the common law courts, and equitable law in the chancery courts, and conflict between them had grown. The former courts were concerned with the plaintiffs 'legal interests', and the latter courts with his 'equitable interests', and this conflict was resolved in the reign of James I (1603–1625) when the King decided that where there was a conflict between common law and equity, equity would prevail, and this decision increased the importance of equity in English law.

The problem of overlapping jurisdiction, outdated procedures and other factors, culminated in the reign of Queen Victoria in the Judicature Acts

1873–1875, which abolished several courts and set up the Supreme Court of Judicature which comprised the High Court of Justice and the Court of Appeal. The High Court was divided into five Divisions, these being the Chancery, the Queen's Bench, the Common Pleas, the Exchequer, and the Probate, Divorce, and Admiralty Divisions. There was now only one court administering common law and equity. In 1880 the Common Pleas Division and the Exchequer Division merged with the Queen's Bench Division.

The Administration of Justice Act 1970 reorganized the High Court of Justice into three Divisions, namely the Queen's Bench (including the Admiralty and Commercial Court), the Chancery and the Family Divisions (*see* page 7).

In 1907, in the reign of King George V, the Court of Criminal Appeal was introduced, and the reform of land law culminated in 1925 in the Law of Property Act, the Land Registration Act and the Land Charges Act all of which affected ownership and tenure of land and the rights of adjoining owners, etc. The Law of Property Act 1925 was amended in 1969.

1.1.2 The process of English law

Law is of two kinds, public law and private law. The first concerns the whole community, being divided into constitutional and administrative law, e.g. (planning law), and criminal law. Constitutional law deals, *inter alia*, with the functions of Parliamentary Ministers and their respective powers, also civil liberties, voting rights, local government, and relationships with Commonwealth countries.

Criminal law is concerned with containing any behaviour that disturbs the peace and well-being of the community, its object being to deter people from wrongdoing and to punish those who transgress the law, and is derived from statutes and judicial decisions applied in the criminal courts (*see* page 7).

Private, or civil law, covers a very wide field and is concerned mainly with the rights and duties of persons towards each other. It is applied in the civil courts (*see* page 7). Some of the more important branches of civil law are the law of contract, the law of tort, family law, the law of succession, the law of trusts. A person may be subject to the rigours of both public and private law at the same time, depending upon the misconduct alleged to have been committed; the outcome of this is that the offender has to appear before two courts.

The greater part of English law, both common law and equity, consists of rules and principles emanating from previous judicial decisions made over centuries, termed 'case law', past decisions of the courts being used as guides to future decisions and termed 'judicial precedents'.

The English common law doctrine is that precedents are binding, this being termed *stare decisis*, i.e. 'let the decision stand', judgements being based upon authoritative summation of the law, including *ratio decidendi*, or grounds for the decision based on facts, and *obiter dicta* being remarks by the way. These decisions are followed by Judges in subsequent cases. Generally, lower courts are bound by the decisions of higher courts, the Court of Appeal being bound by its own decisions, but the House of Lords may rescind its previous decisions.

Case law depends upon accurate and reliable reporting of cases (*see* page 5), and since 1865 official law reporting has come under the jurisdiction of the Council of Law Reporting.

To define 'law' is almost impossible; philosophers centuries before Christ and throughout the ages since have attempted to define it, from the philosophy of 'natural justice' to the more modern concepts among which is 'the body of principles recognized and applied by the State in the administration of justice', this last definition being attributed to Sir John Salmond. This branch of knowledge is known as 'jurisprudence'.

The Courts

Courts have two levels of seniority:

Superior Courts:		House of Lords Court of Appeal High Court of Justice
Inferior Courts:		County Court Magistrate's Court Coroner's Court
and either:	Civil	County Court High Court
	Criminal	Magistrate's Court Crown Court

The House of Lords

There are two divisions of this Court, civil and criminal, and appeal from the Court of Appeal to the House of Lords is available only if the Court of Appeal certifies that a point of law of general public importance exists. Leave to appeal is granted by either of the Courts.

The House of Lords deals only with points of law; the proceedings are not a re-hearing of the case, as they are in the Court of Appeal.

The Court comprises the 'Law Lords', or 'Lords of Appeal in Ordinary', who are salaried life peers appointed to hear appeals. Normally the number is five, or may be more, but a quorum may be three.

House of Lords Judges must be Barristers of at least 15 years' standing or those who have held high office for two years.

The House of Lords is no longer the highest court of law in England, since Great Britain is a member of the European Economic Community. The Court of Justice of the European Communities (CJEC) sitting in Luxembourg adjudicates upon the law of the EEC, and its decisions bind British Courts by reason of the European Communities Act 1972.

The Court of Appeal

There are two Divisions of this Court, civil and criminal, the Criminal Division hears appeals from persons convicted on indictment in the crown Court either against conviction or sentence. The Court of Appeal has the power to quash the conviction or amend the sentence or, in rare circumstances, order a re-trial. The Court comprises the Lord High Chancellor, the Lord Chief Justice, the Master of the Rolls, President of the Family Division, the Law Lords, the Justices of Appeal. In practice, of the *ex-officio* Judges only the Master of the Rolls and the Lord Chief Justice sit, a quorum of three being usual.

The Civil Division of the Court hears appeals from the County Court, all Divisions of the High Court, and various tribunals. The appeal is the re-hearing of the case and the Court may make any award outside the jurisdiction of the original court.

The High Court of Justice

This Court comprises the Queen's Bench Division and the Chancery Division.

The Queen's Bench Division

This Division has civil and criminal functions.

Civil

(1) Original: most major civil actions, e.g. contract and tort.
(2) Appellate: adjudicial views, administrative tribunals and certain civil proceedings in Magistrates' Courts.

Criminal

(1) Original: except perhaps when trying a case of contempt of the High Court, the trial of cases by the QBD is now obsolete.
(2) Appellate: hearing a point of law from a Magistrate's Court.
(3) Supervisory: writs of Habeus Corpus. There may also be a civil remedy, e.g. in immigration cases.

The jurisdiction in Probate, Divorce, etc, now comes within the Family Division of the High Court. There is also an Admiralty Court and a Commercial Court within the Queen's Bench Division.

The Chancery Division

There are three main areas of jurisdiction within this Court.

(1) Original: contentious probate of wills, trusts, mortgages, partnerships, winding-up of companies.
(2) Appellate: from the Commissioners of Inland Revenue.
(3) Family Division: matrimonial cases, guardianship, adoption, divorce, family property, etc.

County Courts

Established in the nineteenth century to deal with small claims, these try some 1½ million cases each year, or about 85 per cent of all civil cases.

Claims may be made in contract or tort up to a prescribed maximum, hire purchase actions, landlord-and-tenant matters, adoption of children, and undefended divorce cases. Judges sitting in Crown Courts also sit in the County Courts as part of their function. They are Barristers of at least seven years' standing.

Each Court has an office and a Registrar who is legally qualified and may try small cases within prescribed limits, and if these sums are smaller than the prescribed limits then leave to appeal is required.

Magistrates' Courts

These are presided over mainly by lay Justices of the Peace (JPs or Magistrates) who normally sit three to a bench, two being the minimum allowed. Some Magistrates' Courts are presided over by Stipendiary Magistrates who are full-time salaried Magistrates recruited from the ranks of Barristers or Solicitors.

Coroners' Courts

These Courts come within the Coroners' Act 1887, and the Coroners' (Amendment) Act 1926, but do not apply to Scotland and Northern Ireland.

Coroners are usually Barristers, Solicitors, and/or Doctors who are empowered to enquire into deaths of a violent or unusual nature in their areas. In certain cases a Coroner may summon a jury to attend the Court. If the members of the jury decide that a death was caused by murder or other crime, they have to say that the deceased was 'unlawfully killed'. The Coroner must then refer the case to the Director of Public Prosecutions.

Crown Courts

These Courts were established by the Courts Act 1971 to replace the former Assize Courts, and they are to be found in most centres of population. They are presided over by either full-time Judges called 'Circuit Judges', or 'Recorders' recruited from Barristers or Solicitors of at least 10 years' standing. The Central Criminal Court, the Old Bailey, is the Crown Court for the City of London. Crown Courts hear all cases on indictment, i.e. serious criminal cases. Trial is by jury of twelve lay persons drawn from the Register of Electors between the ages of 18 and 65 who have been resident in this country for a minimum of five years. Various persons are either excluded or excused for jury service including policemen, lawyers, doctors, nurses, MPs, etc.

1.1.3 The legal profession

The term 'lawyer' may be applied to a Barrister or Solicitor, a custom which may be unique to this country and the Commonwealth.

Barristers are primarily Advocates, but some may be engaged in the drafting of reports, papers, etc, in which pursuits they may be subject to actions for negligence. Barristers have a right of audience in all Courts, but a Solicitor's right is confined to Crown Courts, County Courts, and Magistrates' Courts. Solicitors deal with the preparatory stages of an action before litigation. Barristers may not form partnerships with each other, but Solicitors may. Solicitors may sue a client for fees, but a Barrister who looks to the Solicitor for payment of his fees cannot sue a Solicitor for default of payment.

Solicitors are Officers of the Supreme Court and they may be committed for contempt if they disobey an Order of the Court. Barristers are not Officers of the Supreme Court, and their duties depend upon professional etiquette; they cannot be either committed for contempt of court or sued for professional negligence arising from their work in court. They take their instructions from Solicitors (clients may not approach them directly), and they cannot interview witnesses.

Solicitors are governed in their professional life by the Law Society, this being a statutory body which makes rules governing qualifications, conduct, practice, handling of clients' money, administration of legal aid, compensation funding, etc. All communications between a client and a Solicitor are subject to privilege.

Barristers are members of one of the four Inns of Court, i.e. the Middle Temple, Inner Temple, Gray's Inn, Lincoln's Inn, each of which has three classes of membership, Benchers (the Governors of the Inn), Barristers (called to the Bar by Benchers), and Students.

A Queen's Counsel is a Senior Barrister of at least 10 years' standing who has been called upon to 'take silk', i.e. a silk gown as court apparel instead of other material. He must appear in court accompanied by a Junior Barrister.

In Scotland Solicitors belong to the Law Society of Scotland and may also be members of the ancient association of Writers to the Signet, and Solicitors to the Supreme Court. Scottish Solicitors have the right to conduct first instance stages of important cases, and may also defend in serious criminal charges.

Scottish Barristers are members of the Faculty of Advocates, and only they have right of audience in the Court of Sessions and the House of Lords.

In Northern Ireland Solicitors are members of the Incorporated Law Society of Northern Ireland. Barristers are members of the Honourable Society of the Inn of Court of Northern Ireland.

Law Officers

The Attorney General

Is Head of the English Bar assisted by junior Counsel to the Treasury. His political appointment is vacated with the outgoing Government. He is the Crown's representative in proceedings involving a political or constitutional matter. In Scotland the Lord Advocate corresponds to the Attorney General.

The Solicitor General

Is the Attorney General's deputy; there is a Solicitor General for Scotland.

The Director of Public Prosecutions

Is an eminent Barrister or Solicitor of ten years standing; though appointment is by the Home Secretary, this is not a political appointment. He is Head of the department responsible for dealing with the most important criminal proceedings. In Scotland there is no equivalent as prosecutions are not brought by the police but by the Procurators Fiscal. There is a Director of Public Prosecutions for Northern Ireland.

Master of the Rolls

This title is derived from the days when the holder of the title was concerned with the preservation of Court records. He is still Head of the Records Office, and also presides over the Court of Appeal, Civil Division.

The Lord Chancellor

This appointment is both judicial and political, and it is made on the recommendation of the Prime Minister and he is a member of the Government. He

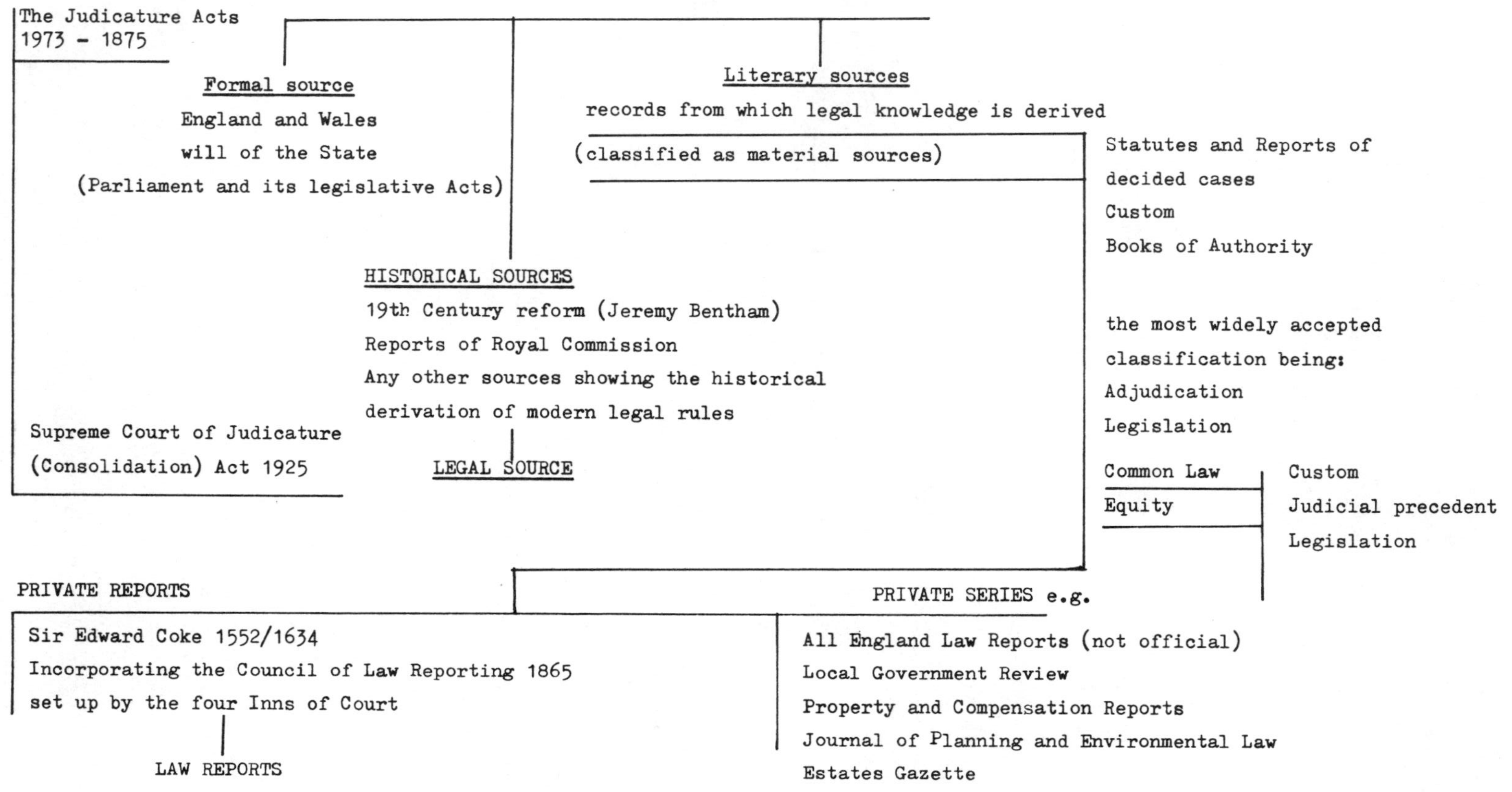

Diagram 1: Sources of law in England and Wales

is Speaker of the House of Lords and ranks highest among all Judges. When the House of Lords sits as a court of law, the Lord Chancellor presides. The incumbent changes with a change of Government.

The Vice Chancellor

This office was revised by the Administration of Justice Act 1970, he acts as Head of the Chancery Division in place of the Lord Chancellor.

Judges

The Lord Chief Justice is Head of the Queen's Bench Division and he presides over the Court of Appeal (Criminal Division) and the Divisional Court of the Queen's Bench Division.

High Court Judges may be dismissed only by direct application to the Sovereign by both Houses of Parliament, though this has not happened in Great Britain since the Act of Settlement in 1701. Circuit Judges may be removed by the Lord Chancellor by reason of infirmity or misconduct. Judges normally retire at the age of 75, and circuit Judges at the age of 72.

Appointments

High Court, Crown Court, and County Court Judges, Recorders, and Stipendary Magistrates are appointed by the Crown on the advice of the Prime Minister or Lord Chancellor.

1.1.4 The United Kingdom

England and Wales, Scotland, and Northern Ireland together constitute the United Kingdom which is a single, independent, legal State administered and governed under the rules of the British Constitution. Since the UK is also a member of the European Community it is subject, through the European Communities Act 1972, to the Treaty of Rome and its laws, rules, and directives.

There is no single document containing all the rules of the British Constitution, and it is said therefore to be 'unwritten'.

By the will of the people, supreme power in the State is at present vested in HM 'The Queen in Parliament', i.e. the Queen, the House of Lords, the House of Commons, acting in unison and being free to make, change, or repeal any law.

HM The Queen ascended the throne by virtue of the Act of Settlement 1701, being in direct line of succession to her late father King George VI. The House of Lords is an entity in itself, its members being raised to the peerage either by the Sovereign or by inheritance.

The House of Commons consists of members elected by vote of the people following a general election or a by-election, the majority party forming the Government, the minority party the Opposition. The elected Government usually governs for a period of five years, but this may be less. In Great Britain the principle is 'one man/woman, one vote'.

Following a general election the Sovereign selects the Leader of the majority party to be Prime Minister; although there is nothing written down to say that this shall be so, it is a convention of the Constitution to do so.

The Prime Minister chooses members of the majority party to be Ministers of the various government departments, which in turn are administered by the Civil Service irrespective of the current government. About 20 of the more important Ministers are invited to become Cabinet Ministers who will attend meetings in the Cabinet Room at Number 10, Downing Street.

The Cabinet will make such govermental decisions and propose such changes in the law as they think desirable.

The Sovereign, who is consulted by the Prime Minister on all major political issues, must give Royal Assent to all changes in existing statute law and to new statute law passed by the two Houses of Parliament, but not to Statutory Instruments or other forms of 'delegated legislation', unless the legislative power has been delegated to 'the Queen (or King) in Council'.

A statute is a law that has passed through both Houses of Parliament and received the assent of the Sovereign, having passed through the following stages:

(1) A bill originated either by the Cabinet or a Member of Parliament and drafted in 'clauses' is introduced into Parliament.
(2) Except for money bills (which must first go to the House of Commons) the bill must be passed by both Houses of Parliament.
(3) *First Reading*: the title of the bill is read out together with the name of the Member introducing it. Printing is then ordered.
(4) *Second Reading*: the principle of the bill is debated. If it is unopposed, or there is a majority vote for it, it passes to the Committee stage.
(5) *Committee stage*: an appointed Committee considers the bill in detail. The whole House may sit as a Committee if the importance of the bill warrants it.
(6) *Report stage*: the Committee reports to the House on its assessment of the bill with any proposed amendments.
(7) *Third Reading*: the general principles of the bill are debated and a vote taken. If the majority vote is in favour of the bill, it is passed to the House of Lords where a similar procedure is followed.

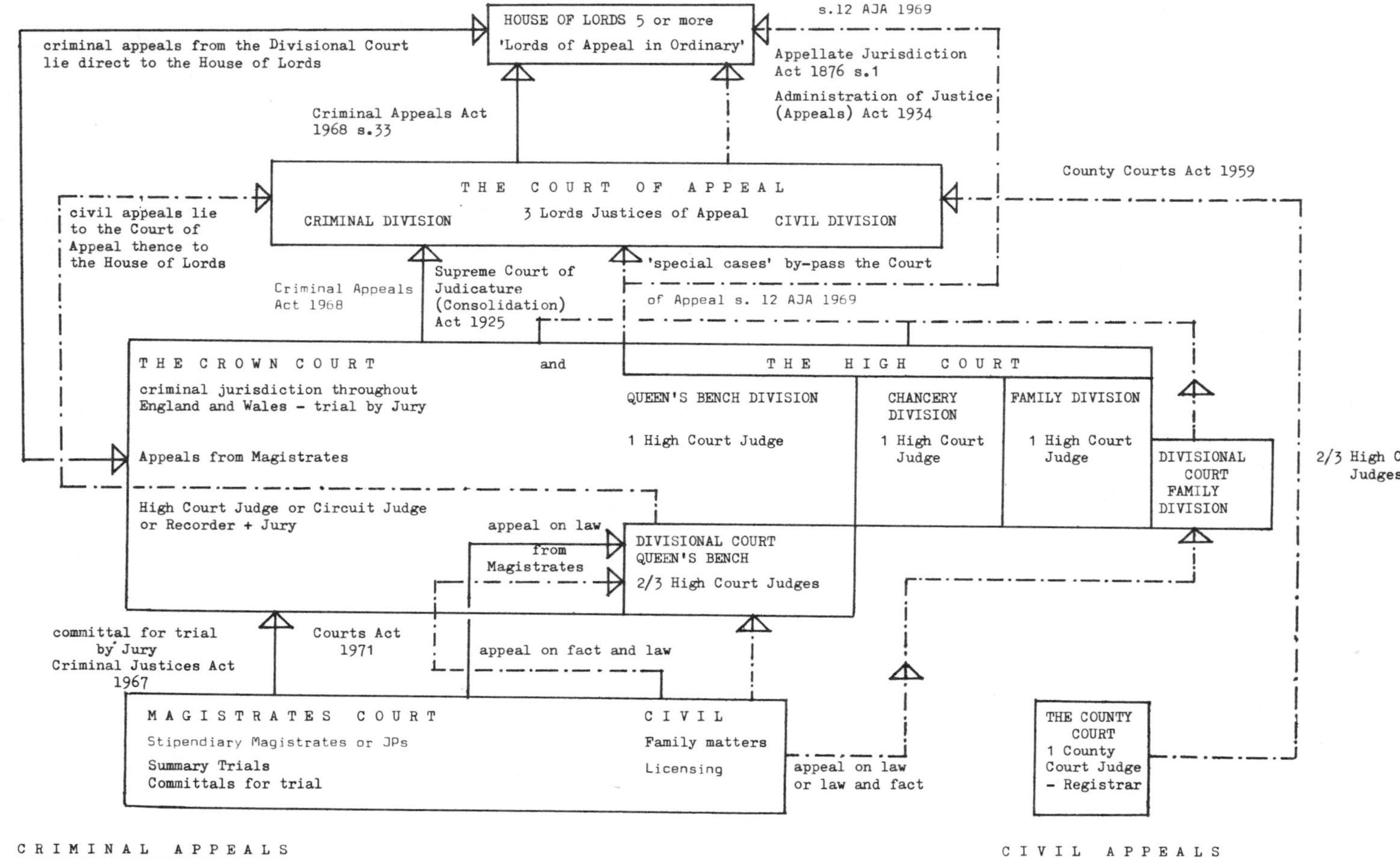

Diagram 2: The structure of the legal system in the UK

When both Houses have passed the bill, it goes to the Sovereign for the Royal Assent. This has not been given personally by the Sovereign since 1854. Assent is notified to each House by the Speaker of that House according to the Royal Assent Act 1967. Previously it was given to an assembly of both Houses by Commissioners acting on behalf of the Sovereign.

The Bill is then an Act of Parliament, becomes law, and is placed on the Statute Book; references such as *Halsbury's Statutes* lists them, and synopses of current Acts can be read in books of reference such as *Stone's Justices Manual*. The Act has an appointed day written into it when it will become effective, and each Act has a Chapter Number in the year in which it becomes a Statute.

Parliament has to make many laws concerned with technical and other matters which for reasons of time are precluded from the stages given above. Parliament, therefore, has to delegate power to make such legislation to Departments, and these are usually produced in the form of Statutory Instruments, e.g. the Building Regulation 1976. Since these documents emanate from central government they are called 'Regulations', or may be 'Rules' or 'Orders'. By transference of function these are then administered by local authorities, or such other bodies as the Government defines, the Minister or Secretary of State concerned retaining the overall central government jurisdiction and control, e.g. the Secretary of State for the Environment, etc.

Local authorities or corporations make bye-laws such as the London Building (Constructional) Amending Bye-laws 1979, the Thames Water Authority Bye-laws, etc. The Greater London Council, being a local authority, produces bye-laws in pursuance of its powers under its General Powers Acts and the London Building Acts 1930/39.

References

AJ Legal Handbook, A. SPEAIGHT and G. STONE (Architectural Press)

'O' Level English Law, D. M. M. SCOTT (Butterworths)

Questions and Answers on 'A' Level Law, V. POWELL-SMITH (Butterworths)

2

A summary of the law as it relates to Architects

2.1.1 Generally

An Architect has been defined as 'one who possesses, with due regard to aesthetic as well as practical considerations, adequate skill and knowledge to enable him to originate, design, arrange for and to supervise the erection of such buildings, or other works, calling for such skill in design and planning as he might, in the course of business, reasonably be asked to carry out, or in respect of which he offers his services as a specialist'. (R *v* Architects' Registration Tribunal. *Ex parte* Jaggar 1945 citing the adopted test of the Architects' Registration Council.)

More particularly, an Architect is one who is registered as such under the Architects' Registration Acts 1931/69, for no one else can use the title professionally.

The Architect has a four-fold duty:

(1) To act as agent for the employer, overseeing the work which the employer has commissioned, and ensuring value for money from the contractor.
(2) To exercise professional skill and foresight, diligence, both under his contract with the employer and towards anyone who might be injured by his negligence or neglect.
(3) To act impartially between the employer and the contractor when considering the extent and quality of the work done, and issuing certificates or other notices.
(4) To act without fraud, negligence, or false agency towards the contractor.

Whoever fulfills the functions of the Architect is subject to the same duties, whether he is an 'Architect' or an 'Engineer' or given any other title.

2.1.2 The Architect as agent

An Architect usually has an express or implied authority to employ a Quantity Surveyor (RIBA Architect's Appointment 1, 1.4). An Architect does not, merely by sending out plans and documents for tender, imply on behalf of the employer that they are accurate. He has no implied authority to guarantee the accuracy of the plans as an implied term of the contract (Scrivener *v* Pask), but if the Architect has been negligent in drawing up the plans or other documents, the contractor may sue him for any loss incurred as a result. The Architect does not have any implied authority to accept tenders, or pledge credit, on the employer's behalf, neither can he vary the contract without express power to do so, nor waive any of its terms, except with the employer's consent (Sharpe *v* San Paulo Railway).

Note: Most building contracts include a clause giving the Architect *express* power to authorise variations, and generally to make decisions on behalf of the employer (*see* JCT Standard Form of Building Contract 1980, Clause 13).

If the Architect represents, innocently or otherwise, that he has the authority of an agent when he has not, then he is personally liable to anyone whom he deceives. If the Architect guarantees the debt of his employer, he cannot be sued on this guarantee unless he has put his signature to some written evidence of that guarantee (S.4 Statute of Frauds 1677); but if the Architect uses any words than can reasonably lead the contractor or supplier to believe the Architect is placing the order himself, no written evidence will be necessary, and the Architect will be personally liable for the debt (Lakeman *v* Mountstephen).

If an Architect signs any contract, e.g. a sub-contract, in his own name without disclosing his agency, he risks personal liability (Beigtheil & Young *v* Stewart).

If the Architect signed a contract on behalf of a limited company, which at that time was not yet incorporated, the Architect will be personally liable for the debt, unless he has made some provision for himself to the contrary in the contract, known as a 'pre-incorporation contract', for without such provision for himself he will be personally liable even if he does not use his own name, but signs in the name of the company, for as yet it does not exist (Section 9, European Communities Act 1972).

If the Architect is bribed, or prevented by secret dealings from being a faithful servant to his employer, he can be dismissed, sued, and prosecuted under criminal law. If, without actually being corrupt, the Architect's duty as agent conflicts with some personal interest elsewhere, he may be dismissed without a fee.

2.1.3 The Architect as expert

Like any expert, the Architect is required to exercise professional skill, being no better or no worse than his reasonably competent brethren. He does not have to be the best Architect in the profession, for by definition there can be only one such person, but an Architect must not ignore apparent dangers no matter who has ignored them in the past (Clay *v* Crump; Bolam *v* Friern Hospital).

The Architect must not delegate his duties for which he was principally retained, for 'a delegate must not delegate'; he must either admit the limitations of his skill at the outset, or pay for the advice himself. If he elects to take, or pay for, the advice or services of someone else, he nevertheless remains liable to the employer for the full discharge of his duties (*see* Chapter 14 – Surveys and Reports).

The Architect's particular duties are many; in sum, he must know building law and any changes made to it, and he should bear this knowledge in mind when he inspects the site, noting the legal as well as the natural risks involved.

He should be honest and careful in his work, and recommend contractors and sub-contractors with similar honesty and care. He should be a timely and diligent checker of foundations and structures before later building work conceals them.

The death of the Architect brings the contract to an end, unless some method of appointing a replacement is provided for. The death of the employer does not affect the contract because it is not dependent on his skill.

The plans and drawings prepared by the Architect belong to the employer upon payment of the Architect's fees, but the copyright in the design remains with the Architect unless he agrees to sell it, i.e. grant a licence for its use (Meikle *v* Maufe).

A report by a Committee to consider the Law of Copyright and Designs under Mr Justice Whitford, March 1977, suggested under Article 551, page 139, 'the view was urged upon us that it is fair and just that the copyright in any work ordered and paid for by a customer or client should belong to the customer or client'. The British Copyright Council strongly opposed this viewpoint, and the provisions of the Copyright Act 1950 still appear to obtain at the present time.

The client has the right to use the Architect's drawings to build the building, but only on the site for which it was designed (Architect's Appointment Part 3, 3.15, 3.16, 3.24 – SW 3.6).

2.1.4 The Architect as an issuer of certificates

Certificates are issued, among other things, to show completion of work, and to entitle the contractor to payment for that work. certificates may be interim or final. Interim certificates are issued from time to time on the basis of the work already done, and include for materials on and off the site as provided for in the contract to ensure the Contractor is kept in funds. The employer usually deducts a percentage, sometimes with a limit on the total deduction (called the 'retention sum') from the amounts due to the contractor; this is to encourage completion of the work. The Architect issues all these certificates but in so doing he does not act as a servant of the employer. He must act fairly between the parties to the contract and certify the proper amounts due, including payments to nominated sub-contractors and suppliers.

The employer cannot escape liability to pay a debt either by ordering the Architect not to certify that it is due (Molloy *v* Liebe) or by preventing access to the site for the purpose of making valuations.

Prior to the decision in Sutcliffe *v* Thackrah it was argued that an Architect issuing a certificate was acting like an Arbitrator delivering his award, and that as such he could not be sued for negligence, any more than could a Judge or an Arbitrator. This was because the Architect was considered to be an impartial person, fairly deciding questions of work and value between the contractor and the employer. The phrase used was 'quasi-arbitrator' (*quasi* = as if).

In this case the Architect had negligently certified too great a sum of money to the contractor. The employer paid the money, but on finding out the truth, he sued the Architect for negligence. The Architect claimed that he could not be sued for negligence, but on appeal the House of Lords gave

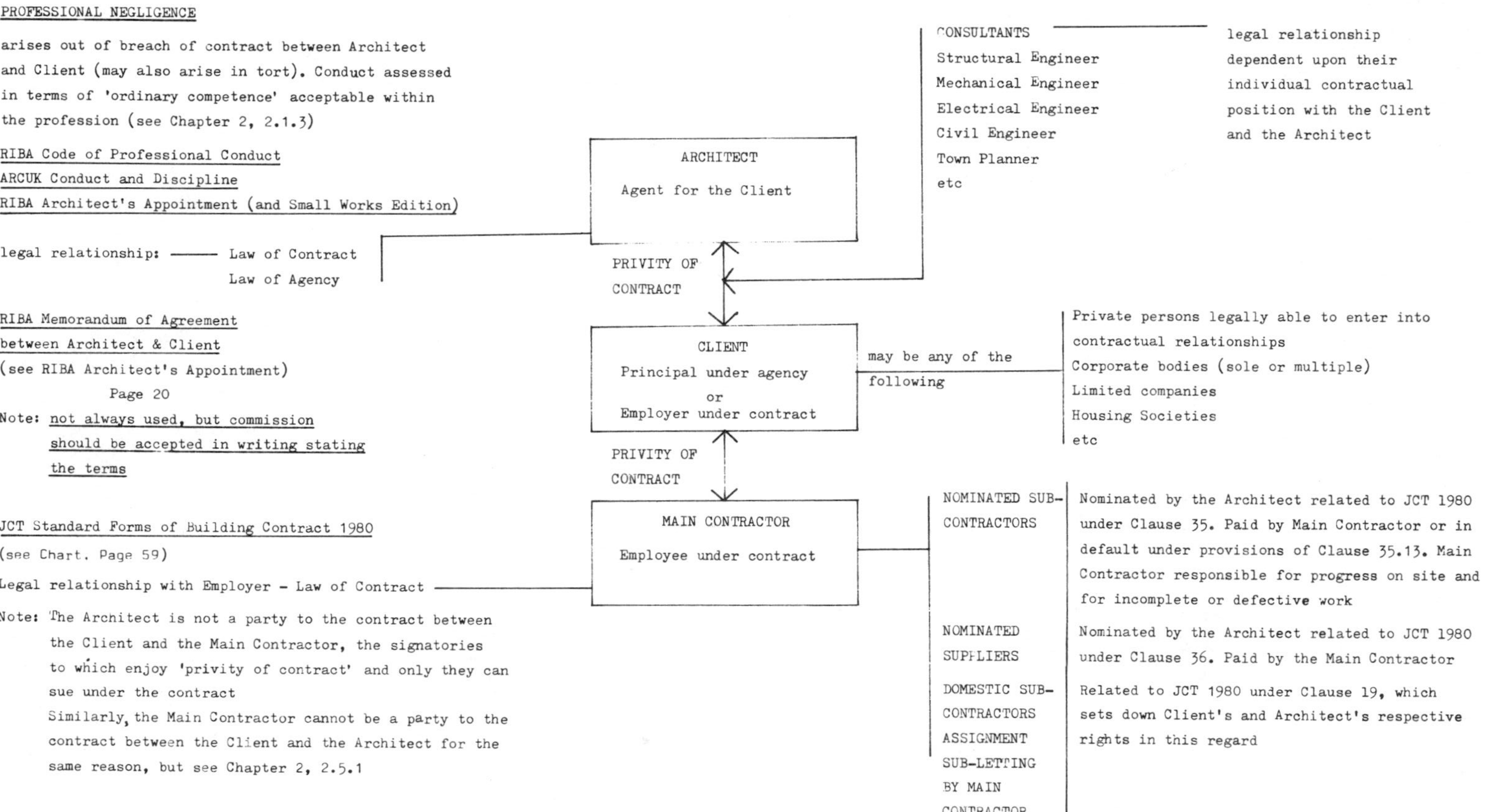

Diagram 3: Professional relationships – 1

judgement for the employer. All Arbitrators have to act fairly, but not all persons who have to act fairly are Arbitrators; if they were so then nobody with a duty to act fairly could be taken to court for acting unfairly.

An Architect is not immune from actions for negligence, because he investigates evidence and does not have to hear opposing arguments as does a Judge.

Sutcliffe *v* Thackrah is the authority for the view that there is no such person as a quasi-arbitrator. It is possible for a contract to stipulate that someone's opinion be final, or that his certificate shall not be questioned. Such provisions may well be valid but their validity depends upon the wording of the contract, and the Unfair Contract Terms Act 1977, and not upon any general protection given to Architects by law (*see also* Arenson *v* Casson).

2.1.5 The Architect and the contractor

As to whether the Architect has any contractual liability to the contractor, *see* Section 2.1.3 (3) above. Even though the Architect usually has no contract with the contractor, he does owe him certain duties at common law.

The Architect may be liable for negligent mis-statement to the contractor, as when the contractor relies upon the Architect's apparently expert advice. In such a case, the Architect will be under a duty of care to the contractor, unless he makes it clear that he is giving the advice without legal liability (Hedley Byrne *v* Heller & Partners).

The tort of negligent mis-statement also applies to erroneous predictions outside the control of the person giving the advice, if it is implied, without truth, that professional skill and care had been used in making the prediction (Esso *v* Marden).

If the Architect, by agreement or common practice, has assumed the duty of complying with bye-laws on behalf of the contractor, and then fails in this duty, he is liable to the contractor for any loss incurred (Townsend (Builders) *v* Cinema News).

As a general rule, however, it is up to the contractor to see that bye-laws and regulations are complied with.

2.1.6 Breach of Warranty of Authority and Ostensible Authority

If, innocently or otherwise, the Architect claims powers of agency he does not possess, and thereby induces the contractor to deal with him as an agent, he is personally liable for what the law calls 'breach of warranty of authority' (*see* Section 2.1.2 (3) above) but if the Architect has previously had authority to act as agent for the employer, that employer should notify the persons with whom he regularly deals that the Architect's authority has ceased. If the employer neglects to do this, the Architect will have 'ostensible authority' to bind him to future contracts with the same suppliers and contractors.

2.1.7 Misrepresentation by the Architect

If the Architect makes a misrepresentation which induces the contractor to enter into a contract with the employer, this representation will bind the employer if the Architect has an express or implied authority to make it (*see* Section 2.1.2(3) above). If the Architect has no authority to make the representation, it will have to be considered whether or not he can be sued for 'breach of warranty of authority' (*see* Section 2.1.6 above). If the Architect never gave any warranty that he had the Employer's authority to make the representation, it will have to be considered whether the representation was made (a) fraudulently, (b) negligently, (c) innocently.

In the case of fraud, the Architect can be sued for the tort of deceit, for all men are treated as Principals in a case of fraud. In the case of negligence, the Architect may be liable for negligent mis-statement at common law, but will not be liable under the Misrepresentation Act 1967, as this Act applies only when misrepresentation has been made by the 'other party' to the subsequent contract.

If the Architect's misrepresentation has induced the contractor to enter a contract with the employer, the Architect himself will not be the 'other party' to the contract, but the 1967 Act will be relevant against the employer if the Architect's misrepresentation has bound the employer in accordance with the ordinary rules of Principal and Agent.

An action for negligent misrepresentation under the 1967 Act is much easier to sustain than an action for negligent mis-statement at common law, but it has been seen above that the latter cause of action may be the only one that can be brought against the Architect personally.

References

AJ Legal Handbook, A. SPEAIGHT and G. STONE (Architectural Press)
'O' Level English Law, D. M. M. SCOTT (Butterworths)
Questions and Answers on 'A' Level Law, V. POWELL-SMITH (Butterworths)
The Law Relating to Architects, RIMMER (revised GILL) (Batsford)
Building Contracts, D. KEATING (Sweet & Maxwell)

3

Building regulations and procedures

3.1.1 The Architect and building controls

The Architect's responsibility in these matters is concerned firstly with the legal implications as previously discussed. These responsibilities emanate from the contractual relationship between the Architect and his client which exists from acceptance of the commission.

The RIBA Architect's Appointment, Part 1, describes the Preliminary and Basic Services which an Architect will normally provide, and building controls are initiated in Work Stage B, 1.8, Work Stage D, 1.12, Work Stage E, 1.15, and the Small Works edition SW1.5, SW1.8. Part 2 of both documents deals with exceptional negotiations which may arise as a result of these preliminary applications.

Under the terms of Clause 6.1 of the JCT Standard Form of Building Contract 1980 the contractor is responsible for obtaining all statutory notices and paying all fees and charges in connection therewith, and has the further duty to bring to the attention of the Architect any divergence between the statutory requirements and the contract documents, including any variation or instruction subsequently issued by the Architect to the contractor.

The Architect equally has a duty to inform the contractor of any changes made to the contract documents which impinge upon and affect the statutory requirements, and to ensure that the contractor is provided in good time with any notices, awards, licences, etc, which may affect the statutory position and impede the general progress of the works (*see* JCT Standard Form of Building Contract 1980, Clause 26).

The amount of legislation affecting building works is enormous; in England and Wales there exist about 170 national Acts, and more than 200 local Acts which may have some bearing upon the construction of buildings, but this book deals only with those statutes as would reasonably affect the normal building process.

The Bibliography lists a number of publications, books, and other sources of information which will assist in expanding the basic information in this book.

Four basic systems of building regulation exist in the United Kingdom at the time of writing, these being:

(1) The Building Standards (Scotland) Regulations 1981 made under The Building (Scotland) Acts 1959/70.
(2) The Building Regulations 1976, and amendments, made under the Public Health Acts 1936/61, applying to England and Wales, but only outside the Inner London Boroughs of the Greater London Council and the City of London.
(3) The London Building Acts 1930/78 and the London Building (Constructional) Amending Bye-laws 1979 applicable to the Inner London Boroughs of the Greater London Council and the City of London.
(4) Building Regulations (Northern Ireland) 1977, and the Building (Amendment) Regulations (Northern Ireland) 1982.

The building regulations in Northern Ireland were made under powers conferred by the Northern Ireland (Temporary Powers) Act 1972, and these have since been amended.

Building regulations in Scotland were instituted in 1957 by the Guest Committee who advised that an Act of Parliament should be instituted to empower a Minister to make regulations applying to the whole of Scotland, with administration and enforcement being under the control of local authorities; this culminated in the Building (Scotland) Act 1959. This Principle Act was subsequently amended by Section 75 of the Health & Safety at Work etc Act 1974, and Section 1 of the Building (Scotland) Act 1972, which has since been further amended.

Anyone wishing to demolish, construct, or change the use of any building must first obtain a warrant from the building authority, who will assure themselves that the proposals conform with the building operations regulations authorized under the Act, and that the building as constructed is in accordance with the drawings submitted for approval. The building authority must issue a Certificate of Completion before a building constructed under a warrant is occupied. Fees are charged for the issue of warrants under the Building (Procedure) (Scotland) Amendment Regulations 1980.

In 1972 the Department of the Environment issued a consultative document entitled *Proposals for a Building Bill*, the object of which was to extend the scope of the building regulations in England and Wales, and bring closer together the Scottish, Welsh and English regulations, as well as those of the Inner London Boroughs of the Greater London Council; it was also meant to improve and rationalize the existing building control systems.

As mentioned in the law synopsis, because of lack of time for proper Parliamentary discussion and procedure, the Bill became an addition to the Health & Safety at Work etc Act 1974 (hence the 'etc' in the Act's title) and was embodied in Part 3 of the Act, and Schedules 5, 6, 7, 8.

The extent of these provisions is yet to be fully realised, particularly Section 70 of the Act. The present Conservative Government has stated its intentions to remove the Greater London Council as a metropolitan authority with a projected date of 1986 as the time when this would happen. The Government has also pursued its proposals eventually to produce a 'building code', a bill being before Parliament at the time of writing.

In *Building Regulation – Practice and Procedure*, page 101, (15.18), the author F D Entwisle wrote, *inter alia*, 'The Inner London area district has long set an example of high quality service, and one would hope that the combination of Local Government Reform (which took effect from April 1974, under the Local Government Reform Act 1972) and the coming into operation of the Building Bill (*see* page 8) bring quick change throughout the country which will ensure that the quality now existing in the Inner London area, and a few other areas, will become widespread throughout the whole of the United Kingdom. It is hoped that the Building Regulation Advisory Committee (BRAC), which operates under the provisions of the Public Health Act 1961 to advise the Government in these matters, will play a more active and positive part towards achieving this desirable end'. Though these sentiments were expressed in 1974, little has happened since that time, but proposals before Parliament at the time of writing will bring changes, though not necessarily as expressed in the above extract.

3.1.2 Historical background to building regulations and bye-laws

An Act for the rebuilding of the City of London – applicable only to the City of London and Westminster, Sir Christopher Wren, *et al*, appointed Surveyor	1667
The Act extended to St Pancras and St Marylebone, Paddington, Chelsea, but Surveyors appointed only in the City	1725
Act amended to extend the appointment of surveyors outside the City	1764
Further amendments in	1766, 1772
Wider powers introduced and extended to City of London, Westminster, St Pancras, St Marylebone, Paddington	1774
The Metropolitan Building Act introduced the term 'District Surveyor', who qualified through a Board of Examiners of three Architects under	1844
The Nuisance Removal and Prevention of Disease Act	1848
The Metropolis Management Act	1855
The Metropolitan Building Act repealed the Act of 1844 and transferred powers to the newly-created Metropolitan Board of works	**1855
Nuisance Removal and Sanitary Act	1866
Artisans' and Labourers' Dwellings Act	1868
Metropolitan Buildings – (Amendment) Acts	1868–1871
Public Health Act	**1875
Local Government Act established in the County of London	1888
City Councils and Rural District Council Act	1888–1894
London County Council formed – inherited all the powers of the Metropolitan Board of Works	1889

New bye-laws introduced	1891
culminating in the London Building Acts	1894, 1898
Fire protection and means of escape introduced	1905
Cubical extent and uniting of buildings	1909
London County Council under its General Powers Act, Part IV, introduced the Cinematograph Act	1909
LCC General Powers Act	1909
steel-framed building and reinforced concrete construction controlled	1916
London Building Act	1930
London Building Act (Amendment) Act	1935
Public Health Act	*1936
Public Health (London) Act	1936
Housing Act	1936
Model bye-laws for all councils (county, district, rural, etc) made under the Public Health Act 1936	
Factories Act	1937
Construction and Conversion of Buildings	1937
London Building Acts (Amendment) Act	1939
London Constructional Bye-laws	1952
London Building (Constructional) Amending Bye-laws	1964, 1966, 1970, 1972
London Building (Constructional) Amending Bye-laws	1979
Building Regulations made under the Public Health Act 1961	1965
Amended to present Building Regulations	1976
Housing and Building Control Act	1984

Town & Country Planning controls

The Housing, Town Planning Act (first Act)	1909
The Housing, Town Planning Act	1919
The Town & Country Planning Act	1932
Restriction of Ribbon Development Act	1935
The Town & Country Planning (Interim Development) Act	1943
The Town & Country Planning Act	1944
The Town & Country Planning Acts	*1947, 1953, 1954, 1962, 1968, *1971
Town & Country Planning Use Classes Order	1972
Town & Country Planning (Amendment) Acts	1972, 1977
Town & Country Planning (Amenities) Act	1974
Town & Country Planning General Development Order	1977
Town & Country Planning General Development (Amendment) Orders	1980, 1981
The Local Government, Planning & Land Act	1980
The Housing & Building Control Act	1983

Note: numerous other Regulations and Orders not quoted.

*Consolidating Acts **Principal Acts

3.1.3 The object of building regulations and bye-laws

Building regulations and bye-laws are made for the purpose of public health and safety, and more recently to improve environmental conditions and to conserve energy.

They are made in accordance with the provisions of the Public Health Act 1936, Part 2, Sections 61 and 62 (as amended by Part 2, Section 4, and Schedule 1 of the Public Health Act 1961), and by Schedule 10 of the Health & Safety at Work etc Act 1974.

Administration

The central government authority is the Secretary of State for the Environment in exercise of his powers under Sections 4 and 6 of the Public Health Act 1961, and under the Public Health Act 1936 (the

Principal Act). Part 2, Sections 61 and 62 and Section 24 of the Clean Air Act 1956, (each amended by Part II, and Part 3 of Schedule 1 of the Public Health Act 1961), and all other powers enabling the Minister in that behalf, after such consultations with the Building Regulations Advisory Committee, and such other bodies as may appear to him to be representative of the interests concerned, as required by Section 9 (3) of that Act.

Local administration is effected by local authorities, but areas excluded from these regulations are:

> The City of London and the Inner London Boroughs of the Greater London Council, which are Camden, Islington, Hackney, Tower Hamlets, Greenwich, Lewisham, Southwark, Lambeth, Wandsworth, Hammersmith, the Royal Boroughs of Kensington and Chelsea combined, the City of Westminster.

In these areas, and the City of London by adoption, the London Building Acts 1930/78, and the London Building (Constructional) Amending Bye-laws 1979 obtain (*see* London Building Act (Amendment) Act 1935, Sections 1–8). These Acts and Bye-laws are administered by the Superintending Architect of the Greater London Council, in association with the Building Regulations Division, and the District Surveyors (*see* Appendix), and in these areas the Building Regulations do not apply.

3.1.4 Applications

The Building Regulations 1976 (with amendments to date)

Applications are made to the local authority in whose area the work is to be carried out (Section IV, A10, of the Act). An appropriate form is obtainable from the local authority which is completed and returned with the requisite number of copies of the drawings. Where reinforced concrete or structural steelwork is proposed it is necessary to submit calculations with the application for approval; this also applies to special foundations. The applications, for which a handling fee is charged, are dealt with by the Building Regulations Enforcement Office (*see* page 21 for typical Enforcement Office arrangement). When approval is given, the applicant receives a copy of the approved drawings together with a set of cards relating to the stages of the work on the site. These are given to the contractor at commencement and he sends one periodically to the local authority when inspection of the work is required from foundations through to completion of the building.

3.1.5 The duties of the Building Inspector

The title 'Building Inspector' is something of a misnomer, since to qualify for the post one takes an examination titled 'Examination for the office of Building *Surveyor* under Local Authorities'. This examination was for many years administered by the RIBA, but it ceased in 1984 when its administration was taken over by the Business and Technician Education Council (BTEC).

The Chief Building Control Officer has overall responsibility for the enforcement team, and the Building Inspector who comes to the site is usually a Junior Building Inspector, or one who has passed the qualifying examination above. It is possible that a District, Senior District, or Principal Surveyor may also come to the site, but this will vary with the district concerned, and the complexity of the work to be supervised, and the technician level of supervision is most commonly employed (*see* page 22).

It follows that the authority of the Building Inspector is directly related to his position in the enforcement team, and supervision on behalf of the local authority by its Inspectors has had a profound legal significance since the cases of Dutton *v* Bognor Regis UDC and Anns *v* London Borough of Merton.

3.1.6 The London Building Acts 1930/78 and the London Building (Constructional) Amending Bye-laws 1979

Part IX, Sections 73 and 74, of the London Building Acts (Amendment) Act 1939 makes provision for the appointment of a Superintending Architect of Metropolitan Buildings for the purpose of aiding in the execution of the London Building Acts and bye-laws made thereunder.

Section 75 of the Act makes provision for the appointment of District Surveyors, who qualify by examination as discussed later, and the allocation of their districts and duties.

Formal submission of plans and details and approvals is not the same in the Inner London Boroughs of the GLC as in areas controlled by the Building Regulations, there is no requirement for the District Surveyor to approve proposals submitted to him in accordance with the provisions London Building Act (Amendment) act 1935, Section 4(2)(b), and as described in the London Building (Constructional) Amending Bye-laws 1979, Part 2. The Building Acts require the serving of a Building Notice on the District Surveyor of the intention to commence operations, such Notice being accompanied by plans and other supporting details two clear working days before work is begun, as required by the London Building Acts (Amendment) Act 1939, Part IX, Section 83 (a), or as provided for in (b) and (c) of the same Section. In practice, plans and details are submitted for comment before the serving of a Building Notice, e.g. where means of escape in case of fire is concerned.

On receipt of plans and details the District Surveyor may issue a Notice of Objection under Section 87 of the Act. If the District Surveyor discovers work on site that does not conform with the bye-laws, whether or not a Building Notice has been served, he may serve on the Builder a Notice of Irregularity under Sections 88, 89 of the Act. Such Notices must be complied with immediately since penalties for failure to do so are incurred, as Section 90 of the Act.

It is imperative that any alterations to drawings or documents, upon which consent has been given by the Council, be notified to the Building Regulations Division and the District Surveyor at once, in order that delays and irregularities may be avoided.

Fees are payable to the Council for the services of the District Surveyor LB Acts (Amendment) Act 1939, Sections 91, 92, 93.

The District Surveyor may request the builder to send him a Statement of Cost of the completed works, Section 84 (3) of the Act, the definition of 'cost' being as described in Section 93 (2) for the purpose of fee calculation. Do not forget to advise the client that such fees will have to be paid by him as they may be substantial.

Dangerous Structures Notice may also be served by the District Surveyor in respect to dangerous and neglected structures. The essential thing in such cases is to know the procedure under the LB Acts (Amendment) Act 1939, sections 61, 62, 63, and to cause to have removed any immediate danger to the public. Note that failure to comply with such notices may result in the Council's workmen entering onto the premises and doing such work of hoarding, shoring, etc, as the District Surveyor may deem necessary. After the removal of the immediate danger seven days must elapse to enable the owner to serve a written requirement that the matter be referred to arbitration, and at the same time give to the Council the name of an independent Surveyor to act for him jointly with the District Surveyor. Section 63 (2) a, (i) requires the independent Surveyor and the District Surveyor to appoint a Third Surveyor to act in the capacity of arbitrator, or a court of summary jurisdiction may so appoint a Third Surveyor in the event of disagreement over such an appointment. This procedure is similar to that discussed under party-wall procedure in Chapter 7, Section 7.1.1 (page 46).

3.1.7 The duties of the District Surveyor

The duties of the District Surveyor are set down in the LB Acts (Amendment Act) 1939, Part IX, Section 82.

He is an appointed officer of the Greater London Council, and by examination holds a certificate of competence to practise his duties. The examination, held annually at the County Hall by the Greater London Council, comprises written papers and an oral examination.

There are 28 District Surveyors appointed in the City of London and the Inner London Boroughs of the Greater London Council, which are: Camden, Islington, Hackney, Tower Hamlets, Greenwich, Lewisham, Southwark, Lambeth, Wandsworth, Hammersmith, the Royal Boroughs of Kensington and Chelsea combined, the City of Westminster.

The prime duty of the District Surveyor is to ensure that all works to buildings and structures within his designated area conform in all respects with the London Building Acts 1930/78, and the London Building (Constructional) Amending Bye-laws 1979, and that any consents issued under the Acts with respect to the works in his area are complied with.

There is provision for a Tribunal of Appeal against decisions of the District Surveyor to which any aggrieved person may apply, but it is very important to remember that Section 86 (3), Part IX, of the LB Acts (Amendment) Act 1939, precludes any applications to the Tribunal of Appeal with respect to matters of structure, and the protection of elements of construction against the action of fire, thus in effect giving to the District Surveyor absolute power in these matters. It should also be remembered that the Act provides for methods of construction and the use of materials to be carried out 'in a workmanlike manner' and 'to the satisfaction of the District Surveyor'.

The District Surveyor and his staff are also advisers to the public, and the earliest consultation is advised as this will do much to obviate irregularities and to ensure that correct applications are made. Do not be afraid to ask for advice, you cannot be expected to know the regulations, or their interpretation as well as the District Surveyor and his staff who use them constantly.

It is possible that the Greater London Council may delegate some of their work to local authorities within their jurisdiction, and presumably the overall jurisdiction of the District Surveyor obtains (London Building Acts (Amendment) Acts 1939, Sections 86, 109) in case of appeal.

It is wise on completion of the works to have a final inspection made by the District Surveyor, accompanied by the Architect or his representative, and if the District Surveyor is satisfied that all is in order, to confirm this in writing.

In this capacity you are acting as agent for the client and the letter should make this clear. It could be couched in something like the following terms:

FIRM LETTER HEADING

date

Nos 224/226, Coronation Grove, Wandsworth, London SW4 MM6

The London Building Acts (Amendment) Acts 1930/78

The London Building (Constructional) Amending Bye-laws 1979

The District Surveyor,

Dear Sir,

Further to our meeting on site at the above premises today, I confirm on behalf of my Client, Mr J N Willoughby, that the work has been completed to your satisfaction in accordance with the above-named Acts and Bye-laws and the drawings Nos. XYZ and ABC submitted to your Council on the 23 May 1983.

I further confirm that all fees due to your Council under the London Building Acts (Amendment) Act 1939, First Schedule, as amended, in respect of these works have been fully paid. Thank you for your assistance and advice in the pursuance of these works which is appreciated.

Yours faithfully,
A N Architect

Address of District
Surveyor

Guidance Notes and Explanatory Memoranda on the Building Regulations are available from Government bookshops.

The Greater London Council issues a number of useful Codes of Practice:

Code of Practice for Building of Excess Height or Cubical Extent under Section 20 of the London Building Acts (Amendment) Act 1939.

Code of Practice for Means of Escape in Case of Fire.

Code of Practice for Means of Escape in Case of Fire – Houses in Multiple Occupation – Section 16 of the Housing Act 1961.

See Appendix for District Surveyors Forms DS 1–5 and Party-Wall and Structure Forms A–G.

3.1.8 Modifications and waivers

Provision is made for modification of building regulations and bye-laws as follows:

The Building Regulations 1976–1983

The Minister has the power under the Public Health Act 1961, Section 6 (1), to dispense with or to relax any regulations.

The first amendment to the Building Regulations 1972 removed any previous limitations and enabled all local authorities to relax the regulations in all cases except their own development. (Part E), Large buildings of over 7000 m^3, large developments including shopping precincts, and air-supported structures. Regulation A12 and Schedule 3 apply to local authority application for relaxation, and Part B of the same Schedule to other applicants.

It should be noted that the Department of the Environment has produced a document listing all applications for waivers and modifications and the decisions made in each case. The Building Regulations 1965 Selected Decisions. Relaxation of Building Regulations.

The London Building Acts (Amendment) Act 1939, and the London Building Constructional (Amending) Bye-laws 1979

Upon receipt of an application the Council may modify or waive any bye-law under the terms of the London Building Act (Amendment) Act 1935, Section 9 (1), and a register of all such applications and decisions made under this section is kept at County Hall for public inspection under Section 9 (5) of the Act.

3.1.9 Estate and Crown Surveyors

Some areas of land are held in trust estates and administered by Estate Surveyors (e.g. Hyde Park Estates, Portman Estates, Howard de Walden Estates, etc) representing the ground landlords or freeholders. Agents are appointed to deal with large areas of land and buildings under the ownership of the Ecclesiastical Commissioners.

It is essential in such areas, in addition to any other statutory consents required, that the Architect obtains consent of the Estate Surveyors to the proposed works, no matter how minor they may seem, by submitting proposals to the Estate Office and obtaining a licence for the work to be carried out, which usually involves payment of a fee. Other interested parties, e.g. Head Lessees must also be informed of any work proposed to be carried out in premises in which they have an interest. it is a mistake to assume that the person commissioning the work has the sole interest or rights in the land (*see* notes on ownership, page 52).

For work in connection with Crown buildings or land (e.g. land or buildings held in trust for the Sovereign, the Duchy of Cornwall, the Duchy of Lancaster, etc) applications are made to the Crown Commissioners Office since these buildings and

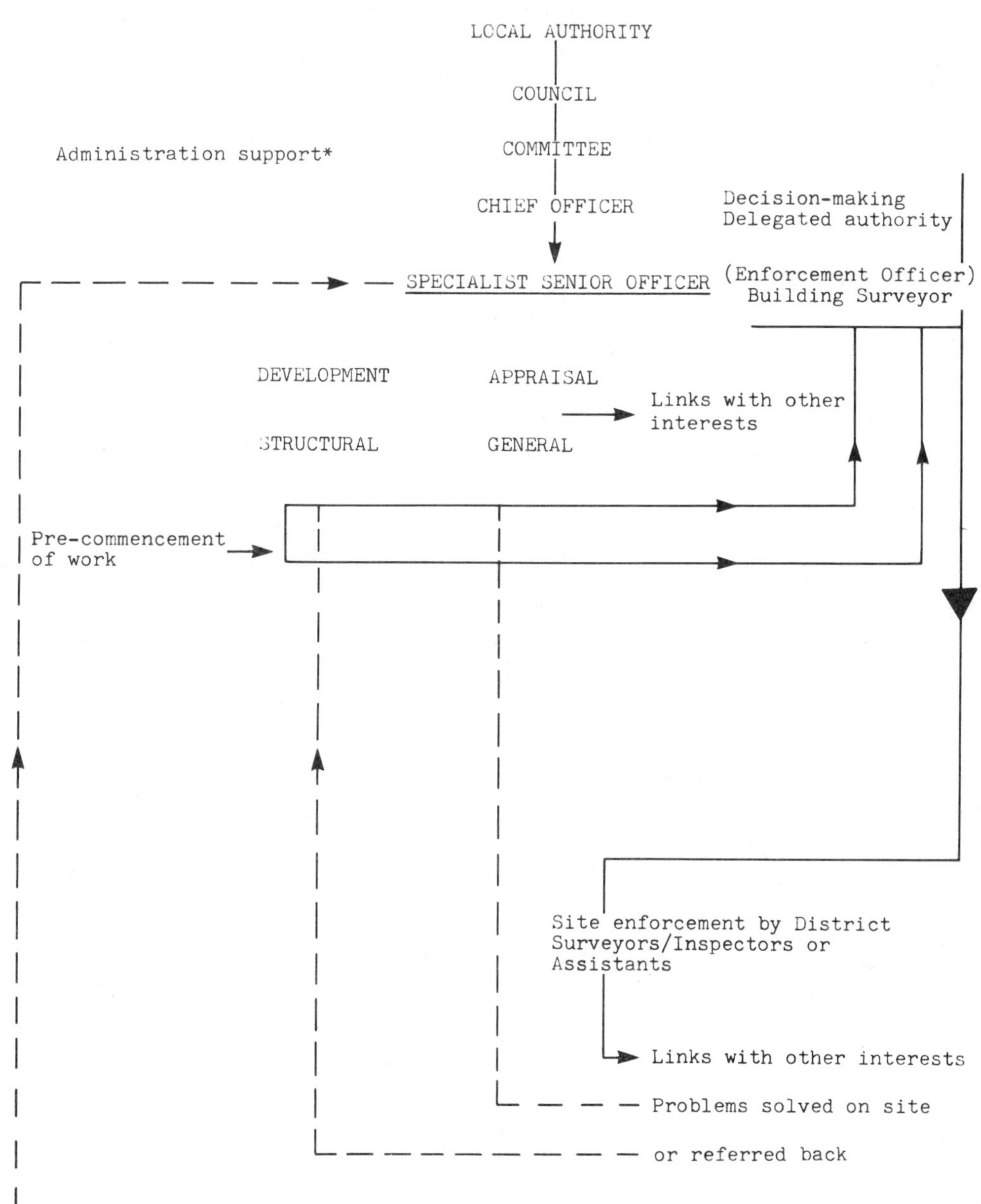

*'Administration support' means skilled qualified administration assistance as part of the major department organization

Diagram 4: The progress of an application for Building Regulation approval – Building Regulation responsibility procedure

DATES AND DEADLINES	PROGRESS OF APPLICATION
Prior to this date there may have been preliminary discussions for large or complex projects, and for some unauthorized work informal enforcement action leading to suitable plans being deposited to regularize the position	Deposit of plans Acknowledge with request to contact
Open day for other departments to see all plans on deposit	Plans considered 3/21 days, depending upon work load
Committee deadline generally to within a period of 35 days (most plans dealt with well within 35 days)	Other interests submit comments: Main drainage, sewage disposal, fire prevention, Public Health, Petroleum Officer, Licensing Officer Final discussions with developer to clear matters to enable a favourable recommendation to be made. If not possible extension to prescribed period granted, otherwise rejection recommended. Application may be made for relaxation of regulations, if appropriate Check with town planning development control before final clearance
	End prescribed period of 35 days or two calendar months
	Official notices despatched
Any or no period may elapse between approval and commencement of work on the site	Work on site commences, notice received, District Surveyor checks plans and details and queries any outstanding points. Site visits
Work on site proceeds. Time depends on size and complexity of job	Discussion with agents, Clerks of Works, Resident Engineers, liaison with other staff involved
Satisfactory completion. Habitation Certificate for dwellings. Information of completion to interested parties	Towards completion, Health and Fire Prevention Officers, or other special interests, introduced to site. Careful check relating plans approved to actual job, before clearing as satisfactory

Appraisal Surveyor (Deposit of plans to end of prescribed period)

Structural Engineers involved (Official notices despatched to discussion with agents)

District Surveyor involved (Work on site commences to satisfactory completion)

Diagram 5: Progress of an application

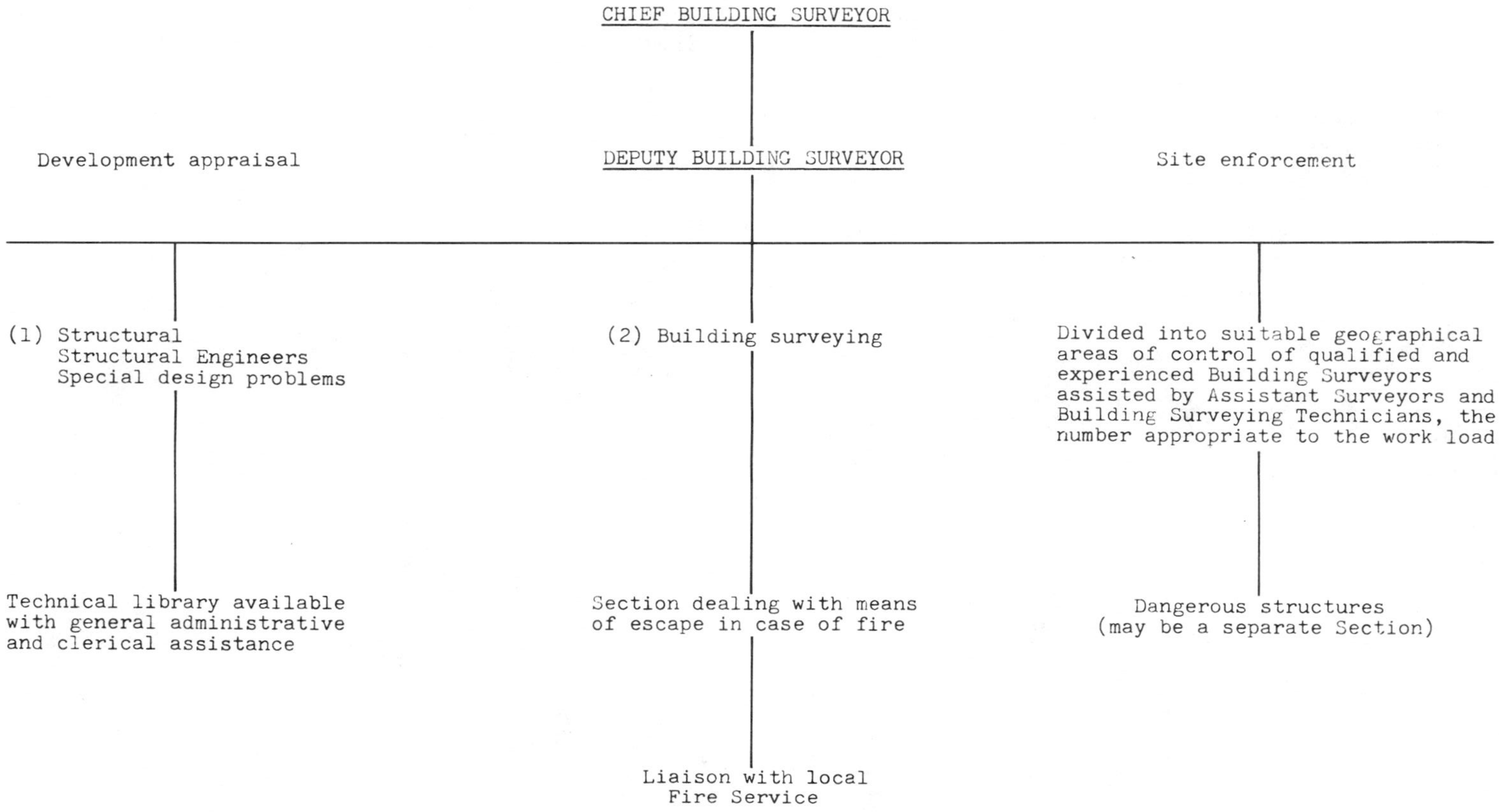

CHIEF BUILDING SURVEYOR

DEPUTY BUILDING SURVEYOR

Development appraisal

Site enforcement

(1) Structural
Structural Engineers
Special design problems

(2) Building surveying

Divided into suitable geographical areas of control of qualified and experienced Building Surveyors assisted by Assistant Surveyors and Building Surveying Technicians, the number appropriate to the work load

Technical library available with general administrative and clerical assistance

Section dealing with means of escape in case of fire

Dangerous structures (may be a separate Section)

Liaison with local Fire Service

Diagram 6: Building regulation enforcement office – typical arrangement

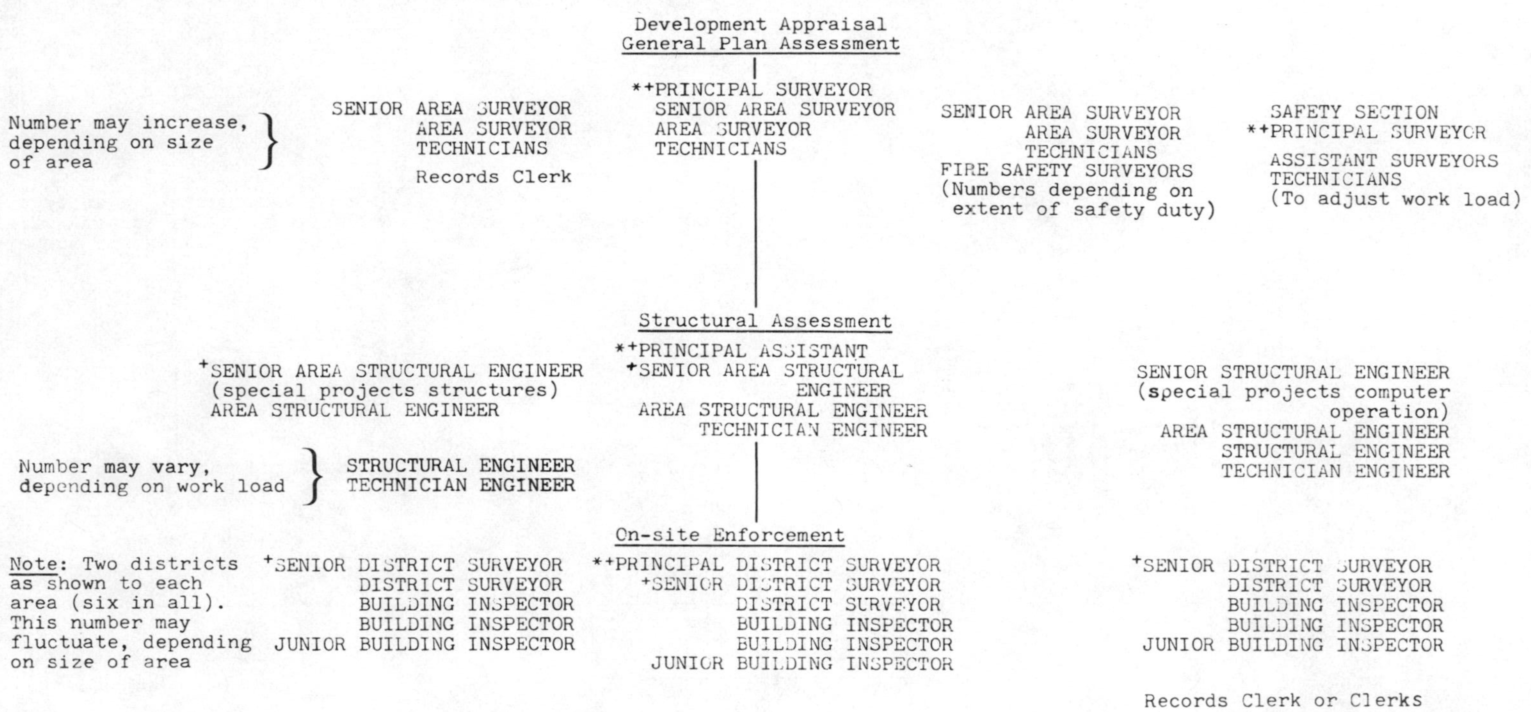

Diagram 7: Detailed arrangement of a complete Enforcement Unit

land, among others, may be exempt from building regulations or bye-laws. Refer to London Building Acts (Amendment) Act 1939, Section 149 *et seq*, the Building Regulations 1976, Part A, (A5), the Town & Country Planning Act 1971, Sections 266/268, but *see* the provisions of Public Health Act 1936, Section 341 (1).

3.2.1 The Environmental Health Officer

Formerly this office was held by Sanitary Inspectors and Health Officers, but the powers of these officers are now wider than hitherto.

Under the Public Health Acts 1936/61, which are the fount of building regulations, and former bye-laws, applying to all areas of England and Wales (except the Inner London Boroughs of the Greater London Council), there is a wide range of controlling legislation of which the Architect should be aware.

Central government control is shared between the Department of the Environment and the Department of Health and Social Security, while local control is administered through the local authority; but central government is empowered through Section 322 of the Public Health Act 1936 to investigate, on receipt of a complaint, a local authority's failure to carry out its function.

In the Public Health Act 1961, Section 26, 'defective premises', and procedures which may be followed in this regard, it it opportune to mention a small Act which is sometimes overlooked, particularly when architects are engaged on housing work. This is the Defective Premises Act 1972, especially Section 1, 'duty to build dwellings properly'. The Act binds the Crown as described in Section 1 (5), but it is not to be considered as retrospective; it is statute barred after six years either from the completion of the dwelling or from when remedial work was finished. The Act does not apply to Northern Ireland and Scotland.

Whilst discussing causes of action which are statute barred under the Limitations Act 1939, the Law Reform (Limitation of Actions, etc) Act 1954, and the Limitations Act 1963/80, it is important to consider the case of Sparham Souter and Others *v* Town & Country Developments and Benfleet RDC (Court of Appeal), since this case had a profound effect upon Architects, and others, and their statutory liability.

In 1964 planning permission was granted subject to compliance with the building regulations.

In May 1965 the works were inspected and passed by the Building Inspector.

In November 1965 the plaintiff purchased the property.

In 1968 cracks appeared in the brickwork due to inadequate foundations and the house subsequently became uninhabitable.

In October 1971 the plaintiff issued writs against the builder and the local authority.

The specific issue was whether the claim against the local authority was at the time statute barred.

In the House of Lords, Lord Denning reminded himself of the decisions in Bagot *v* Stevens and Dutton *v* Bognor Regis UDC, and said 'This does make me pause, but now, having thought it over time and again, and been converted by my brethren, I have come to the conclusion that, when building work is badly done and covered up, the cause of action does not accrue and the time does not begin to run until such times as the plaintiff discovers that it has done damage, or ought with reasonable diligence to have discovered it'.

He concluded, therefore, that the damage occurred when the cracks appeared in the brickwork, and as this date was less than six years before the writ was issued, the claim against the Council was not statute barred.

Limitation on causes of action was originally six years for contracts under hand and 12 years for contracts under seal from the completion of the works. Limitation seemingly was to prevent the bringing into court of actions based upon dubious evidence and unreliable or absent witnesses, which is bound to occur with the passage of time.

3.2.2 Nuisances

The Environmental Health Officer (EHO) has become more involved in this matter.

There are two kinds of nuisance, 'public' and 'private'. The former is a crime, being an act or omission causing discomfort or inconvenience to a class of Her Majesty's subjects, for which the perpetrator is liable to prosecution. Lord Denning described a public nuisance as 'one which is so widespread in its range, or so indiscriminate in its effect, that it would not be reasonable to expect one person to take proceedings on his own responsibility to put a stop to it, but that it should be taken on the responsibility of the community at large' (Attorney General *v* PYA Quarries Ltd).

Private nuisance is much more common and is a tort, not a crime, and may be committed against a person or persons. It consists of an unlawful interference with an occupier's use of his land. In order to succeed in a cause of action a plaintiff must prove these three things:

(1) An indirect interference with the use of his land.

(2) Damage; there must be an injury to the soil or interference with the use of the land causing discomfort or inconvenience.
(3) Unlawfulness, among other things, reasonableness, malice, duration. locality, sensivity.

Locality is important, e.g. 'What would be a nuisance in Belgrave Square would not necessarily be so in Bermondsey' (Sturgess *v* Bridgeman).

Probably the most common complaint of noise nuisance between neighbours is loud music, and as long ago as 1950 a government-sponsored investigation into noise in dwellings listed, among other things, audible conversation, toilets flushing, loud music, car noises during the night, and milk deliveries as some of the more unacceptable nuisances. Noise, smoke, fumes, vibration, from industrial premises, tree roots and overhanging branches are also common sources of complaint.

In dwellings, especially semi-detached and terraced properties, and flats, the nature of the construction of the party walls and floor is an inherent source of noise transmission, particularly in older premises converted from single dwellings into self-contained flats where old timber floors are inadequately treated to reduce noise transmission (the subject was investigated by the Building Research Establishment (formerly BR Station) many years ago, and the BRS *Digests* 88/89 suggested methods of construction to reduce noise transmission). Since these methods were suggested in the late 1950s the situation has been exacerbated by the use of hi-fi and other high-volume equipment transmitting both airborne and structure-borne sound at high decibel levels.

The EHO is able to help such problems to be alleviated, if not entirely removed, and the Control of Pollution Act 1974 provides him with statutory powers in this regard. He can take noise-level readings, and some local authorities undertake night patrols after 10.30 pm in an effort to control noise levels from music, etc, and may serve Abatement Notices on the offenders for any private nuisance which may be injurious to health or cause discomfort to the occupants of premises. The problem is that Abatement Notices have a statutory time in which to become effective, which can be as long as 21 days, and it may take much longer if subsequent court action is taken where there is a breach of Notice to abate a nuisance.

Owners may apply directly to the court for an injunction to prevent others committing alleged nuisances. An approach in the first instance to the instigators of the noise may achieve results, failing which the advice of the EHO should be sought. There appears to be little one can do about fractious and noisy children.

The author once had a neighbour in a flat above who installed two full-size pin-ball machines in his living room; the consequent noise was horrendous and the disturbance was resolved only by enforcing the terms of the lease. This action solved the initial problem but brought in its train a series of petty and unpleasant nuisances too numerous to describe.

In the case of industrial premises, noise zones are set up around the premises and these must not be exceeded, otherwise Abatement Notices may be served (*see* also Section 51, T & C Planning Act 1971).

The Public Health Act 1936, Section 94, makes provision for local authorities to take action in the event of nuisances, particularly where such nuisance may render a building unfit for habitation. The Public Health Act 1961, Section 30, and the Housing (Underground Rooms) Act 1959, Section 18, deal with habitable rooms below ground level, and the requirements of the local authority are very stringent in terms of light, ventilation and damp penetration (*see* Chapter 5).

Whilst discussing nuisances it is appropriate to mention the Rylands *v* Fletcher case of 1868, House of Lords, where the ruling was directed at occupiers who engage in hazardous activities on their properties. 'The person who, for his own purpose, brings onto his land and collects and keeps there anything likely to do mischief if it escapes, must keep it at his peril, and if he does not do so, is *prima facie* answerable for all damage which is the natural consequence of its escape'.

Liability involves:

(a) A bringing and accumulation on the land.
(b) The accumulation of things in a non-natural manner on the land, e.g. it is natural to store water on land for domestic purposes, but to do so on a large scale is unnatural.
(c) The storage of dangerous chemicals, electricity, gas; and would be likely to include anything stored in bulk which would cause damage if it escaped.
(d) There must be an escape of the thing from the land where it is kept and it must cause damage.

Animals are natural things and are not included; they are dealt with in the Animals Act 1971, and the Animal Boarding Establishments Act 1963. The EHO is also concerned with matters of public health in wider terms, e.g. the preparation and consumption of food and drink, toilet facilities, control of communicable diseases, and he is concerned with the Offices, Shops and Railway Premises Act 1963, and the Health & Safety at Work etc Act 1974.

In matters of plumbing and drainage installations, and alterations to existing systems, applications are made to the local authority on special forms accompanied by drawings of the proposals made on durable material for permanent record purposes. There is an overlapping of jurisdiction between the public health and building regulations, and the procedures vary. For example, the Greater London Council issues its own drainage bye-laws made under Section 34 (1) of the Public Health (London) Act 1936, and Section 87 (1) of the London Government Act 1963.

3.2.3 HM Factory Inspectorate and the Health & Safety at Work Executive

In work concerned with factories (*see* Factories Act 1961, Part XIV, Section 175, for definition of 'factory') the Architect is required to be cognizant of those sections of the Act which are applicable in the design and alteration of factory premises, or premises converted to factory use.

HM Factory Inspectorate is one of a number of inspectorates operating under the Health and Safety at Work Executive (*see* Sections 19, 20, of the Act), the Health & Safety Commission being responsible for policy making and legislative ammendments. The central Government control is through the Secretary of State for Employment and the Department of Employment.

There are 21 regional areas of the Factory Inspectorate, each under an Area Director who is a Senior Factory Inspector.

3.2.4 Water supply legislation

Water supplies for domestic, industrial, commercial, and public utility purposes, come from three main sources:

(1) Upland sources, or 'catchment areas', remote from towns drained by small streams which form natural lakes, or man-made lakes formed by means of dams, both of which are termed 'impounding reservoirs'.
(2) Lowland sources of large rivers fed from catchment areas.
(3) Deep wells.

The areas in (1) above are remote to avoid pollution, and rely upon natural gravity to supply water to 'service reservoirs' near to towns and cities to avoid costly pumping. Rivers drawing upon large 'catchment areas' are also a source of supply, and a high degree of pollution treatment, plus pumping costs, is off-set by a reduction in long pipe lines and dams. The river authorities play a large part in determining how much water is taken from the rivers after the requirements of the riparian owners (riparian = of, or on, a river bank) below the draw-off point has been met. The following is an example of a notice which might appear in the local press:

WATER RESOURCES ACT 1963

Notice of Application for a Licence to Abstract Water

Notice is hereby given that an application is being made to the Anglian Water–Great Ouse River Division by Mr J Smith, White House Farm, Routon, Norfolk, for a licence to extract water in the following quantities from the chalk strata at the following points of abstraction:

> For spray irrigation April/September 15 000 gallons per hour, 330 000 gallons per day, 18 800 000 gallons per year, on or near grid reference 000/111 in the parish of Routon.

A copy of the application and any map, plan, submitted with it may be inspected at the office of .... at all reasonable hours during the period beginning 12:12:83 to 9:1:84.
Any person wishing to make representation etc....

It is the duty of the river authorities, in collaboration with the water authorities, to test the water in rivers and to control their pollution.

Deep well holes are sunk by water authorities into permeable strata such as sand and limestone, and the well-water is then pumped into the 'service reservoirs'; it is usually unpolluted, but very hard water.

Artesian wells (the name originated from the French province of Artois) are sunk into natural valleys or basins, and the static head of water pressure provides water without pump assistance.

Water is distributed to the consumer in these two phases:

(1) Source to service reservoirs.
(2) Service reservoirs throughout the areas of supply by means of service mains.

The demand for water varies during the day from 15 to 40 per cent over the average demand, these peaks of demand being met by the service reservoirs which provide a local supply source without affecting the demand at source. The service reservoirs normally carry a three-day supply to meet local demand including emergencies such as fire fighting.

Legislation

Reservoirs – impounding and service reservoirs

Water Resources Acts 1945/63, with amendments to date, administered through the Water Resources Board.

Note: Not applicable to either Scotland or Northern Ireland.

Land Drainage Act 1950/76 relates to the Water Act 1945, with amendments to date.

Rivers and water courses

Water Resources Acts 1945/63, with amendments to date, River authorities administering model bye-laws from the Minister.

Note: Not applicable to either Scotland or Northern Ireland.

Rural Water Supplies and Sewerage Act 1944 (relates to the Public Health Act 1936).

Rivers (Prevention of Pollution) Acts 1951/61, with amendments to date.

Land Drainage Acts 1950/76.
Control of Pollution Act 1974, Part 2.

Note: The Secretary of State for the Environment was empowered under the Countryside Act 1968 Section 22, to encourage and control the use of impounded water, lakes and reservoirs, rivers, etc, for recreational purposes.

Service reservoirs to consumers

Water Act 1945, with amendments to date. This is the Principal Act as far as water supply is concerned.

From the Public Health Acts 1936/61 other legislation stems with regard to the specific requirements of water as follows:

(1) Housing Acts 1959/80.
(2) Offices, Shops and Railway Premises Act 1963.
(3) Factories Acts 1937/61.
(4) Public Utilities Street Works Act 1950.
(5) Local Government (Miscellaneous Provisions) Act 1953, Section 12.

Local bye-laws made by water authorities are usually directed towards the proper installation of piping and fittings, and the general control of water wastage; e.g. Thames Water Authority Bye-laws, formerly the Metropolitan Water Board Bye-laws 1964, made under Section 17 of the Water Act 1945, for preventing the waste, undue consumption, misuse, or contamination of water supplied by them.

References

Building Law for Students, K. MANSON, (Cassell)
Building Regulation – Practice and Procedure, F. D. ENTWISLE, (*Estates Gazette*)
London Building Acts 1930/78, GLC
London (Constructional) Amending Bye-laws 1979, GLC
The Building Regulations 1976 (HMSO)
Defective Premises Act 1972 (HMSO)
Factories Act 1961 (HMSO)
Fire Precautions Act 1971 (HMSO)
Health and Safety at Work etc Act 1974 (HMSO)
Highways Act 1980 (HMSO)
Housing Acts 1959/80
Offices, Shops and Railway Premises Act 1963 (HMSO)
Public Health Acts 1936/61 (HMSO)
Public Health (London) Act 1936 (HMSO)
Note: This list is not comprehensive and the list given in the RIBA Guidance Notes for the Final Examination in Architecture, Part 3, should be referred to.
Questions and Answers on 'A' Level Law, V. POWELL-SMITH, (Butterworths)

4

Town and country planning legislation and procedure

4.1.1 Historical synopsis

Unlike building regulations and bye-laws, town and country planning is a child of the twentieth century. The Housing, Town Planning etc Act 1909 introduced the concept of 'planning law'. Local Councils were authorized to prepare a town planning scheme for their own areas showing land in the course of development or to be developed. The plan had to be approved by the Local Government Board, and subsequently by the Minister concerned. This Act had little impact, it merely laid down what type of development would be allowed to continue.

The subsequent Act, the Housing, Town Planning etc Act 1919, made it obligatory for boroughs whose population exceeded 20 000 to submit a scheme for town planning; interim development permission was provided whilst plans were prepared, with compensation being paid to persons affected by the plan.

The Housing etc Act 1923 stated that once a scheme for development had been prepared, and within a month of a claim for compensation, the scheme could be modified.

The Local Government Act 1929 made the county council the local planning authorities, and also provided for county district councils to delegate their authority (under the Town Planning Act 1925) to county councils.

The Town & County Planning Act 1932 secured control of development by making planning schemes compulsory, with interim orders permitting certain types of development to continue during the preparation of the schemes, but no penalties were imposed for failure to apply for permission to develop.

The Town & Country Planning (Interim Development) Act 1943 brought all areas under control, and introduced Enforcement Notices. The Ministry of Town & Country Planning was formed.

The Town & Country Planning Act 1944 dealt with the redevelopment of blitzed and blight areas, overspill and compulsory purchase. Designated Orders were introduced covering areas which eventually would be compulsorily purchased.

The Town & Country Planning Act 1947 (the then Principal Act) set down the existing use of all land as on the appointed day as the authorized use, and prohibited any landowner from developing his land other than as authorized under the Act. Land which changed hands after the appointed day was also restricted to the use authorized on the appointed day. Development charges were introduced which the developer was legally obliged to pay on completion of the development.

The Town & Country Planning Act 1953 abolished development charges and negated the intentions of the 1947 Act to nationalize land.

The Town & Country Planning Act 1954 made provision for compensation to be paid if the applicant was refused permission to develop, and if he did not already have a development charge application.

The 1947 Act introduced the 'development plan' which every local authority had to prepare for its own area and which were renewable every five years. The Act also conferred on local authorities wider powers to undertake their own developments; compensation for redevelopment was stated.

It would seem that the involved legal ownership of land coupled with opposing ideological views of the Socialist and Conservative governments, has resulted in a lack of comprehensive and positive town and country planning policy, thus creating anomilies in decision making. The Socialist government introduced the Land Commission Act 1967 and the Community Land Act 1975, both of which intended to take land under the control of central government and to impose 'betterment levy' against the development of land. However, both these Acts were shortlived; the first was repealed in 1970 and the second in 1980.

Whatever system of government is in power, the original intentions of the Town & Country Planning Act 1947 still obtain, i.e.

(1) To replace former systems of planning schemes with a new system of flexible development plans (now called 'structure plans'), subject to continuous review by planning authorities, and ministerial approval.
(2) With certain exceptions, to prohibit development being undertaken without planning permission being obtained from the local planning authority.
(3) To continue with compulsory purchase of land by local authorities, and to give them wider powers in their own developments.
(4) To provide for financial assistance to local planning authorities to enable them to increase and discharge their functions under the Acts, including acquisition, development, and redevelopment of land.

4.1.2 Planning blight

The allocation of land for compulsory acquisition for whatever reason where this is stated in the structure plans, gives rise to problems for owners within these areas. The possibility of selling property at the current market value is seriously affected by 'planning blight'; in many such cases proposals may not take place for many years, but the effect upon the area is profound. Provision is made in the Town & Country Planning Act 1971, Sections 192–207, for Purchase Notices, (commonly called 'blight notices') to be served upon the planning authority. This can be done only if the proposals in the structure plan have been approved by the Minister, and fall within the specified descriptions in Sections 192 (6) of the Act.

Notices may be served by:

(a) the resident owner/occupier of the hereditament
(b) the owner/occupier of any hereditament with a net annual rateable value not exceeding the prescribed limit
(c) the owner/occupier of an agricultural holding

'Owner/occupier' means a freeholder, or a lessee with at least three years unexpired lease to run. 'Hereditament' means all the land included in the valuation for rating purposes, Section 207 (1) of the Act.

The Purchase Notice requires the authority to purchase the property forthwith, but the authority may serve a counter-notice within two months, and the matter is then referred to the Lands Tribunal who may reject or uphold the Notice. If the original Notice is not contested, or the Lands Tribunal uphold the Notice, then the authority must purchase the interest.

4.1.3 Aims and objectives of planning law

To provide for planning the development and use of land, the terms 'development' and 'land' have the meanings as described and defined in the Town & Country Planning Act 1971, Part III, Section 22 (1).

'Development' is divided into 'operations' and 'uses', the former being described as 'the carrying-out of building, engineering, mining or other operations, in, on, over, or under the land', and the latter as 'the making of any material change in the use of any buildings or other land'.

When development is proposed the T & C Planning General Development Order 1977 and the Amendment Orders 1980/81 should be consulted to ascertain if planning permission is required for a proposed development involving operations, and Schedule 1, Class III for change of use, subject to Article 4 of the Order. The T & C Planning General Development Order 1977 lists 23 classes of permitted development related to Section 24 of the T & C Planning Act 1971, but caution should be exercised as they are still subject to the definition of 'development' within the meaning of the Act, and may also be subject to limitations and conditions which must be observed, failing which, enforcement action may be taken by the planning authority.

Similarly, the T & C Planning (Use Classes) Order 1972 gives 18 use classes grouped into similar-use classes, whereby changes of use within the same group does not constitute a 'material change of use' and, other things being equal, are considered as permitted development not requiring application or planning permission.

If there is any doubt as to whether planning permission should or should not be applied for, application should be made to the planning authority under the T & C Planning Act 1971, Section 53, to determine this.

Administration

The central government administration is under the jurisdiction of the Secretary of State for the Environment through the Department of the Environment, in association with the Secretary of State for Wales, and the Secretary of State for Trade and Industry, (*see* page 29).

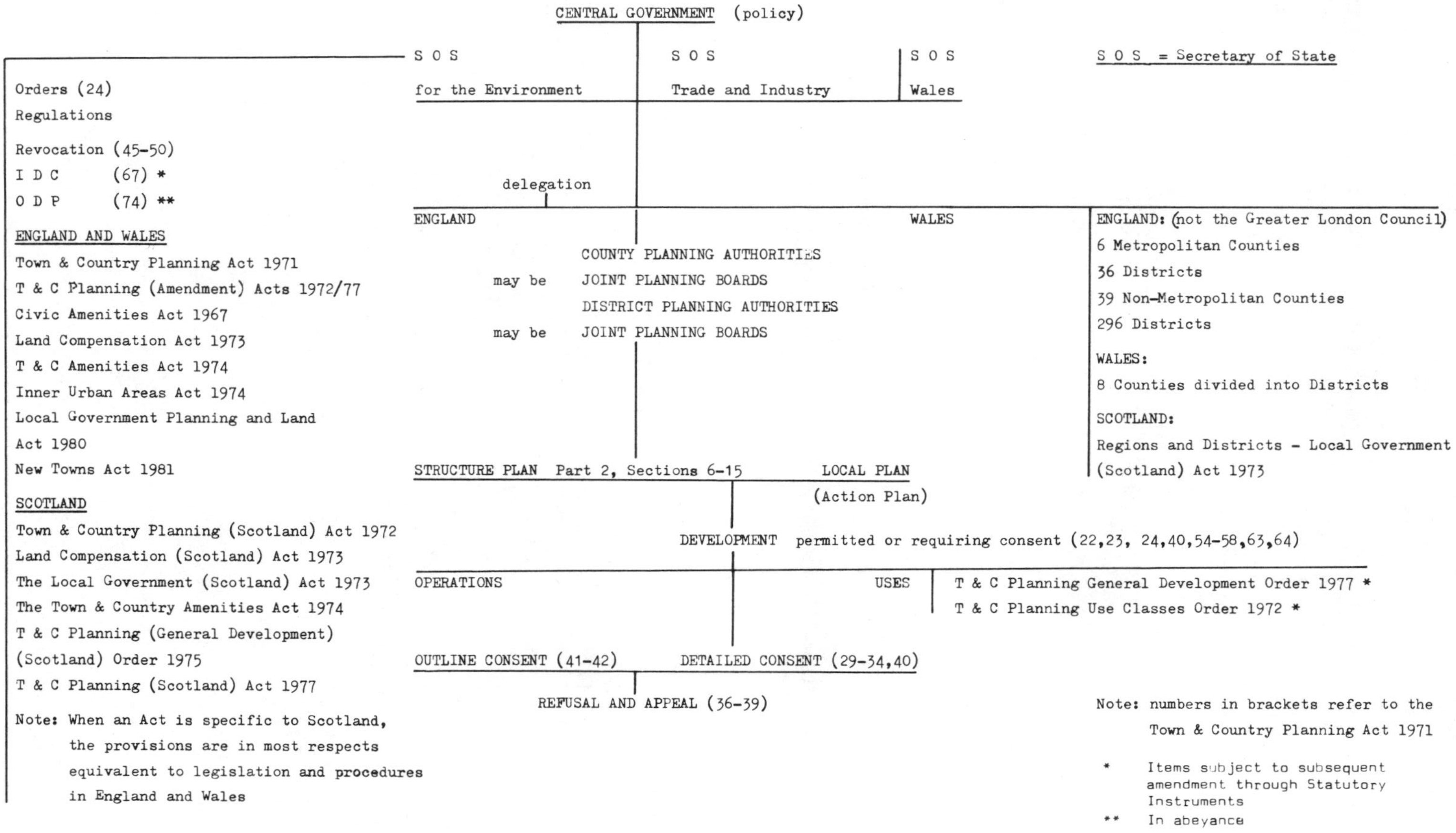

CENTRAL GOVERNMENT (policy)

S O S for the Environment | S O S Trade and Industry | S O S Wales

S O S = Secretary of State

Orders (24)
Regulations

Revocation (45–50)
I D C (67) *
O D P (74) **

ENGLAND AND WALES

Town & Country Planning Act 1971
T & C Planning (Amendment) Acts 1972/77
Civic Amenities Act 1967
Land Compensation Act 1973
T & C Amenities Act 1974
Inner Urban Areas Act 1974
Local Government Planning and Land Act 1980
New Towns Act 1981

SCOTLAND

Town & Country Planning (Scotland) Act 1972
Land Compensation (Scotland) Act 1973
The Local Government (Scotland) Act 1973
The Town & Country Amenities Act 1974
T & C Planning (General Development) (Scotland) Order 1975
T & C Planning (Scotland) Act 1977

Note: When an Act is specific to Scotland, the provisions are in most respects equivalent to legislation and procedures in England and Wales

delegation

ENGLAND | WALES

COUNTY PLANNING AUTHORITIES
may be JOINT PLANNING BOARDS
DISTRICT PLANNING AUTHORITIES
may be JOINT PLANNING BOARDS

ENGLAND: (not the Greater London Council)
6 Metropolitan Counties
36 Districts
39 Non-Metropolitan Counties
296 Districts

WALES:
8 Counties divided into Districts

SCOTLAND:
Regions and Districts – Local Government (Scotland) Act 1973

STRUCTURE PLAN Part 2, Sections 6–15 | LOCAL PLAN (Action Plan)

DEVELOPMENT permitted or requiring consent (22,23, 24,40,54–58,63,64)

OPERATIONS | USES

T & C Planning General Development Order 1977 *
T & C Planning Use Classes Order 1972 *

OUTLINE CONSENT (41–42) | DETAILED CONSENT (29–34,40)

REFUSAL AND APPEAL (36–39)

Note: numbers in brackets refer to the Town & Country Planning Act 1971

* Items subject to subsequent amendment through Statutory Instruments
** In abeyance

Diagram 8: Town and country planning structure and administration in England and Wales

The local administration is either the county council as the local planning authority for a county (which may be a Joint Planning Board), or a district council as the planning authority for a district (which might also be a Joint Planning Board).

After the local government reform in 1972 the former borough, urban, and rural district councils may still exist as towns or parishes, except in larger urban areas, together with former parishes, and in Wales as communities or sub-divisions of districts, again except in larger urban areas.

4.1.4 The Architect's responsibilities

Within the RIBA Architect's Appointment the Architect undertakes in Work Stage B, 1.8, to advise on the need to obtain planning permission, and under Work Stage D, 1.12, to make application for planning permission. Similar provision being made in the Small Works Edition Part 1, 1.5 and Part 2, 2.14.

The Architect is absolved from guaranteeing that planning consent will be granted, and the provisions for revocation in the T&C Planning Act 1971, Section 45 should be remembered.

Provision is also made in the RIBA Architect's Appointment, Part 2.29, for the Architect to undertake 'exceptional negotiations' with a planning authority, and under 2.32 to make submissions to the Royal Fine Arts Commission, or other non-statutory bodies; fees for these services are negotiable and in addition to the preliminary and basic services.

Since 9 January 1982, the Minister has made the T&C Planning (Industrial Development Certificates) (Prescribed Classes of Building) Regulations 1981 (SI 1981 No 1826) removing special control over industrial buildings as described in the T&C Planning Act 1971, Sections 66–72. These relaxations, however, are not retrospective. The Local Government, Planning and Land Act 1980 made new provisions for the setting up of enterprise zones in which, in effect, automatic planning permission would be granted subject to limitations laid down in the enterprise zone scheme. (*see* 'Enterprise Zones', Inner Cities Directorate, Room P2/102, Department of the Environment, Marsham Street, London SW1P BE).

Diagram 8 on page 29 shows both Office Development Permits and Industrial Development Certificates as 'in abeyance' but are included to show that interim controls for specific areas of development can be introduced as deemed necessary by central government.

4.1.5 Applications (Form TP1)

Application for consent in principle, or 'outline consent' is possible under the T&C Planning Act 1971, Section 42. This is made in the normal way, but the application is marked 'outline', and must be accompanied by a site and block plan to required scale sufficient to identify the land and its immediate environs, together with a written description of the development proposed. When granted, outline consent is valid for a period of three years from the date of approval, and will usually contain 'reserved matters' which must be resolved with the planning authority within this period (Section 42, 2 (b) of the Act) and a detailed planning application made. When detailed consent is granted it is valid for a further two years, making a total of five years from the date of the outline consent. A substantial start must be made on the works within the two-year period from the granting of the detailed consent as required by Section 43 (1) of the Act.

These two important points arise from outline consents:

(1) They apply only to operations and not to changes of use.
(2) They are consents in principle only, and full detailed consent must be obtained, including the resolution of any 'reserved matters', before any building work to which the consent relates commences on site.
(3) Detail consent is normally valid for five years (Section 41.1).

Consultation with the planning authority at an early stage in any proposed development is strongly advised, although this is informal discussion, it does 'test the temperature of the water' in planning terms, but it should always be borne in mind that this is informal guidance only, and the granting of planning consent rests with the planning committee concerned which may not necessarily concur with the informal advice given to the applicant.

4.1.6 Refusal of planning permission

The RIBA Architect's Appointment, Part 2.29 or SW 2.13, deals with this aspect of the Architect's services. When an application for planning permission results in a refusal by the planning authority, the Architect must carefully consider what course of action to advise his client to take, since the Architect is the client's agent in this regard, and will require permission from the client to proceed with such course of action as is decided. The reason for refusal is normally given, and may possibly be resolved by making such changes to the submitted proposals as will satisfy the planning authority, either by possibly a letter of agreement to the changes or by a re-submission of amended proposals.

If, however, the refusal is a more serious matter regarded by the planning authority as being development contrary to the planning policy for the area concerned, it may be necessary to appeal to the Secretary of State who, under Section 36 of the 1971 Act, has power to determine an appeal against the decision of the local planning authority; and Section 36(8) and Schedule 9 of the 1971 Act provide for certain appeals to be heard and determined by an Inspector appointed by the Minister for the purpose. When the appeal has been decided by the Inspector, the decision becomes that of the Secretary of State. An Inspector's decision may, however, be challenged in court under Section 245 of the 1971 Act.

Since the T&C Planning (Determination of Appeals by Appointed Persons) (Prescribed Classes) Regulations 1981, SI 1981 No. 804, from 1 July 1981 all appeals under Sections 36, 37 of the 1971 Act, i.e. appeals against refusal of applications for planning permission, and all appeals against enforcement notices (Section 88 of the 1971 Act) are to be determined by Inspectors on behalf of the Secretary of State. This does not apply to statutory undertakers where development of land relates to Section 225(1) of the 1971 Act.

Appeals have to be lodged with the Secretary of State within six months of the local planning authority's decision or the expiry of such other period of time when such a decision ought to have been given (Section 36(2) 1971 Act).

Although as has been said, the Secretary of State has the power to determine an application referred to him for decision following a refusal by a local planning authority (Section 36 of the 1971 Act), he is also empowered under Section 35, and GDO 1977, to ask for an application to be referred to him for decision (termed 'called-in' applications) and may include an application for approval by a local planning authority of 'reserved matters' in an outline planning consent granted by the authority under Section 35(1) of the 1971 Act. Section 35(6) of the Act states that 'the decision of the Secretary of State on any application referred to him under this section shall be final', but may be challenged in the High Court on a point of law.

4.1.7 Listed buildings

Listed buildings are buildings of special architectural or historic interest, including not just the building itself but also any feature of its exterior contributing to the architectural or historic interest of any group of buildings of which it forms a part (Section 54(1) 1971 Act).

Similar control is exercised over ancient monuments by the Ancient Monuments and Archeological Areas Act 1979, as well as the T&C Amenities Act 1974.

4.1.8 Conservation areas

Control of demolition in conservation areas is effected under the T&C Planning (Amendment) Act 1972, which includes Scotland, Sections 8, 9, and the T&C Amenities Act 1974; Section 10 of the former Act provides for grants and loans for the preservation and enhancement of character and appearance in conservation areas.

Although painting of houses and other premises is permitted development under the T&C Planning General Development Order 1977, Schedule 1, Class 2(3), the planning authority has the power to control painting of premises where the general character and amenity of the area so dictate.

It is also possible that covenants attached to land control the colour and type of paint to be used and the frequency of painting. This is quite strictly adhered to in trust estates, as discussed in Chapter 3, 3.1.9.

4.1.9 Demolition, generally

There would appear to be a number of factors to be considered in demolition, operations, and uses, insofar as compliance with the planning authority's requirements is concerned.

Demolition has not been considered as 'development' *per se* within the meaning of the Act; on the other hand, partial demolition has been, in certain circumstances (Coleshill & District Investment Ltd *v* Minister of Housing and Local Government).

In terms of 'operations' it would appear that demolition or destruction negates any previous use rights (Gray *v* Minister of Housing & Local Government).

In terms of 'uses' the important issue seems to be whether the 'use' has been continuous in planning terms, and whether limitations on this use have been imposed from the outset (Guildford RDC *v* Fortescue; Same *v* Penny).

An excellent report by George Dobry, QC, titled *Control of Demolition* (HMSO), was instigated by the Department of the Environment in 1974.

Apart from the control of demolition under Section 55(1) T&C Planning Act 1971, in the City of London and the Inner London Boroughs of the GLC the District Surveyor must be notified before any demolition work is carried out, under the provisions of the London Building Acts (Amendment) Act 1939, Section 83. Elsewhere in England and Wales a Notice under Section 29 of the Public Health Act 1961 must be served on the local authority before any demolition work takes place.

If demolition works are likely to exceed a period of six weeks in operation, HM Factory Inspectorate must be notified under the Factories Act 1961, Section 127(7). (HM Factory Inspectorate is now embodied into the Health & Safety at Work Inspectorate).

In Scotland a warrant must be in accordance with the Buildings Authority, and the work must be in accordance with the Building Regulations under the Building (Scotland) Act 1959, as amended to date.

Adjoining owners also have rights under both statutory and common law provisions, and notices where applicable must be served on them as required by law so that agreement may be reached on matters such as rights of support, rights of light, disturbance, noise, nuisance, protection of property, etc.

Failure to comply with the foregoing provisions may result in injunctions or other legal actions being pursued by persons so affected.

In the City of London and the Inner London Boroughs of the GLC the provisions of the London Building Acts (Amendment) Act 1939, Part VI, will obtain, and should be referred to for proper service of notices (*see* Appendix and page 47 for outline procedure).

For the Architect it is important to ensure, particularly where demolition works are to be carried out under a separate contract from the general building works, that such contracts contain clauses adequately covering the client's interests in matters of insurance for all those matters which are embodied in the JCT Standard Form of Building Contract 1980, and also to take cognizance of any other insurances which may be prudent to consider.

The British Standard for Demolition is BS 6187.

The problem of bonfires on demolition sites is covered in the British Standard, and are also dealt with under the Clean Air Act 1968, Part 1, (5). One should also consider the provisions of the Control of Pollution Act 1974.

4.1.10 Enforcement and Stop Notices

Development undertaken without planning consent or contrary to planning legislation, where it is not 'permitted development' as previously discussed, will, upon discovery of the infringement by the planning authority, be countered by an Enforcement Notice under Section 87, Part V, T & C Planning Act 1971, where the planning authority considers the circumstances warrant it; also, within the time required for the Enforcement Notice to take effect, they may serve a Stop Notice to prevent further operations being proceeded with.

The correct serving of the Notices by the planning authority would appear, from cases heard on appeal, to be a critical factor in the force of their success.

It should not be assumed that the two Notices are synonymous in their action; indeed, at the time of the introduction of Stop Notices the Minister issued a Circular 4/69 giving guidance on their use.

4.2.1 Advice and information

Within normal working hours everyone has access to the structure plan, or local plan, for an area; these are held by the planning authority and may be seen on request.

Also, the following information can be obtained concerning any site or land within the Planning authority's jurisdiction.

(1) *Zoning:* The designation of land for a particular use, e.g. domestic, light industrial, commercial, agricultural, 'white land', etc.
(2) *Plot ratio:* The permissible area of a building which may be built in relation to the total site area, e.g. 1:1, 4:1, etc.
(3) *Density:* Relates to the number of dwellings per hectare for a given area which is permitted by the planning authority and which must not be exceeded.
(4) *Angles of light:* The permitted light angles related to a particular site in terms of heights of buildings, the angles being taken from the roads, paths, boundaries, etc, adjacent to the site.
(5) *Improvement lines:* Lines of building frontage (building lines) may be set back in new development to provide for future road widening schemes in association with the highway authority (*see also* Highways Act 1980, Sections 73, 74).
(6) *Listed buildings:* Buildings which are of architectural or historic interest (*see* page 31) may be listed under the T & C Planning Act 1971, Part VI, Sections 54, *et seq*, to protect them from demolition or alteration.
(7) *Sight lines:* Where corner sites are concerned the planning authority in association with the highways authority will insist upon adequate sight lines at the road junctions (Highways Act 1980).

As with building regulations and bye-laws, planning applications are dealt with by committees; in the case of planning controls, application dates are even more important as the statutory time, two months, may be extended as the planning authority may deem necessary. It is essential that application dates be adhered to otherwise lengthy delays can ensue. You should advise your client of the statutory times required for dealing with applications, and also the possibility of extensions.

If you are asked by your client to proceed on the basis of a planning consent, either outline or detailed, through a source other than your own practice, do not accept it at face value; check the validity of the consent in terms of time, and ensure that in the case of an outline consent the 'reserved matters' are capable of resolution before making a detailed application. In both cases ensure that the proposed development conforms with the terms of the consent, and also that those items in (1)–(7) above have been properly considered.

Do not forget to advise your client that fees are payable by him with respect to planning applications in accordance with the T & C Planning (Fees for Applications and Deemed Applications) Regulations 1982, which is a Statutory Instrument.

4.2.2 The Highways Acts 1959–1980

These Acts are of significance for the Architect in that in a number of ways they impinge upon matters affecting the construction of buildings in relation to highways. The latest Act of 1980 consolidates previous legislation.

Some of the salient points are as follows:

(1) The design of housing estates and other developments intending to create new roads.
(2) The creation of footways and bridle paths.
(3) The adoption of roads by local authorities.
(4) Improvement lines for road widening (these may be seen upon application to the highways authority, also the planning department of the local authority).
(5) The designation by the highways authority of lines of building frontage, i.e. building lines. Where prescribed, no new building, other than a boundary wall or fence may be erected in advance of this line without permission. This applies to extensions and additions to buildings.
(6) Where access to premises is required the highways authority will invoke Section 184, i.e. crossing over the carriageway, and may carry out the work themselves and charge the building's owner accordingly.
(7) Miscellaneous works to highways including, *inter alia*, improvement, safety, widths, levels, corners, trees, shrubs, verges, lighting, fences, boundaries, etc.
(8) The projection over the highway or public footway of obstructions, e.g. fire doors, canopies, shop blinds, etc.
(9) Construction and subsequent alteration of building constructed over highways maintained at public expense, requiring a licence from the highways authority, which is registered as a local land charge (*see* page 53).
(10) Section 168 deals with accidents occuring in or near a street during the course of carrying out building works and giving rise to serious bodily injury to persons in the street. The building's owner may be subject to a maximum fine of £500.
(11) Section 174 relates to the foregoing, requiring safety measures such as shoring, etc, to afford protection and support to buildings adjoining streets.
     This section also deals with builders' skips placed on highways and is read in conjunction with Sections 139 and 140.

Space does not permit of more than a resumé of this important Act which it is recommended should be read *in toto*.

References

An Outline of Planning Law, SIR D. HEAP (Sweet & Maxwell)
Planning Law and Procedure, A. E. TELLING (Butterworths)
Highways Act 1980 (HMSO)
Town and Country Amenities Act 1974 (HMSO)
Town and Country Planning Act 1971 (HMSO)
Town and Country Planning (Amendment) Act 1972 (HMSO)
Town and Country Planning General Development Order 1977 and (Amendment) Order 1981 (HMSO)
Town and Country Planning Use Classes Order 1972 (HMSO)

Note: This list is not comprehensive and the list given in the RIBA Guidance Notes for the Final Examination in Architecture, Part 3, should be referred to.

5

Housing law

Housing law, in general terms, deals with housing conditions and the several duties of local authorities in this respect.

One must carefully distinguish between housing law and public health law, as the Building Regulations 1976 and the Greater London Council (GLC) bye-laws are issued under Section 4, and Schedule 1 of the Public Health Act 1961 (as amended by the Health & Safety at Work etc Act 1974, Section 61), and the London Building Acts 1930/78 respectively (*see also* the Health & Safety at Work etc Act 1974, Section 70).

With the exception of public sector housing, i.e. local authority housing, the law of landlord and tenant is not considered to be part of housing law as such.

The principal Act in housing law is the Housing Act 1957 which was amended in 1961, 1964, 1973, 1980; this last had, *inter alia*, very important implications for housing societies who were, within certain limitations, given the right to sell their properties.

The financial implications of implementing these Acts has given rise to other legislation in excess of that provided for in the Acts themselves, e.g. the Housing (Financial Provisions) Act 1958 and the Housing Finance Act 1972.

5.1.1 Administering authorities

Central government control is entrusted to the Secretary of State for the Environment, this control being administered by the local authorities.

Local housing authorities are district councils, except for the Inner and Outer London boroughs of the GLC, where the responsibility is divided between the GLC and the London boroughs. The London boroughs have responsibility for the whole range of housing, but the GLC may exercise power under Part V of the Housing Act 1957, i.e. the provision of housing accommodation.

Powers are also limited in respect to county councils outside London.

5.1.2 Private sector housing law

Houses unfit for human habitation: Housing Act 1957, Section 4

Every local authority must ascertain whether all houses in its area of jurisdiction are fit for human habitation, and in the event of any premises being considered unfit the Medical Officer of Health must make official representations.

Under Section 4 of the Act, as amended by the Housing Act 1969, Sections 5 and 18, a premises must be considered only in respect of the following:

> repair, stability, freedom from damp, internal arrangement, natural lighting, ventilation, water supply, drainage and sanitary conveniences, disposal of waste water, facilities for the preparation and cooking of food.

The question to be considered in any of these matters is degree, as of themselves they do not individually or collectively render a house unfit for occupation, only if one or all of them is considered to be capable of rendering the premises unfit in its present condition. 'Back-to-back' houses were prohibited under Section 5 of the Act, but this ban was repealed by the Housing Act 1980, Schedule 25 (4).

Basement rooms, i.e. where the floor level of the rooms is more than three feet below the level of the adjoining street, are dealt with in Section 18 of the Housing Act 1980, and also in the Public Health Act 1961, Section 30. The matters dealt with encompass ventilation and lighting, dampness, effluvia, or exhaltation of fumes.

The local authority deals with the person having control of the house, i.e. the owner/occupier, landlord, or long-term lessee where only a nominal ground rent is paid; in the last case it is the lessee who is assumed to have control of the premises (Housing Act 1961, S.16).

The local authority procedure in the case of unfitness for habitation is, in the first instance, to consider whether the premises can at reasonable expense be made fit for habitation, and if so, issue a 'repair notice' which specifies the work to be done not less than 21 days from the service of the notice. If the work is not done there is no penalty, but the local authority has the power to enter upon the premises and to carry out repairs and look for the owner for immediate recompense, or in instalments over a period of up to 30 years. The debt is a charge on the premises registered with the local Land Charges Registry, and this can be conveyed with the property in the event of sale. The local authority has all the rights of a mortgagee, and may obtain permission and sell the property to recover the debt. (*See also* Dangerous Structures Notices, page 17).

If the local authority considers that a premises cannot be made fit for human habitation at a reasonable cost, they must invite the owner (i.e. the person in control) to discuss the problem; within 21 days thereafter the owner may undertake to do work as may be necessary to make the house fit, the local authority having jurisdiction to agree a specified period in which this work may be done.

In the absence of any such undertaking the local authority may take any of three courses of action:

(1) Issue a 'Demolition Order', giving notice to vacate the premises within a reasonable period, not less than 21 days, and to demolish the premises within six weeks thereafter. These periods may be extended. Failure on the part of the owner to demolish within the prescribed period may result in the local authority demolishing the property and selling the materials of any value, and sueing the owner for the amount of any balance resulting from the demolition operations and costs.

(2) Issue a 'Closing Order' which would be used in the following circumstances:

   (a) Where demolition would result in the removal of support from adjoining premises.
   (b) Where the premises could be used for a purpose other than human habitation, e.g. storage.
   (c) Where only part of the premises, say the basement, is unfit for human habitation.
   (d) If the building is a listed building of historic or architectural interest.

(3) The local authority may issue a Compulsory Purchase Order.

The Act provides for a right of appeal to the County Court by any interested person within 21 days following any one of these actions by the local authority.

Having issued either a Demolition Order or a Closing Order the local authority has an imposed duty under Section 39 of the Land Compensation Act 1973 to provide suitable alternative accommodation. Re-housing may be assumed by the GLC, or be imposed on a development corporation, or the Commissioner for New Towns. However, the responsible authority for the displacement must defray any net loss incurred by the re-housing authority (Section 42 of the Act). Only the person residing in the house at the time of the service of the Order is entitled to re-housing obligation, and no one else.

Houses in multiple occupation

These are premises occupied by persons who do not form a single household or hereditament (Section 59 of the Housing Act 1969; *See also* Section 16 of the Housing Act 1961, Means of Escape in Case of Fire). The Housing Acts 1961, 1964 and 1969 give to local authorities certain powers with respect to houses in multiple occupation. (*See also* GLC Code of Practice).

Registration

The Housing Act 1961, Section 22, empowers local authorities to submit to the Secretary of State a scheme of registration of houses which, or part of which, are let in lodgings, or which are occupied by members of more than one family, and of buildings which comprise separate dwellings, two or more of which do not have a sanitary convenience and personal washing facilities accessible only to those living in the dwelling.

The authority may, on certain grounds, refuse to register a house, or require that specific work be carried out before registration. Infringements of registration schemes carry penalties on summary conviction.

Code of management

The Housing Act 1961, Section 13, authorizes the Secretary of State to make regulations prescribing a code of management for any house in multiple occupation, and such a code was issued in 1962 titled

Housing (Management of Houses in Multiple Occupation) Regulations SI 1962/668.

Control order

Any house found by the local authority to be in an unsatisfactory condition may be brought under control by the issue of an order applying the code conditions for occupation. Appeal against an order may be made to the County Court within 21 days of the service of the order. The local authority may also prescribe the maximum number of persons to be housed in multiple occupations, and may also order specified works to improve the premises.

Overcrowding

Abatement of overcrowding under the Housing Act 1957, Part 4

A dwelling-house is deemed to be overcrowded where the number of persons sleeping on the premises are either

two persons being more than ten years old and of opposite sex, not being persons living together as husband and wife, sleeping in the same room.

OR

In excess of the number permitted by either of the following tables (Schedule 6).

Note: Table 1 prescribes the number of persons per room (normally two) in relation to the number of rooms.
Table 2 prescribes the number of persons allowed in a room in relation to its size (*see* Parker Morris Standards 1961). Only a room with an area of 110 sq. ft. or more is considered to be a 'full unit' providing accommodation for two persons. A smaller room may accommodate one or 1½ persons; a child under the age of ten years is classified as half a person; an infant under the age of one year is ignored.

5.1.3 Special areas

In general improvement of housing, there are three designated areas: clearance areas, housing action areas, general improvement areas. The Housing Act 1974 created 'priority neighbourhoods', but these were repealed under the Housing Act 1980, Section 109 (3).

Clearance areas

A local authority may effect a clearance area, either by agreement with the owners or by compulsory purchase (*see* Covenants, Chapter 7, 7.1.4).

Before this is done the local authority must pass a Resolution to create a clearance area, and must satisfy the following:

That all houses are unfit for habitation by reason of their bad arrangement or environs, and are injurious to the health of, or are a danger to, the inhabitants.

Buildings in the area, other than those for habitation, would have to be considered in the same terms.

The most satisfactory method of dealing with the area is the demolition of all the buildings contained in it.

That the local authority can provide alternative accommodation for those displaced by the demolition.

That the local authority has the resources to finance the plan.

The Secretary of State must receive, for information only, a copy of the Resolution which must be accompanied by a statement of the number of persons involved in the displacement.

Houses may be retained within the area 'for the time being', which means making them wind and weatherproof, a condition which may last for some years. The expression 'twilight housing' is sometimes applied to such premises, and schemes by organizations such as 'Shelter' may prevail upon local authorities to release these houses as temporary shelter for the homeless. They also become subject to 'squatters' and more undesirable elements of society.

Under the Land Compensation Act 1973, persons displaced by reason of clearance areas may be entitled to a 'home loss payment' which a sum of money equivalent to three times the rateable value of the premises, subject to a minimum of £150 and a maximum of £1500, but under Section 30 of the Act the Secretary of State is empowered to vary these amounts and the rateable value multiplier.

Caravan dwellers on caravan sites may also claim home loss payments unless an alternative site is provided on reasonable terms, the caravan being the only or main residence and having a qualifying interest or right in the site.

Tenants in furnished accommodation are also entitled to claim home loss payments, as are tenants under contracts of employment.

Housing action areas

The Housing Act 1974, Section 36, provides for areas to be declared as 'housing action areas' by the local authority if the general living conditions within the area are unsatisfactory. They must be dealt with within five years to bring them up to a satisfactory standard, and to ensure proper and effective management and use of the accommodation. The Secretary of State may extend the five-year period by a further two years if the circumstances warrant it.

General improvement areas

These areas are created by the Housing Act 1969 as amended and consolidated by the Housing Act 1974. The local authority prescribes a 'Preliminary Resolution' for submission to the Secretary of State, who may veto it; otherwise the local authority may confirm the scheme in two local newspapers as designated, ensuring that all persons in the area are informed.

The effect of this designation is that larger sums by way of grants are made available for the improvement of the houses in the area concerned.

5.1.4 Grants for improving, converting and repairing houses

Types of grant available

The Housing Act 1974 consolidated previous provisions for grants and extended them for improvement, conversion, and repair of houses.

This stems from previous government policies to use resources on repairing and improving existing housing stocks rather than demolishing and rebuilding them.

Four basic types of grant are available:

(1) Intermediate grants in respect of works required for the improvement of dwellings to a modest standard by the provision of 'standand amenities' listed in Part 1, Schedule 6 of the Act as
  - a fixed bath or shower
  - a hot-and-cold water supply at a fixed bath or shower
  - a wash-hand basin
  - a hot-and-cold water supply at a wash-hand basin
  - a sink
  - a hot-and-cold water supply at a sink
  - a water closet

(2) Special grants in respect of houses in multiple occupation by reason of works for standard amenities and escape from fire.

(3) Improvement grants for conversion of dwellings or other buildings into dwellings or self-contained living units to a standard higher than that provided by only standard amenities. The improvement of dwellings for the disabled is included in this category.

(4) Repair grants for works of repair not included in the previous three categories.

Provision with respect to the application for and approval of grants falls within the following:

(5) No grant may be given in respect of a dwelling erected after 2 October 1961 (subject to exceptions).

(6) The applicant should be a 'freeholder', or a 'leaseholder' with not less than five years unexpired lease, or a 'protected' or 'secured' tenant.

(7) The initial grant is not sacrosanct, but may be extended at the discretion of the local authority.

(8) All grants are based upon an 'appropriate percentage' of the cost of the works; grants may be 50, 60 or 70 per cent or in some cases as much as 90 per cent depending upon the nature of the improvement. Percentages may be changed by the Secretary of State.

(9) All applications must be accompanied by either a 'certificate of future occupation', or a 'certificate of availability for letting', whichever is appropriate. In the first case the applicant must intend to live in the house for five years, and in the second case that the house will be available for letting as a residential property for five years, not including letting as holiday accommodation or bed-and-breakfast accommodation. In the event of these requirements being trangressed, the applicant may be required to pay back the whole of the grant or such portion as may have been received. This requirement protects properties against get-rich-quick developers using grant aids to carry out conversions. The grantee's family or his successors after death may occupy the premises as stated in the Housing Act 1980.

Intermediate grants

The payment of intermediate grants is not discretionary but mandatory on the local authority who have to pay it after they are satisfied that when the works have been completed in accordance with the grant application:

(a) The house will be provided with all the standard amenities exclusive to the use of the occupants.

(b) The house will be in good repair, excluding internal decorations, having due regard to its age, character, and the locality.

(c) That thermal insulation standards will comply with the requirements of the Secretary of State (i.e. Building Regulation standards).

(d) That in all other respects the house will be fit for human habitation, as stated on page 34, or as may be at the discretion of the local authority.

(e) The premises will be available for use for a period of 15 years as a dwelling-house, or such other period as may be specified by the Secretary of State.

Eligible expenses or maximum amount of costs

These are expressed by Statutory Instrument – Grants by Local Authorities (Eligible Expenses Limits) Order (SI 1980/1736). The limits per unit are £3500 in London and £2500 elsewhere, but these limits are subject to changes by SI issued by the Secretary of State.

Special grants

This is a discretionary grant for houses in multiple occupation, and provides for standard amenities for shared rather than for individual usage of occupants. The standard is higher than the ordinary standard amenity grant.

Improvement grants

These are also discretionary, and provide for the following:

(a) The house will provide all the standard amenities for the exclusive use of the occupants.
(b) The premises will be in good repair, excluding internal decorative condition, having regard to its age, character, and locality.
(c) That the premises will conform to the twelve points as set down in the Secretary of State's Circular 160/74, para 11, which are as follows:

    Be substantially free from dampness.
    Adequate lighting and ventilation in each habitable room.
    Safe and adequate artificial lighting, with sufficient socket outlets for safe and proper functioning of domestic appliances.
    Have adequate facilities for drainage of the premises.
    Be in stable structural condition.
    Have satisfactory internal arrangements (planning).
    Satisfactory facilities for the preparation and cooking of food.
    Be provided with adequate facilities for heating.
    Have proper fuel storage provision (where required).
    Proper storage for refuse.
    Comply with the Building Regulations requirements in respect of thermal insulation current at the time of the grant approval.
    That after improvement the premises will provide satisfactory accommodation for housing for a period of 30 years, which period may be decreased by the local authority but not to less than 10 years.

There are limits on rateable value and eligible expenses, but both are subject to change from time to time. Such limits do not apply to action housing areas or for premises improved for disabled persons.

Repair grants

A repair grant is discretionary, and may be paid on proof of the following:

(a) The works proposed are of a substantial structural character, or other prescribed requirements.
(b) In the case of an owner-occupied dwelling that it is situated outside a housing action area, and falls within the prescribed rateable value limits. Houses in housing action areas are not limited in this respect.
(c) That on completion of the works the dwelling will have attained a reasonable standard of repair commensurate with its age, character, and locality.

5.1.5 Compulsory improvement of dwellings

This normally applies only to Housing Action and General Improvement areas, but it may be extended to leasehold houses if the tenant makes a formal application to the local authority for improvement where the house is without some of the standard amenities and can be improved or repaired at reasonable cost.

The local authority issues a Provisional Notice to the owner to discuss the necessary works and any other relevant matters. If the owner fails to do anything to implement the works, the local authority may serve an Improvement Notice, which is not applicable to owner-occupied premises, since compulsory improvement of dwellings is primarily directed towards houses in tenant occupation.

Appeals against compulsory improvement may be made to the County Court. Where enforcement is necessary, the local authority may carry out the work, recovering expenses from the person in default. The local authority may also grant loans to owners for carrying out improvement works.

5.1.6 Conversion of property

In undertaking conversion, alteration, or extension of property it is essential that a comprehensive survey be carried out as discussed in Chapter 14, Surveys and Reports.

The broad issues which have to be considered are as follows:

(a) Covenants, easements, and licences (*see* Chapter 7, 7.1.4).

(b) Rights of adjoining owners (*see* Chapter 7, 7.1.1).
(c) Town and country planning controls (*see* Chapter 4).
(d) Building regulation and bye-law controls (*see* Chapter 3).
(e) Rights under controlled and other tenancies.
(f) Protection against fire and means of escape requirements (*see* Chapter 6).
(g) In premises other than dwellings, e.g.
    licensed premises, the Licensing Act 1964
    food preparation and/or sale, Food Hygiene Regulations 1970 Food & Drugs Act 1955.
(h) Housing Acts 1957/74/80.
(i) Highways Acts 1959/80, especially lines of building frontage, 'building lines', and any projection over or onto the public highway, e.g. fire-escape doors, shop blinds, etc.
(j) Public Health Acts 1936/61.
    Public Health (London) Act 1936.
(k) Fire Precautions Act 1971 where a fire certificate is required (*see* Chapter 6).
(l) Building Regulations 1976 and London Building Acts 1930/78, London Building (Constructional) Amending Bye-laws 1979.

Strict compliance with Building Regulations and Bye-laws is often difficult to achieve, and proposals are dealt with on their merits, not following hard-and-fast rules; this is particularly so in the case of fire precautions and means of escape, and thermal and sound insulation requirements (*see* Chapter 13, page 94).

The following extracts from the London Building Acts (Amendment) Act 1939, Sections 134, 135 indicate the generality:

'No person shall without the consent of the Council make any alteration of any building in such a manner that when so altered it will by reason of the alteration not comply with the London Building Acts or with any bye-laws made in pursuance of those Acts'. (Section 134).

'Every addition to or alteration of a building or structure and every other work made or done for any purpose in to or upon a building or structure (except necessary repair not affecting the stability or construction of the building or structure or any part of the building or structure) shall be subject to the provisions of the London Building Acts and of any bye-laws made in pursuance of those Acts'. (Section 135).

'No person shall without the consent of the Council convert a building or structure or part of the building or structure in such a manner that the building or structure or part of the building or structure will after being so converted not comply with such of the provisions of the London Building Acts or any of the bye-laws made in pursuance of those Acts as may be applicable to the building or structure or part thereof as so converted'. (Section 139).

Part V, Section 35, of the Act deals with means of escape from old buildings. Conversion from a single dwelling to self-contained flats will involve considerable cost in the subsequent protection of staircases, provision of smoke lobbies, party separation, etc, and possibly provision of secondary means of escape in case of fire, if dwellings or other premises are above the prescribed heights from the pavement adjoining the premises.

London Building Act (Amendment) Act 1935, Section 4
Power of the Council to make bye-laws, Section 4(2)
Power of the Council to waive or modify bye-laws, Section 9(1), (5).

Building Regulations 1976
Part A (General)
Parts B, C, D, E, Section 2, G, H, K, L, M, N, P
Schedules 2 to 12 inclusive

Housing Act 1974
Part VII, Grants by local authorities

Limitation Acts 1939 to 80
Responsibility for latent defects

Defective Premises Act 1972
Especially Part 1. Responsibility to build properly dwellings for human habitation

Town & Country Planning Acts 1971/72 (see Chapter 4)

Town & Country Planning General Development Order 1977
Has 23 Schedules of 'permitted development' not requiring planning applications or consents

Town & Country Planning Act 1971
Schedule 8, Part 1, extensions to dwellings

Town & country Planning Use Classes Order 1972
Material change of use (*see* Chapter 4)

Trust Estates
See Chapter 3, 3.1.9 for licences to carry out works of alteration and conversion in these areas

References

Alteration and Conversion of Houses, J. F. GARNER (Oyez Publishing)
Housing, Tenancy, and Planning Law made Simple, A. J. LOMNICKI (Heinemann)
Housing Acts 1957/80 (HMSO)
Land Compensation Act 1973 (HMSO)
London Building Acts (Amendment) Act 1939 (HMSO)

6

Fire and buildings

In architectural practice the consideration of fire in buildings (ignoring its cause, propagation, growth and decay) falls under three broad headings:

6.1.1 The design aspects

(a) The site and its immediate environs including access for fire-fighting purposes.
(b) The mass of the building(s) in relation to the proximity of the site boundaries, height of the building(s), materials of construction and their resistance to the action of fire.
(c) Fire loading of the building(s) considering special hazards, e.g. storage of explosive and/or flammable material, etc.
(d) Compartmentation and separation of the various volumes of the building both vertically and horizontally, including fire stopping.
(e) Circulation horizontally and vertically in relation to means of escape access points.
(f) Provision of fire-fighting equipment within the building, including wet and dry risers, hose points, fire buckets, sprinklers, smoke detectors, extracts, alarm systems, notices, signs and other directives.

6.1.2 The legislative aspects

(a) Building regulations and bye-laws.
(b) Fire certificates.
(c) Codes of Practice and BS specifications.
(d) Agrément Board certificates.
(e) Research and advisory organisations.
(f) Acts of Parliament.
(g) Home Office regulations.
(h) Department of Education and Science.
(i) Scottish Education Department.
(j) Scottish Development Department.

6.1.3 The contractual aspects

(a) The contract drawings:
  consents under Building Regulations, bye-laws, and other regulations.
(b) Insurances under the contract:
  the contractor's responsibility to insure the works
  the Employer's responsibility to insure the works
  the Architect's responsibility to inspect the insurance policies and premium receipts, and instruction for additional insurance as provided for in JCT Standard Form of Building Contract 1980, Clause 21.2.1
  to advise where necessary on transference of insurance on partial or complete occupation by the Employer.

The Architect's duties in this regard are determined under Architect's Appointment, Work Stage J, 1.20, and Work Stage K, 1.21, or SW1.12, and JCT Standard Form of Building Contract 1980, Clause 22, and the Clause 22 Perils as described in the Conditions, Part 1, General Definitions, 1.3. The Architect has to determine:

(a) Who is to insure the works, the contractor or the employer?
(b) Assess any additional risk over and above the normal contract requirements which the Architect should advise the Employer to insure against under Clause 21.2.1.
(c) Does the Architect approve of the insurers as proposed by either the employer of the contractor? (Clause 22.A.2).
(d) Are the Architect's and other Consultant's fees included in the policies in the event of partial or complete rebuild being necessary after a fire?

(e) In the event of extensions to existing building, is the employer also insured for the existing building and contents against all risks incurred by the works.
(f) Is the sum insured in the policy commensurate with the total cost of the works?

In the case of (b) above, the Architect would have to arrange for an insurance assessor to attend the site and advise on the additional insurance cover and the premium charge for the indemnity.

In all insurance negotiations the policy may be preceded by a Cover Note which is equally binding upon the insurers, but the terms of which should be carefully scrutinized, as the terms of the policy are the essence of the indemnity. When the policy is to hand it is wise to have it scrutinized by an expert source as to the precise meaning of any terms which may be obscure to the lay reader. Insurance brokers are experts in this field, and the ABS Insurance Agency under the auspices of the Architects' Benevolent Society offers to Architects advice and reduced terms on insurances for all purposes.

The Architect may elect, if he is competent to do so, to negotiate the insurance claim with the insurers on behalf of the client, and some of the points to be considered in this course of action are as follows:

In new buildings

(1) Notify the insurers immediately the fire has been reported.
(2) Go to the scene of the fire and carry out the following matters:
    (a) Once the fire is out, get the site secured against intruders and pilfering.
    (b) Instruct the Contractor to remove any debris, remove any work in danger of immediate collapse, shoring up and supporting any part of the structure as necessary. (*see* Dangerous Structures, page 17).
    Seal off any damaged services.
    Notify as soon as possible the statutory and service undertakers to ascertain any flooding or damage to their respective systems.
    (c) Instruct the contractor to weatherproof the building as necessary (claims may take a long time to settle).

Note: In any case where there may be danger to the public, the first duty of the Architect is to ensure that the danger is removed. In this he may act of his own volition but must notify the client as soon as possible of the action taken.

When immediate matters have been dealt with, subsequent actions will be as follows:

(d) Arrange for a Quantity Surveyor's estimate of the cost of reinstatement as a basis for claim.
(e) Arrange to meet the insurer's Assessor on the site to discuss the claim; it is wise to have the QS present at this meeting.

    It follows that the claim may not be merely related to the reinstatement of the damaged building, but may also include for real and personal damage suffered by others as a result of the fire, including smoke damage and damage caused by the fire brigade in fighting the fire.

    There may also be unfixed materials and stored materials and components on the site to be included, and possible damage to the contractor's plant and machinery, some of which may be hired. Also tools and effects belonging to site operatives. Damage may also extend outside the site to other buildings, cars parked in adjoining streets etc.

Claims must be accurate and exclude anything which cannot be substantiated, or anything which may be construed as fraudulent, otherwise all claims under the terms of the policy could be negated.

The main contractor may exercise his right not to continue and rebuild the damaged or destroyed building if the delay is likely to be protracted, even though the Architect may exercise his right under the terms of the contract (Clause 25) to agree to an extension of the contract period for this purpose. In this event, the Quantity Surveyor will have to assess the value of the works completed at the time of the fire, and any incidental costs incurred in 2(b) or 2(c) above, making due allowance for all unfixed materials and components either on site or in workshops off site which the client has not yet paid for, and for any loss-of-profit claim the contractor may make. Sub-contractors, both nominated and domestic, will have their contracts terminated with that of the main contractor, and any monies due to them will also have to be assessed.

The Architect will then have to advise the client on the best method of selecting a new main contractor to complete or rebuild the works as required and negotiating a new contract, which may be on the 'cost-plus' basis as discussed in Chapter 8; this will include making new contracts with nominated sub-contractors and suppliers through the new contractor, and adjusting new prices, or re-nominating.

In the event of the original contract having been a fixed-price contract, this will have to be carefully considered and negotiated in terms of the original contract insurance cover, as in such contracts time for completion is critical for the contractor, and the new contractor's premium rate may be substantially higher depending upon the lapse of time since the original contract was let.

The degree of complication in the event of fire claims depends upon the severity of the fire and its possible cause, as well as the extent of third-party claims for injury or damage to persons or property.

Depending upon the size of the claim, and to some extent on the insurance company dealing with it, settlement may be either very quick or a protracted affair dragging on for months. The Architect should advise the client of the possibilities as soon as possible and obtain his authority to proceed with the claim, and assisted by the Quantity Surveyor, obtain a settlement and undertake reinstatement of the works. Any additional fees resulting from the negotiations and subsequent additional works, which should be met out of the fire insurance, should be dealt with under Architect's Appointment, Part 4, 4.37 or SW4.1, and the method of payment agreed with the client from the outset.

6.1.4 Reference sources in the design of buildings

Code of Practice:

BSCP 3, 1948 *Code of basic data for the design of buildings*
- Chapter IV Precautions against fire
- Part 1, 1971 Flats and maisonettes (in blocks of over two storeys)
- Part 2, 1968 Shops and department stores

BSCP 110 *The structural use of concrete*
- Part 1, 1972 The structural use of concrete, design, materials and workmanship

BSCP 153 *Windows and rooflights*
- Part 4, 1972 Fire hazards associated with glazing in building

BSCP 121 *Walling*
- Part 1, 1973 Brick and block masonry

BSCP 413 *Ducts for building services*

British Standards

BS 459 *Doors*
- Part 3, 1951 Fire check flush doors and wood and metal frames (half-hour and one-hour types)

BS 476, 1953 *Fire tests on building materials and structures*
- Part 7, 1971 Surface spread of flame tests for materials
- Part 8, 1972 Test methods and criteria for the fire resistance of elements of construction

BS 1635, 1970 *Graphic symbols and abbreviations for fire protection drawings*

BS 2560, 1978 *Specification for exit signs (internally illuminated)*

BS 4422 *Glossary of terms associated with fire*
- Part 1, 1969 The phenomenon of fire
- Part 2, 1971 Building materials and structures
- Part 3, 1972 Means of escape
- Part 4, 1975 Fire protection equipment
- Part 5, 1976 Miscellaneous terms

BS 5266 *Emergency lighting*
- Part 1, 1975 Code of practice for the emergency lighting of premises other than cinemas and certain other specified premises used for entertainment

BS 5268 *Code of Practice for the structural use of timber*
- Part 4 (4.1) 1978 Fire resistance of timber structures (Amendment 2947 July 1979)

BS 5378 *Safety signs and colours*
- Part 1, 1980 Specification for colour and design

BS 5395 *Code of practice for stairs*

BS 5422 *Specification for the use of thermal insulating materials*

BS 5499 *Fire safety signs, notices, and graphic symbols*
- Part 1, 1984 (revision) Specification for fire safety signs

BS 5502 *Code of Practice for the design of buildings and structures for agriculture*
- Part 1 (1.3) Fire protection

BS 5588 *Code of Practice for fire precautions in the design of buildings*
- Part 1.1, 1984 Code of Practice for single-family dwelling houses
- Part 3, 1983 Code of practice for office buildings
- Part 4, 1978 Smoke control in protected escape routes by pressurization

International Organization for Standardization (ISO)

ISO 834, 1975 *Fire Resistance Tests – Elements of Building Construction*

ISO 1182, 1979 *Fire Tests – Building Materials – Non-Combustibility Tests*

ISO 1716, 1973 *Building Materials – Determination of Calorific Potential*

ISO 3008, 1976 *Fire Resistance Tests – Door and Shutter Assemblies*

ISO 3009, 1976 *Fire Resistance Tests – Door and Shutter Assemblies*

ISO 3261, 1975 Fire Tests – Vocabulary

Agrément Board

Agrément Certificate *Fire resistance of materials and components*

Department of the Environment

Circular 17/68 *The Building Regulations 1965 – Multi-Storey Car Parks*

Circular 19/69 *The Building Regulations 1965 – Town Centre and Shopping Precincts*

Circular 67/71 *Public Health Act 1961, Building Regulations. Notes for Guidance on Relaxations or Dispensation of Part E Requirements for Private Dwelling Houses in the circumstances set out in Case B of Regulation A8 (1)*
Circular 96/71 *The Building Regulations 1965, Air-Supported Structures*
Circular 91/73 *Public Health Act 1961. Building Regulations, Appendix 1, Notes for Guidance on the Relaxation or Dispensation of Part E requirements*

(Covers portal frames, raised storage areas, new institutional buildings, canopies over petrol pumps, provision of sprinklers, basement conditions, surface spread of flame, historic buildings, space separation)

Department of Education and Science
Building Bulletin 7, 1975 – Fire and the design of schools

Fire Offices Committee
Rules for the Construction of Buildings – Standards 1–5 1979
Rules for the Construction of Buildings – Grades 1–2 1978
Rules for the Construction and Installation of Fireproof Doors, Lobbies and Shutters 1967

The Greater London Council
London Building (Constructional) Bye-laws 1972
London Building (Constructional) Amending Bye-laws 1979
Code of Practice Means of Escape in Case of Fire 1976
Code of Practice Means of Escape in Case of Fire – Houses in Multiple Occupation – Section 16 of the Housing Act 1961

Addendum in respect to houses used as Hostels, Lodging Houses, and similar establishments (1981)

Code of Practice for buildings of excess height and/or additional cubical extent requiring approval under Section 20 of the London Building Acts (Amendment) Act 1939 (1974)

Places of Public Entertainment – Technical Regulations 1972
Play Safe – A guide to standards in halls used for occasional stage presentations (1980)
A Guide to Fire Safety in Exhibitions and Similar Presentations in Hotel Buildings (1972)
Code of Practice for Pop Concerts (1977)

The Home Office
Guides to the Fire Precautions Act 1971
No. 1 Houses and Boarding Houses
No. 2 Factories 1979
No. 3 Offices, Shops and Railway Premises 1977
Old People's Homes 1983 } draft guides
Hospitals 1982 }

Fire Prevention Guides
No. 1 Fire precautions in Town Centres and Re-development Areas
No. 2 Fire precautions in new Single-Storey Spirit Storages and Associated Buildings 1973

The author is advised at the time of writing that several changes are taking place in the form of new British Standards, Development Documents, Draft Guides, and the proposed new Building Regulations etc, thus making an up-to-date list of information difficult to achieve. The reader is advised to consult the current Year Book of the British Standards Institution, and Practice Notes in professional journals.

6.1.5 The Fire Precautions Act 1971

If there is any doubt as to whether a premises falls within the jurisdiction of the Act then the local fire authority should be consulted. Premises which are affected by the Act and require a Fire Certificate are those

(a) Used as sleeping accommodation, i.e. hotels, inns, etc.
(b) Used as, or as part of, an institution providing treatment or care, i.e. hospitals, nursing homes, clinics, etc.
(c) Used for purposes of entertainment, recreation or instruction, or for the purposes of any club, society or association.
(d) Used for purposes of teaching, training or research.
(e) Used for any purpose involving access to the premises by the public, whether by payment or otherwise.
(f)* Formerly covered by the Factories Act 1961.
(g)* Formerly covered by the Offices, Shops, and Railway Premises Act 1963 (*see also* GLC Code of Means of Escape in Case of Fire – FPL Procedure).

* *see* Fire Certificates (Special Premises) Regulations 1976
Fire Precautions (Factories, Offices, Shops and Railway Premises) Order 1976, SI 1976 No. 2009
Fire Precautions (non-Certified Factories, Offices, Shops, and Railway Premises) Regulations 1976, SI 1976 No. 2010.

Premises exempted are those

(h) Covered by the Mines & Quarries Act 1954.
(i) Used solely or mainly for public worship.
(j) Used as a single private dwelling, or any premises consisting of or comprising a single house occupied by persons not forming a single household.

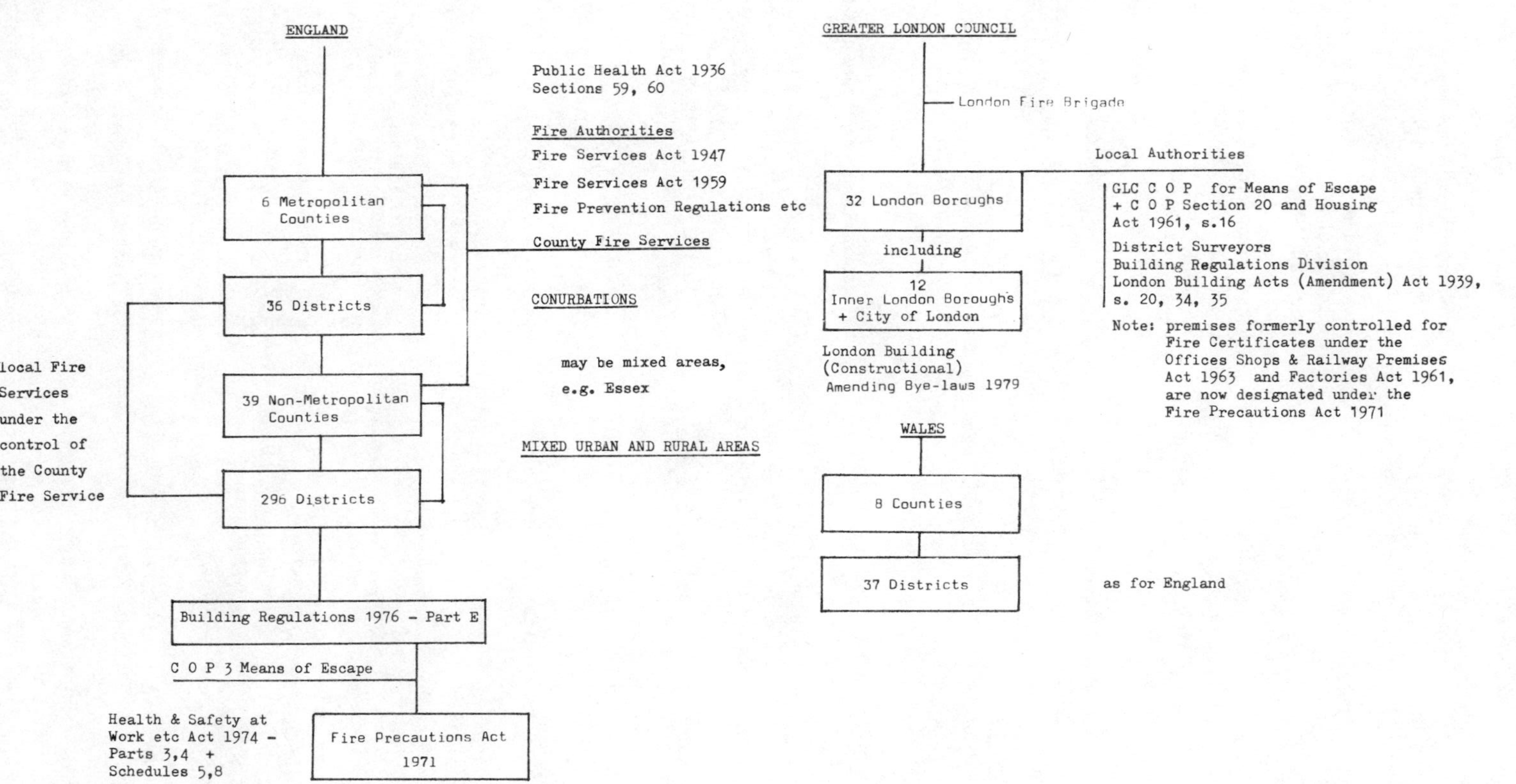

Diagram 9: Fire authorities and legislation in England and Wales

Premises not exempted if there is living accommodation, except as aforesaid:

(k) Below ground-floor level of the building which constitutes or comprises the premises.
(l) Is two or more or more floors above the ground floor of that building.
(m) Is a room of which the floor is six metres or more above the surface of the ground on any side of that building.

Enforcement

Enforcement of the Act is by the fire authority under Section 18 of the Act, with provision for consultation with the local authority concerning building regulations and means of escape. Fire Officers in pursuance of the Act may enter premises and ask questions requiring sworn answers, the Inspector must produce evidence of the inspection. Penalties and appeals are provided for in the Act, and applications must be made on the prescribed form to the authority concerned. The use of the building must be stated and plans may be called for.

If the fire authority requirements are not met, what is required must be stated in writing and a time limit to execute the requirements imposed upon the owners of the premises.

The Fire Certificate must state (a)–(e) below and possibly (f)–(h) in addition:

(a) the use of the premises
(b) means of escape
(c) maintenance of means of escape
(d) location of fire fighting equipment
(e) means of giving fire warning
(f) instructions what to do in the event of fire
(g) limitations of the number of occupants
(h) any other precautions required

The problem in implementing the Act has been shortage of manpower to undertake the inspections.

The Certificate or a copy of it must be kept on the premises.

Other requirements which may lead to regulations are

(i) Internal construction and materials.
(j) Instruction on what to do in the event of fire.
(k) Positioning and number of attendants.
(l) Record of training and maintenance of equipment to be kept.

See Section 40 of the Act for application to the Crown, etc.

The Act does not apply to Northern Ireland, save Section 40 and part Section 35. For Scotland see Sections 13(6) and 14 and Schedule 1.

References

Aspects of Fire Precautions, R. E. G. READ and W. A. MORRIS Building Research Establishment

Fire and the Architect, RIBA WORKING PARTY Fire Protection Association and the RIBA

Fire Precautions Act 1971 (HMSO)

7

Rights of adjoining owners

This aspect of the Architect's services is dealt with in Architect's Appointment, Part 2, 2.34 and SW2, 2.16, 2.17, 2.18.

An understanding of the rights of adjoining owners is essential if the Architect is to instigate work for building owners, since failure to recognize these rights and take action necessary to ensure they are not trangressed, may give rise to injunctions being granted by the Courts to stop work on site, thus causing long delays to ensue until matters are resolved; and as a result the client may take action against the Architect for negligence.

The three most common rights which arise are: rights of light, rights of support, and party rights. To a lesser degree, but nonetheless important, are rights under convenants, easements, and licences (*see* page 62).

Chapter 1 outlined the law regarding common law and equitable law, and statutory law, and although it is accepted that equity will prevail over common law, equally statutory law takes precedence over the other two. This does not mean that having received town planning and building regulation consents one can go ahead and build ignoring the other rights enjoyed by adjoining owners. Numerous cases in the courts have shown that it is indeed very foolish to do so.

7.1.1 Party rights

For all practical purposes the provisions of the Law of Property Act 1925, Sections 38, 39(5), and Schedule 1, Part V will be referred to for the purposes of 'party wall' and 'party structures' outside the City of London and the Inner London Boroughs of the GLC, where the provisions of the London Building Acts (Amendment) Act 1939, Part VI, Section 44 *et seq* obtain.

Since the Law of Property Act 1925, walls of which two adjoining owners are tenants in common, are deemed to be severed vertically as between the two owners, each party having the right of support and user over the half of the other owner, i.e. each owner grants the other an easement over the full thickness of the wall (*see* drawing 4, facing page)

Where a wall varies in thickness at different points throughout its height, presumably the position of the centre line will vary with that thickness, and in the length of the wall a similar presumption would be made, ignoring such minor features as corbels, off-sets, oversailing courses, etc.

A wall may be a party wall for as far as it is used as such and no further.

A party wall is not necessarily a wall that separates buildings, it may separate a building and an open space, or two open spaces, in which case it would be termed a 'party fence wall'. Where such a wall is wholly on the property of one owner, but there is agreement to maintain it as a separating wall, it would be termed a 'party boundary wall'.

Premises may be separated by party structures such as arches over common access ways, which may also include floors, and Sections 38, 39(5), of the Law of Property Act 1925 obtain.

Where party floors are concerned, the words 'severed vertically' appear to be synonymous with a median plane through the thickness of the floor (*see* drawing 5, facing page).

In the work to party walls where a part or the whole thereof becomes exposed to the weather, there appears to be no legal redress under the Law of Property Act 1925, as the Act provides for rights in support and user, but *see* page 31 for Section 29 of the Public Health Act 1961 for local authority powers in this regard.

The Court has powers under the Law of Property Act 1925 to settle any dispute in respect of interests and rights in a wall on application by an interested party.

The reader should also be acquainted with the 'definitions' of party matters in the London Building Acts (Amendment) Act 1939, Sections 44 *et seq*.

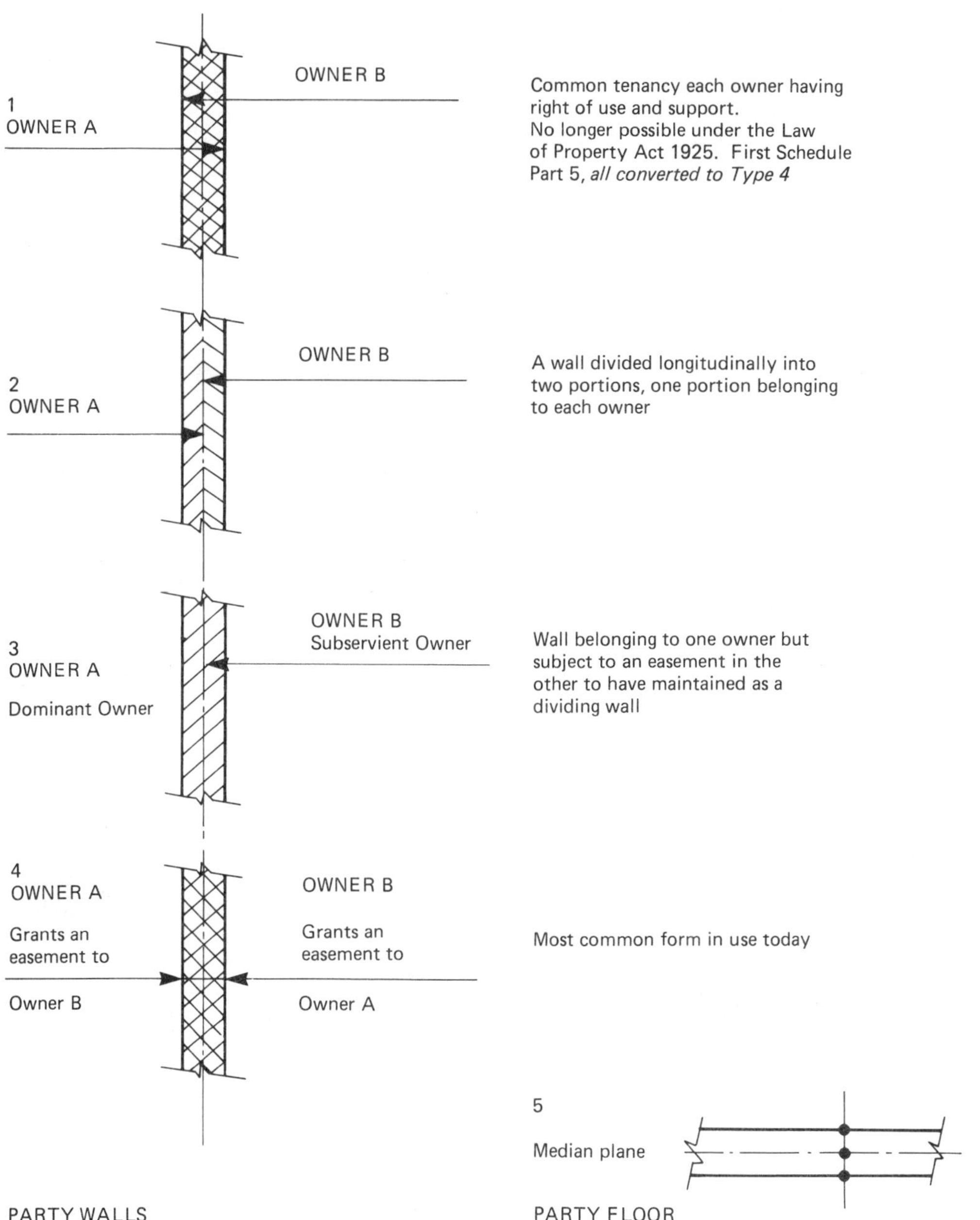

7.1.2 Outline party-wall procedure

Architect's Appointment, Pt 2, 2.35/SW 2.17, 2.18

Applicable to the City of London and the Inner London Boroughs of the GLC under the London Building Acts (Amendment) Act 1939, Part VI, Section 44 *et seq*.

(1) Obtain sets of forms A–G (*see* Appendix) from the RIBA Publications Department.

(2) Check on site whether the wall(s) are 'party' within the meaning of the Act, i.e. party wall, party structure, party fence, party boundary, etc, (read definitions in the Act), or if it is intended to build within 10 or 20 ft of the adjoining owner's premises and at a lower depth (*see* Figures, page 49) read Sections 50 (i)(a) and 50 (i)(b), London Building Acts (Amendment) Act 1939.

Note: If doubt exists as to whether the matter concerned is a party situation, proceed as if it were; it is always possible to revoke the service of a notice, but time will be wasted if it proves to be so and the appropriate notices have not been served (*see* page 52 for ownership of property).

(3) Serve the appropriate notice(s) in accordance with Section 124 of the Act, apply the directions carefully so that the notice is not invalidated due to improper service. Attach to the notice the drawings showing the proposed works to the party wall or structure to amplify the written description of the works in the notices. Note carefully the provisions of the Act with regard to Counter Notices and Dissent from Notices (*see* Sections 48, 49, 50(2)a,b,c.

(4) Assuming a difference has arisen, Section 55, and a Surveyor has been appointed to act for the adjoining owner, prepare the draft Award (*see* typical Award, page 49). It is wise to make a careful survey of the wall or structure together with a Schedule of Existing Condition, with photographic evidence to support it. This can be of assistance if claims are made for alleged damage arising from the works.

Attach the Schedule and photographs to the draft Award.

(5) Meet the adjoining owner's Surveyor on site and agree the draft Award, including the Schedule of Existing Condition and photographs; also agree the appointment of the Third Surveyor (Section 55, (a) (ii) of the Act, and *see* Chapter 8, 8.1.4). Do not forget to contact the proposed Third Surveyor to confirm that he would be willing to act, and if so to send him in due course a copy of the Award and the drawings. Ascertain the amount of the adjoining owner's fees, and notify the client of the amount and when it will be due for payment (*see* (6) below).

(6) When the adjoining owner's Surveyor has agreed the draft Award *in toto*, prepare the final Award, of which at least six copies are needed; and send two copies to the adjoining owner's Surveyor for signature. When he has signed he will normally be entitled to his fees, not on completion of the works.

Notify the client of the cost of the intended works (*see* Sections 55(1), 56(1,a,b,c,d,e,), 56(2,3,4,5,6,), 57, 58, 59, of the Act).

(7) Provide the contractor with two copies of the Award and drawings; the Clerk of Works and the District Surveyor also will need a copy of each; then proceed with the works to completion.

(8) Arrange intermediate and final meetings on site with the adjoining owner's Surveyor by mutual agreement as required.

(9) If disputes arise which cannot be settled between the Building and the adjoining owner's Surveyor, Form G should be used for the appointment of the Third Surveyor who will act as Arbitrator, as provided for in the Act. (*see* Chapter 8, 8.1.4).

Note: The Award is a formal agreement and is legally binding on the parties concerned, but may be challenged in the County Court and High Court as provided for.

It is possible to have several Awards covering different conditions on one site with several adjoining owners. If they can be persuaded to appoint one Surveyor to act for them all it will make for a much easier Award procedure.

As a matter of good management and courtesy, do advise any tenants in the properties and others not served with notices of the intended works, the time of commencement if known, and any scaffolding, shoring, etc, which may have to be erected on their property, remembering that the Award should include for protection of any gardens, greenhouses, etc, on the adjacent property.

In minor works it is not always necessary to adopt the full party wall procedure, an exchange of letters can be used to confirm agreement, but it is better to make a personal approach to the adjoining occupiers first and discuss the proposals with them. (Remember the comments on page 18 with regard to ownership and the right to instigate works to properties.)

In letters to occupiers, it is always advisable to make reference to the Act using a phrase such as e.g. 'In accordance with the provisions of the London Building Acts (Amendment) Act 1939, Part VI, Section 44 *et seq*, I write on behalf of my client(s) to advise you of intended works to the party wall (or structure) separating premises at .... in accordance with the attached drawings ....'.

Remember always that the Architect is responsible, on behalf of the client, for the structural stability, support, and protection of the adjoining land and buildings, and clearing away and making good of all consequent damage and disturbance arising from the works.

London Building Acts (Amendment) Act 1939, Part VI, Section 50

Case 1, Section 50 (i)(a) – Notice on Form C (see Appendix)

If any part of a new building or structure is proposed within 10 ft distance and at a depth lower than the foundations of the existing adjoining building the adjoining owner may require his building to be underpinned.

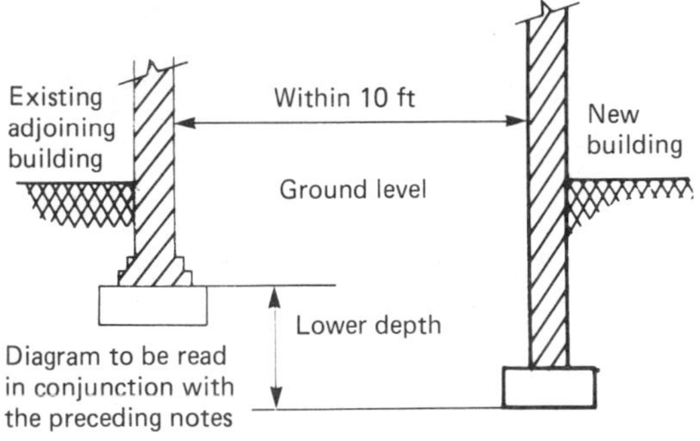

Case 2, Section 50 (i)(b) – Notice on Form D (see Appendix)

If any part of a new building or structure is proposed over 10 ft from but within 20 ft and extending to a depth within the 45° angle from the face of the adjoining existing building the adjoining owner may require his building to be underpinned.

In any case to which Section 50 (i) applies, note the following:

(a) At least one month before commencing to erect a building or structure the building owner (he who proposes to do the work) shall serve on the adjoining owner notice in writing of his intentions. The notice shall state whether he proposes to underpin or otherwise strengthen or safeguard the foundations of the adjoining owner's building.

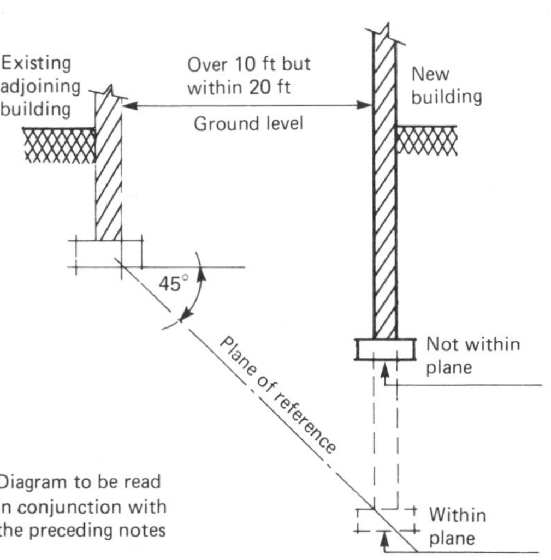

(b) Drawings should accompany the notice showing the site of the building or structure, and plans and sections of the new structure or building and proposed depths of foundations.
(c) Within 14 days the adjoining owner may serve a counter notice refuting the necessity to underpin, or requiring such strengthening as may be deemed necessary, as the case may be.
(d) A dispute is deemed to have arisen.
(e) The building owner shall compensate the adjoining owner, and any adjoining occupier, for inconvenience, loss or damage.
(f) On completion of the work the building owner shall provide the adjoining owner with particulars of the work done, if so requested.

All the work executed under the terms of the Award will be paid for by the building owner; the adjoining owner will only contribute to the costs, either in whole or in part, depending upon his immediate or future use of the wall or structure. This apportioned cost is dealt with under Sections 56 *et seq* of the Act.

Typical party-wall Award

Date: 18th March 1982

PARTY WALL AWARD

made between

Mr.J.Willoughby

and

Mrs.J.K.Nicholls

In respect to premises known as

18 & 19 CHEVALIER MEWS,
LONDON S.W.3

in the Royal Borough of Kensington
and Chelsea

in accordance with

The London Building Acts (Amendment)
Act 1939
Part VI, Sections 44–59

AWARD IN THE MATTER OF the London Building Acts (Amendment) Act 1939 Part VI and in the matter of a certain party structure separating premises known as No.18 CHEVALIER MEWS, S.W.3 in the Royal

Borough of Kensington and Chelsea and the premises adjoining thereto on the West side being known as No. 19 CHEVALIER MEWS in the Royal Borough of Kensington and Chelsea.

WHEREAS Mr.J.Willoughby of No. 18 CHEVALIER MEWS, S.W.3 (hereinafter called the Building Owner) is the Owner of No. 18 CHEVALIER MEWS, S.W.3 and Mrs.J.K.Nicholls is the Owner and Occupier of the premises known as No. 19 CHEVALIER MEWS, S.W.3 (hereinafter called the Adjoining Owner).

AND WHEREAS the said Building Owner did give Notice on the 22nd February 1982 of their intentions AND WHEREAS a difference is deemed to have arisen between the Building Owner and the Adjoining Owner the Building Owner has appointed Mr J J Scott, FRIBA, FBIM of 22 Prior Street, London S.W.4 to act as his Surveyor and the Adjoining Owner has appointed Mr.F.J.Saunders, MA, FRICS, of 46 Parliament Street, London S.W.1 to act as her Surveyor pursuant to and for all purposes mentioned in Section 55 of the said London Building Act.

AND WHEREAS the said J.J.Scott and F.J.Saunders have in pursuance of the said Section 55 of the said Act selected Mr.W.M.Nisbett, FRIBA, of 66 Bessborough Gardens, London S.W.2 to act as Third Surveyor and in the event of the said W.M.Nisbett being unable to act have agreed that if they do not jointly decide upon a substitute the Third Surveyor shall be appointed by the President of the Royal Institute of British Architects.

NOW WE the undersigned Surveyors appointed under the said Act having surveyed the wall referred to the said Notice and duly considered all the matters in connection therewith do hereby in pursuance of the said Act AWARD AND DETERMINE as follows.

1. THAT the wall separating the premises of the Adjoining Owner from the premises of the Building Owner is a party wall for its full height.
2. THAT on the signing of this AWARD the Building Owner may proceed with and complete the following works and exercise all or any of the rights given to the Building Owner by the said Act.

   (a) TO EXCAVATE below the existing ground level on the Building Owner's site to form a new concrete foundation to the satisfaction of the District Surveyor and the Adjoining Owner's Surveyor in concrete mix 1:2:4 cement, fine aggregate, coarse aggregate, including underpinning in concrete mix 1:6 cement, 'all in' coarse aggregate, the existing foundations of the party/fence wall in lengths not exceeding 1.5 metres at any one time.

   (b) TO MAKE GOOD the party/fence wall and structure after demolition of the existing shed and to point the same in mortar mix 1:2:5 lime, cement, sand over the height and the length shown on the attached plan, and to apply to this area two full coats of Elastomeric Compound 227 RIW to act as a vertical damp-proof course between the existing and new walls.

   (c) TO PREPARE AND PROPERLY WEATHER the top of the party/fence wall where this abuts the new wall with a weathered cement fillet and zinc cover flashing to the satisfaction of the Adjoining Owner's Surveyor.

   (d) TO DO ANY OTHER WORK to the party/fence wall or on the Building Owner's land adjacent to the wall as may be rendered necessary by or consequential upon the foregoing works or by the requirements of the District Surveyor.
3. THAT the Building Owner shall give all Notices legally demandable by the properly constituted authorities and shall conform to the London Building Act, One thousand nine hundred and thirty and the London Building Acts (Amendment) Act One thousand nine hundred and thirty nine and all regulations and requirements including those of the District Surveyor and the local Authority and shall pay all fees legally demandable by them.
4. THAT the cost of the Works described herein shall be borne by the Building Owner and any risks involved shall be the Building Owner's responsibility.
5. THAT the said Works shall be carried out with good and proper materials and workmanship and in a manner and strength in accordance with the Building Acts and Regulations and to the satisfaction of the authorities concerned and the District Surveyor.
6. THE BUILDING OWNERS will as far as possible carry out the work from their own premises and keep down dust and make good any work disturbed by them so that nothing disturbed shall be in a worse condition than it is now or as described in the attached Schedule of Condition.
7. THAT THE BUILDING OWNERS shall be responsible for any injury to persons or property which may be occasioned or brought about by the execution of these works and shall indemnify the Adjoining Owner in

respect of any claims which may be made against them in respect to such injuries or damage arising from the Works hereby authorised in this Award.

8. THE BUILDING OWNER shall after the signing of this award forthwith pay the charges of the Adjoining Owner's Surveyor in the matter of this Award and for his inspections in connection therewith in the sum of £150.00 (One hundred and fifty pounds) and will pay also the cost of preparing this Award and its counterpart with the Adjoining Owner's Surveyor.
9. THE BUILDING OWNER shall adequately uphold, maintain, and protect the Adjoining Owner's premises and the party structures during the progress of and at the completion of the Works and shall erect, maintain, and remove as required, hoardings, screens, shoring, and all necessary protections to the entire satisfaction of the Adjoining Owner's Surveyor and cause as little inconvenience as possible to the Adjoining Owners and Occupiers.
10. THE BUILDING OWNER shall at his own expense on completion clear away all shoring, rubbish, and materials, and make good any damage occasioned to the Adjoining Owner's property and to the finishes and decorations thereof so that nothing disturbed is in a worse condition than it is now or as described in the attached Schedule of Condition as a direct result of carrying out the said works and notice of which shall be given to the Building Owner's Surveyor not less than six months after the completion of the Works. The Building Owner shall by Notice give the effective date of completion of the said Works to the Adjoining Owner.
11. NO MATERIAL DEVIATION shall be made from the Works as herein set forth without at least seven days previous notice in writing to the Adjoining Owner's Surveyor, and unless the Adjoining Owner's Surveyor shall give consent in writing to such deviation before the expiry of such notice as aforesaid, a further difference shall be deemed to have arisen and such deviation shall not proceed until such difference has been settled by a supplementary Award agreed between the two Surveyors.
12. THAT THIS AWARD is subject to the rights of the Freeholders and all other parties.
13. THAT all lorries etc delivering or collecting materials etc to and from the works shall at no time be left attended or unattended directly outside the Adjoining Owners's premises. Neither shall any debris or materials be deposited in front of the Adjoining Owner's premises or on the flat roof adjoining the party/fence wall.
14. THAT the Surveyors to the Building and Adjoining Owners shall respectively be allowed reasonable access to the premises of the other during the course of the Works for the purpose of inspecting that portion of the work affected by or referred to in this Award.
15. THAT the Surveyors making this Award reserve to themselves the right to make any further Award in respect to any matters arising out of this Award or not determined by it.
16. IN the event of any difference arising out of this Award or subsequent Awards the matter shall be referred to the Third Surveyor named herein whose decision shall be final and binding and may be made a Rule of the Court on application of either party
    IN WITNESS THEREOF we have hereunto set our hands the........day of..............One thousand nine hundred and eighty two

SIGNED...
Surveyor to Adjoining Owner

SIGNED...
Surveyor to Building Owner

7.1.3 Rights of light

If one has a window in a property which has admitted light into the premises for a prescribed period of time without interruption as required by law, then the owner of that property acquires a permanent right to that light. The legislation dealing with this right is the Prescription Act 1832, and the Rights of Light Act 1959; the latter extended the prescribed period from twenty to twenty seven years to overcome the possibility of property overlooking vacant bombed sites acquiring rights of light that otherwise they would not have enjoyed. Prior to this Act, and before the Town & Country Planning Acts forbade it, the usual method of preventing an acquired right of light was to erect a suitable hoarding in front of the window(s) concerned for a period of time to break the continuity. Interruption of access ways and footpaths etc to prevent an acquired 'right of way' under the Prescription Act 1832 and the Rights of Way Act 1932 is also used.

In the case of rights of light, however, a 'notional obstruction' is lodged with the local Land Charges Registry for the payment of a fee, by means of an accurate drawing depicting the obstruction of the window(s) concerned.

In constructing sites which may give rise to claims for rights of light, the Architect should carefully consider the action to be taken. Past judgements on cases in the courts are based upon the individual circumstances in each case, and it is unwise to apply these judgements to other circumstances. In the author's experience, it is always a good plan to assess the proposed development in terms of the positions of the adjoining property windows, taking into consideration the proximity of the proposed development to the windows and any possible diminution of the light, sunlight being excluded from enjoyment of light. The areas which are lighted by windows may also have some influence on the court's decision, e.g. staircases, bathrooms, and other areas which may be considered less important than the living rooms, bedrooms, or working areas.

There exists a rule of thumb called the 45° rule which has been used in negotiations by Architects and Surveyors for many years as a point of departure in negotiations. This is a 45° plane projected from the level of the lowest window cill in the existing building within which there is a tacit agreement not to encroach so as to obstruct the light of that existing property. This rule has no apparent foundation in law.

The best initial approach, as with all adjoining-owner problems, is first to have an informal talk with them about the proposals, which may prove to be fruitful or not, remembering the comments on the freehold ownership of adjoining properties.

Failure to reach agreement, and proceeding without such agreement, may result in injunctions being sought in the courts to prevent the development taking place, this resulting in long delays and frustration.

There are no hard-and-fast rules in such matters; one must proceed with care and try to assess possible complications which may arise. Compensation awarded by the courts has ranged from removal of the offending development causing the obstruction of light, to payment of compensation assessed by the amount of artificial light required to make up the deficiency. In the author's experience, compensation was offered in the form of a lump sum by the developer which was acceptable to the adjoining owner. This may obtain particularly where the adjoining owner is not occupying the premises but rents it to others.

It is also worth remembering that infringed properties in a development situation may have a limited life themselves in terms of compulsory purchase, or by some other order of the local authority, or by an order under the T & C Planning Act 1971, Section 51, and compensation should be viewed in the light of this where appropriate.

A word of caution, however, on the open-cheque-book approach to such problems; a firm agreement should be legally drawn up and the terms and conditions of the compensation payment to the adjoining owner clearly stated.

Properties can change hands during the course of building development and people can be capricious and change their minds.

7.1.4 The law of property relating to architectural practice

English law divides property into two classes, 'real property' and 'personal property'. Real property, or 'realty', is confined to freehold interests in land, whilst personal property, or 'personalty', is everything else a person may own, being divided into chattels real, i.e. leasehold interests in property, and personal chattels such as books, pictures, jewellery, clothes, etc, including rights of action, which can be protected only by legal action.

Many books have been written on the legal aspects of this subject, and it is intended here to deal only with those aspects of property law which are germane to the Final Examination, Part 3 syllabus, and which impinge upon architectural practice.

The Law of Property Act 1925 together with the Land Registration Act 1925 are the Principal Acts concerned with the ownership of land and rights which are enjoyed by owners and others.

Since the Norman Conquest when William the Conqueror took all the land unto himself, the Crown has owned all the land to this day, granting its subjects an 'estate' in the land, although today this is not considered to be of great importance, and a 'freehold estate' may be treated as absolute ownership, although this is subject to statutory intervention such as compulsory purchase, etc.

The Law of Property Act 1925, under Section 1, states that after this date there would be only two legal estates in land

(a) An estate in fee simple absolute possession.
(b) A term of years absolute.

The phrase 'in fee simple absolute in possession' is defined as meaning that the estate is capable of inheritance without restriction, e.g. to either male or female descendants. 'Absolute' means free from conditions, e.g. 'to my son James in fee simple provided that he becomes a Catholic' is not a legal fee simple. 'Possession' is defined in Section 205 of the Law of Property Act 1925 as including, *inter alia*, 'the receipt of rents and profits or the right to receive them'; thus, the owner of a fee simple absolute in possession may grant a lease of the land itself, but still be in legal 'possession'.

The English law of estates, which is considered by some to be complicated, has the advantage that it permits varying interests in land to exist at any one time.

Real property can in general be transferred only by due form and process, e.g. by Section 52 of the

Law of Property Act 1925 all conveyances of legal estate must be made by deed.

A term of years absolute is granted for the leasehold of a property, which may be anything from a short to a very long term governed by the terms of the lease or tenancy. The weekly tenancy of a property is a legal estate under the control of the Landlord and Tenant Act 1954. Leasehold houses are subject to the Leasehold Reform Act 1967, but this does not include flats or maisonettes or commercial premises.

Not all property is registered under the Land Registration Act 1925; although reference sources have asserted that all land should have been registered by 1980, at present only about 70 per cent of it is registered.

All searches on title are made through the Land Registry Office, where changes of ownership in fee simple are recorded. Parish records may also be a source of information on land ownership and boundaries.

The local Land Charges Register kept by the local authorities records for inspection any charges made against land or property, not against owners, as discussed in Chapter 3.

For the Architect it is important that ownership of the land or property to be developed is clearly determined, and the rights of adjoining owners considered, and that covenants, easements, licences, etc are not trangressed.

Covenants

These are rules by which a parcel of land can be used; they run in perpetuity with the land and are conveyed with it. Restrictive covenants made after 1925 must be registered as a land charge, though this requirement does not apply to lease covenants. Restrictive covenants made before this time, and those in leases, are not registerable and purchasers must have notice of them if they are to be bound by them.

Provision is made under Section 84 of the Law of Property Act 1925 for an application to be made to court for a decision as to whether a restrictive covenant is still applicable to a freehold estate in land, and also for application to be made to the Lands Tribunal for a restrictive covenant to be modified or extinguished. Where houses are converted into two or more tenements, provision is made in the Housing Act 1957, Section 165 for the County Court to set aside restrictive covenants provided that certain conditions can be met.

Covenants may also be extinguished under Compulsory Purchase Orders, T & C Planning Act 1971, Section 118.

It is important to distinguish the relationship of restrictive covenants to consents granted under building control and town planning legislation. Consent granted under the respective Acts does not absolve one from complying with covenants against which the proposals may offend.

It is possible to insure against infringements of covenants, but it is always advisable to seek legal advice before contemplating the infringement of any covenant even though it appears to be out of date and meaningless.

Licences

A licence is permission given to another person by an owner of land permitting another person to do something which otherwise would be an act of trespass on his land, e.g. to grant a right of way. It is a personal privilege and the person to whom it is granted may have no legal interest in the land. (*See* also Chapter 3, 3.1.9).

Natural rights

'Natural rights are not acquired by an owner from the previous owner or from anyone else, but comprise rights which have been attached to land by law, or are naturally incident thereto' – *Law of Easements*, Bowen.

Easements

These are dealt with under the Prescription Act 1832. Definition: 'A right or privilege enjoyed by an owner of land in or over land which belongs to another owner, under which the latter in obliged to submit to a specified use of his land in a particular way' – Bowen.

In order for an easement to exist there must be two parties both of whom are owners of adjoining lands.

(a) The Dominant Owner, i.e. the beneficiary.
(b) The Servient Owner, i.e. the submissive owner.

Easements may be 'positive', i.e. those which can be observed, e.g. the crossing of land, the discharge of water or drainage effluent over adjoining land, etc.

Easements may be 'negative', i.e. those which cannot be observed, e.g. obscuring light from an adjoining owner's buildings, or any other imposition upon the Servient Owner which restrains him from doing something, i.e. one or more rights of his property.

'Continuous easements' are those which operate when the Dominant Owner exercises his right, e.g. a right of way.

Easements may be created by

(a) Express grant: One owner may grant to another an easement over his land.

(b) By means of use: Conveyancing Act 1881.
(c) By implied grant: In conveyancing a person is deemed to convey all easements pertaining to the land.
(d) By prescription: Personal use e.g. Rights of Way Act 1932.

Under the Law of Property Act 1925 the following should be noted:

(a) Easements may be created without use.
(b) Are legal estates.
(c) Bind the lands even in the hands of a purchaser without notice of such easement.

An easement is a right which conveys no profit; where rights are granted to take from the land they are called 'profits *à prendre*' or may be 'rights of common', e.g.

(a) Pasture: the right to pasture cattle.
(b) Estovers: the right to cut timber.
(c) Soil: the right to dig for minerals.
(d) Turbury: the right to cut turf.
(e) Piscary: the right to fish in a river, stream or pond, etc.

7.1.5 Dilapidations

Dilapidations are more within the sphere of the Building Surveyor than the Architect, but a knowledge of them is important within the general knowledge of the law of property which every Architect should know. In 1829 James Elgar wrote 'Dilapidations is the injury which has accrued to houses, buildings or erections, during the temporary possession of one party whereby a successor or reversioner sustains damage, and for which the customs and laws of this realm have proved and pointed out a remedy'. It has been pointed out by subsequent authorities that this definition omitted the word 'land', and therefore was clearly lacking since land is also subject to the law of dilapidations.

All dilapidations arise from the Law of Waste which applies between landlord and tenant. The Law of Waste (wastum) has two important divisions

(a) Voluntary waste, and
(b) Permissive waste.

The first is positive damage to land or dwellings, e.g. pulling down buildings, felling trees, removing railings, opening mines or quarries on land, etc. The second is damage by wilful neglect or omission such as allowing buildings to fall into a state of decay, or allowing arable land to remain overgrown and uncultivated.

Legal liability for civil dilapidations arises under these three heads

(a) The Law of Tort which includes the Law of Waste,
(b) The Law of Contract between landlord and tenant, and
(c) Statute, e.g. failure of landlords to repair property contrary to the Housing Acts, Public Health Acts, London Building Acts 1930/78, etc.

The legal remedies for waste are

(a) Damages at common law, and
(b) Remedies in equity.

'Voluntary waste', which includes alterations to the property by the tenant subject to the Law of Waste may be defined as 'ameliorating waste', i.e. 'to make better'; if as a result of the alterations the property is improved and its value enhanced, it is possible that equity would refuse the granting of an injunction to restrain the doing of something which would cause no injury to the reversioner, and from which no damages could be assessed, but this is only conjecture.

Claims for damages may be brought by the landlord at any time during the currency of the lease if the landlord so wishes, but on expiration of the lease term the landlord must make a claim within six years if the lease is not by deed, and twelve years if it is (cf the Limitations Acts regarding latent defects).

The usual method of arriving at a claim is to have the premises surveyed by a Surveyor who, having regard to the terms of the lease and its covenants, will prepare a Schedule of Dilapidations. Provision is made for legal and survey fees in the Law of Property Act 1925, Section 146(1), and all that is required under an interim schedule of defects for the tenant to repair and make good under the covenants of his lease is a simple list.

In the case of a Schedule on expiry of the lease, however, it is more detailed and every item must be separately measured and valued, or separately priced if on the 'spot item' description, i.e. an item of work described as a sequence of operations in a total clause in the Schedule, not as individual items or under separate trades.

Lessees are bound by the terms of their individual leases, as are the landlords. Lessees may have the right under the terms of their leases to sub-let the premises, and it is not uncommon to find numerous sub-lessees occupying premises, together with tenants on a week-to-week, month-to-month, or at will basis; such tenancies are sometimes very loose in their terms. The subject of the law of landlord and tenant is outside the scope of this book, but a knowledge of it is useful, and a reference is given in the Bibliography.

It is a mistake to assume that the person commissioning work to premises has the sole right or interest in the land or premises (*see* Chapter 3, 3.1.9, page 18).

The Ecclesiastical Dilapidations Measures 1923/29 (as amended 1959) are concerned with properties belonging to the church, and unless one is a Diocesan Surveyor, or holds a similar capacity, it is unlikely that Architects in general will have cause to use these measures.

References

AJ Legal Handbook, A. SPEAIGHT and G. STONE (Architectural Press)
Building Law for Students, K. MANSON (Cassell)
Party Structure Rights in London W. A. LEACH (*Estates Gazette*)
London Building Acts (Amendment) Act 1939, Part VI, s.44, GLC
Prescription Act 1832 (HMSO)
Rights of Light Act 1959 (HMSO)
Rights of Way Act 1932 (HMSO)

8

Architects and the law of contract

The Law of Contract is a difficult area of study, particularly the large number of forms of contract in use, and the adverse legal and general comment which their use has attracted over many years.

Numerous books deal with the legal aspects of the subject, either in whole or in part, and it is dangerous for lay persons to expound upon the legal implications of contracts as this is a matter for lawyers and the Courts.

The Architect needs to know not only the fundamentals of contract law, but also his rights, duties and responsibilities in the administration of the building contract on his client's behalf.

The word 'contract' derives from the Latin *contractum* = to draw together; thus, a contract is the drawing-together of persons who, being entitled to do so, wish to enter into a legal relationship affecting their future conduct towards each other, which must not be contrary to the law; and in the event of alleged breach of that contractual agreement, the plaintiff may seek a remedy through the due process of arbitration or litigation, or may eventually have recourse to both courses of action.

Contracts are basically of two kinds

(a) Specialty Contracts and
(b) Simple Contracts.

The former are written contracts in the form of 'deeds of contract' and must be 'signed, sealed, and delivered', e.g. a conveyance contract for property or land.

The latter may be written in some form, or oral, or implied from the actions of the parties concerned. They do not take any specific form, e.g. an auctioneer may request a bid of £50, a person nods assent; the fall of the auctioner's hammer signifies that the offer is accepted and the contract made.

A seal is used as the identity of the artificial legal entity of a limited company or corporation participating in a contractual agreement, not of the persons who for the time being are responsible for the administration of such organisations.

The written contract, which may take numerous forms, is used as the legal basis of the terms and conditions of the contractual agreement between the parties, setting down their respective intentions at the time when the contract was signed, in the absence of any intentions to deceive, defraud, misrepresent, etc, which may lead to repudiation of the contract, or other action as provided by law.

All contracts are agreements, but not all agreements are contracts. In order to distinguish between these two statements certain legal requirements have to be satisfied. Accepting the legal capacity of the parties, the validity and lawfulness of the contract terms, and the intention to create legal relations, these can be said to be, in simple contracts,

(a) Offer,
(b) Acceptance,
(c) Promise,
(d) Consideration (not essential in specialty contracts).

The proof of the existence of these four actions is necessary to support an assertion that an agreement is a contract within the law.

These principles can be applied to both the Architect's contract with his client, and the contractor's contract with the employer, e.g.

	Architect's contract	*Employer/contractor contract*
Offer:	the commission	the contractor's tender
Acceptance:	the Architect's acceptance of the commission	the employer's acceptance of the tender
Promise:	the Architect's promise to do the work commissioned	the contractor's promise to do the work in accordance with the tender documents as the basis of contract
Consideration:	the client pays the Architect's fees in consideration of the work done	the employer pays the contractor the Contract Sum (tender price) in the absence of any variations thereto

In the case of the employer/contractor contract, it follows that the tender price becomes the Contract Sum in the contract when this is drawn up for signature of the parties, and will become a 'lump-sum' contract (Williams *v* Fitzmaurice), i.e. a sum of money to be paid for a 'whole work', which may be 'fixed-price' or subject to 'fluctuations', or some other form of contract to which the parties agree.

Insofar as the Architect is concerned, in order to avoid misunderstanding and disputes arising from commissioned works, it is advisable to confirm in writing to the client what is to be done from the outset, sending the client the appropriate copy of the RIBA Architect's Appointment booklet. The RIBA also publishes a Memorandum of Agreement for use between the Architect and the client.

It is always a risky business to undertake work for a client without the contractual obligations of both parties being set down from the outset, including the Architect's authority to proceed through the work stages as set down in the Architect's Appointment booklets, since sanction to do one stage does not imply authority or sanction to proceed with other stages without the client's authority.

All professional work carries an element of risk, since clients are taken on trust, and there is sometimes a tendency, particularly with established clients, to proceed with work without formal acceptance of the commission. In times of recession and business failures, it is suggested that in all cases it is prudent that the terms of the appointment be confirmed in writing with the client in order that *bona fide* fees claims can be established in the event of the client's bankruptcy or liquidation of business as the occasion may demand.

In the administration of the contract the Architect has to advise the client in the first instance on the best type of contract to be used according to the prevailing circumstances. Sometimes the client may be loath to enter into a contract at all, relying instead upon the terms of the offer, received as an estimate or tender, as the basis of working.

Criticism of the various forms of contract used for many years in the building industry, and assertions that they are pro-client or pro-contractor documents, have been the subject of much argument and debate. Suffice it to say, in the event of a dispute arising from the works, it is better to have any form of contract than none at all, particularly where the contract terms are related to drawings, specification, or a Bill of Quantities, as the basis for the contractual works.

The contract also gives to the Architect 'warranty of authority' (as has been discussed in Chapter 2, 2.1.6, page 12) making for a firmer professional relationship with the parties to the contract, although the argument propounded that the Architect's judgement in contractual matters is biased towards the client, from whom the Architect derives his fees, is a long-standing one.

The Architect is concerned with the administrative procedures and 'drills' under the terms of the 'warranty of authority' vested in him, e.g. to grant extensions to the contract period, and to issue certificates, etc.

It is not the prerogative of the Architect to interpret the legal implications of the terms and conditions of the contract; it is, however, his duty to attempt to resolve differences between the employer and the contractor as they arise, using impartial, reasoned argument and pursuasive skill, in order that disruptive and costly actions in court may be avoided.

For many years one of the inherent problems of contractual procedure for the Architect has been the increasing pressure from clients to begin works on site with insufficient time to prepare all the necessary documentation and information to obtain firm tenders for the works. To some extent this tendency has been ameliorated by new forms of contract coming into use to meet the demands, such as re-measurement contracts, some with approximate quantities, which are open-ended in terms of the total cost of the works at commencement with perhaps a fixed fee or percentage over and above the total cost of the works to the Contractor on completion.

The building process is a precarious business at the best of times, and fraught with claims for extras over and above the contract sum, more particularly so when the documentation upon which the work is carried out is flimsy and capable of exploitation, albeit with justification in some cases.

The legitimate 'Contingency Sum' to allow for 'unforeseen extras' in the course of the contract works, and the dubious procedure of padding-out Prime Cost Sums to meet increased or unforeseen costs tend to be rapidly swallowed up where insufficient time is allowed for preparation of documents.

8.1.1 Types of contract in use

Lump-sum contracts

The contractor agrees to carry out and complete a whole building work for a pre-agreed sum of money (Williams *v* Fitzmaurice). It may well be that such a contract is *indivisible* i.e. a condition of the contract is total completion of the works before payment is made, but this is uncommon (*see* 2.1.4, page 10).

In the event of non-completion of certain works, but where the work is substantially complete, it would appear that the courts take the view that the contractor is entitled to some payment for the work completed. i.e. a *quantum meruit* payment less a 'set-off' for the incomplete works (Hoenig *v* Isaacs). One can relate this to the Practical Completion date as provided for in the JCT Standard Form of Building Contract 1980, Clause 17, 17.1.

A lump-sum contract may be constructed in various ways, and may also be subject to additions for variations, extra works, adjustment of Prime Cost Sums, contractor's loss and expense, extensions of the contract period, etc, but the contractor's basic legal entitlement is the agreed lump sum as this is the essence of the original contract.

Cost contracts

There are many forms of this contract structure, cost contracts, cost-plus contracts, prime cost plus a fixed fee or percentage contracts, or simply called 'fee contracts'. More recently 'management contracts' have emerged from the cost-contract basis.

There is no pre-agreed lump sum but the total cost of the actual works performed on completion. The contractor must, of course, establish the costs to him on a satisfactory basis, his performance being honest and avoiding frivolous claims and waste. The contractor is then entitled to an agreed fee or percentage over the total prime cost of the completed works to cover his overheads and profit.

Insofar as fluctuations are concerned, a lump-sum contract can also be considered as a fixed-price, but in so doing care must be taken to ensure that the contractor is not frustrated in carrying out the works as speedily as possible from inception to completion, as such a contract disbars him from any increased labour or material costs in the absence of a fluctuations agreement, and in the absence of variations and extra works.

If the lump sum is subject to variations and extra works, these are measured by various means as provided for, e.g.

(a) At the rates upon which the tender was based,
(b) At an agreed rate, or
(c) Daywork rates (Definition of Prime Cost of Daywork Rates in the Building Industry)

In cost contracts the contractor is usually paid for extra works on the same basis as the original contract works, but this is not sacrosanct.

Design-and-build contracts

Contractors now enter into contracts on the basis of design-and-build, and employ Architects (RIBA Architect's Appointment, Part 2, 2.39) and other professionals to undertake the design aspects of the work, taking unto themselves the absolute promise that the works will be fit for their intended purpose (Independent Broadcasting Authority *v* EMI Electronics Ltd (1981) 14 BLR 1), whereas Architects undertake to exercise only reasonable care in design.

Management contracts

These normally take the form of measurement-and-valuation contracts with some person acting for the client as an entrepreneur co-ordinating and administering the building works, employing such specialist skills as may be required for the purpose, and controlling the supply of labour and materials by sub-contractors and suppliers within the framework of the overall building programme, and organizing payment for same.

Architects may engage in this capacity, as provided for in Architect's Appointment, Part 2, 2.38. Such work calls for a high degree of skill and knowledge of site operations, organization and planning, including managerial ability.

8.1.2 Contractual procedures

Preparation of contract documents

It is the duty and responsibility of the Architect under Architect's Appointment, Part 1, 1.20 to advise the client on the appointment of the contractor, and the respective responsibilities of the contractor, client, and Architect under the terms of the building contract (*see* page 11), and to prepare the contract documents and get them signed by the parties to the contract, and to provide such production information as is required under the contract.

The nature of the contract documents will vary with the type of contract to be used, e.g. where quantities are not used, the contract form, together with the contract drawings and the Specification, will be the basis of the contract and termed the 'Contract Documents'. The drawings and the Specification will be signed by the parties to the contract something like the following:

SCOTLAND

Scottish Building Contract + Supplement + Sectional Completion Supplement + Scottish Supplement for use with Approximate Quantities

THE JOINT CONTRACTS TRIBUNAL FORMS

Ref	Description
80/PW	Private Edition(with Quantities)
80/PWO	Private Edition (without Quantities)
80/LAW	Local Authority Edition (with Quantities)
80/LAWO	Local Authority Edition (without Quantities)
80/PWA	Private Edition (with Approximate Quantities)
80/LAA	Local Authority Edition (with Approximate Quantities)
80/SF/P	SFBC 1980 Editions Part 3 - Fluctuations (Private)
80/SF/LA	SFBC 1980 Editions Part 3 - Fluctuations (Local Authority)
80/PN/1-21	Practice Notes for 1980 Editions

TENDER DOCUMENTS FOR NOMINATED SUB-CONTRACTORS 1980 EDITIONS

Scotland	Ref	Description
NSC/1/Scot	80/NSC/1	Nominated Sub-Contractor Tender and Agreement
NSC/2/Scot	80/NSC/2	Employer/Nominated Sub-Contract or Agreement for use where Sub-Contractor tendered on NSC/1
NSC/2a/Scot	80/NSC/2a	Employer/Nominated Sub-Contract or Agreement for use where NSC/1 NOT used
NSC/3/Scot NSC/3a/Scot	80/NSC/3	Standard Form of Nomination of a Sub-Contractor where Tender NSC/1 HAS been used

THE SUB-CONTRACT FORMS 1980

Scotland	Ref	Description
NSC/4/Scot	80/NSC/4	Nominated Sub-Contract NSC/4 (including Amendments 1 & 2) Sub-Contract for Sub-Contractors who have tendered on Tender NSC/1 and executed Agreement NSC/2 and have been nominated by Nomination NSC/3
NSC/4a/Scot	80/NSC/4a	Nominated Sub-Contract NSC/4a (including Amendments 1 & 2) Sub-Contract NSC/4 adapted for use where Tender NSC/1 and Agreement NSC/2 and Nomination NSC/3 have NOT been used
	80/NSC/FL	Supplement to NSC/4 and NSC/4a containing Fluctuations Clauses 35 (Contribution Levy and Tax), 36 (Labour and Material Cost and Tax),37 (Formula Adjustment) for use with each of the above Sub-Contracts

JCT FORMULA RULES

Ref	Description
80/FR/M	Main Contract Formula Rules for use with Clause 40 of the Standard Form of Building Contract, Private and Local Authority Editions with Quantities 1980 Editions
80/FR/SC	Sub-Contract Formula Rules referred to in the Sub-Contract NSC/4 Clause 37.1; in Tender NSC/1, Schedule 1, Appendix B, and In Sub-Contract NSC/4a Clause 37.1 and Appendix Part 2

CONTRACTOR'S DESIGN DOCUMENTS

Scottish Design-and-Build Contract + Scottish Supplement

Ref	Description
81/CD	Standard Form of Contract with Contractor's Design 1981 based on Standard Form 1980 Edition where no Architect/ Supervising Officer is appointed on behalf of the Employer
81/CD/DP	Contractor's Designed Portion Supplement 1918 enables part of the works to be designed by the Contractor, amending Standard Form 1980 Edition with Quantities, Private and Local Authority Editions
81/PN/CD1A & B	PRACTICE NOTES FOR USE WITH CONTRACTOR'S DESIGN FORMS
80/MW	Agreement for Minor Building Works
80/MW/Sup	Minor Works Supplement

JCT TENDERS FOR NOMINATED SUPPLIERS

Ref	Description
TNS/1	Tender for Nominated Suppliers (First Two Schedules)
TNS/2	Warranty for Nominated Suppliers (Third Schedule)

FORMS OF CONTRACT FOR DOMESTIC SUB-CONTRACTORS

Ref: DOM/1/A, DOM/1/B, DOM/1/FR, DOM/2 — New Form of Contract for Domestic Sub-Contractors 1980 and supporting documents

---

Ref: C35 — A Form of Contract for civil engineering works equivalent to the JCT Standard Form of Building Contract in the building industry. Issued with the approval of the Institution of Civil Engineers, the Association of Consulting Engineers and the Federation of Civil Engineering Contractors. The present edition was issued in 1973. It is essentially a re-measurement contract

CENTRAL GOVERNMENT CONTRACTS

Ref: GC/Works/1/Edn 2 — General Conditions of Government Contracts for Building and Civil Engineering Works

Ref: GW/S, GW/S/C — Sub-Contract Forms for use with GC/Works/1/Edn 2

MISCELLANEOUS FORMS OF CONTRACT

A Form of Contract based upon the JCT Standard Form is used by the Association of Consultant Architects

The British Property Federation also issues a Form of Contract 1983 Edition

OVERSEAS CONTRACTS

Ref: FIDIC Form — This form is used by the Federation Internationale des Ingenieurs - Conseils, and the Federation Internationale Europeene de la Construction

Note: At the time of writing a form termed the JCT Intermediate was under discussion as an intermediate form of contract between the JCT Standard Form and the Agreement for Minor Building Works

This chart should not be regarded as a comprehensive coverage of all forms of contract in use, but indicates some of the more familiar forms

Diagram 10: Forms of contract in use, and supplementary documents

This is the drawing No. 000 referred to in the Form of Contract

signed .... Employer
signed .... Contractor
dated ....

This is the Specification marked 'A' referred to in the Form of Contract

signed .... Employer
signed .... Contractor
dated ....

The form of contract provides for witnesses to the signatures on page 9 of the JCT Form 1980, and in the case of local authority forms for 'attestation'. It should be remembered that the local authority is a corporate body signing under seal, except otherwise as provided for in the Corporate Bodies Contracts Act 1960 and in terms of the corporation Standing Orders.

Where quantities are used the Specification is not a contract document *per se*; the Form of Contract, the drawings and the Bill of Quantities are the contract documents, and these will be similarly signed and witnessed, substituting the Bill of Quantities for the Specification. It is suggested that the Specification is a supporting document by implication, since without it, together with the drawings, the Bill of Quantities could not have been prepared. Practice today departs from this ideal for many reasons, but in the event of disputes the Architect should remember his responsibilities in this regard.

If the contract is under seal the Inland Revenue stamp duty is 50p and the contract should be sent through the Post Office, or direct to the Controller of Stamps, Bush House, London. It is always wise to keep a duplicate copy of the form of contract in a safe place away from the office in case of fire.

On the signing of the contract, the site will be handed over to the contractor at the time stated in the contract which is then the beginning of the contract period. It could be said that from this time a licence is granted to the contractor to occupy the site or premises and assume responsibility for it under the terms of the contract until completion of the contract works.

The important thing for the client and the Architect is to avoid any frustration of the contractor's contractual liabilities which may give rise to impossibility of performance, or claims for loss and expense, e.g. if the Architect fails to provide in good time the necessary information on nominated sub-contractors and suppliers, thus affecting the general progress of the works.

Such information as is requested by the contractor is covered by Clause 26.2, JCT Form 1980 where, in essence, the demand for information, etc, must be reasonable.

It is not proposed to comment upon the continued use of the JCT Form of Contract 1963 as amended, or its attendant forms of sub-contract.

8.1.3 The JCT Standard Form of Building Contract 1980

Mandatory duties of the Architect

Clause	
2.3	Instruct the main contractor on divergencies
4.3.1	Instructions to main contractor to be in writing
5.2	Provide the main contractor with the following: copies of the JCT Form of Contract; contract drawings; blank Bills of Quantities (where appropriate)
5.3	Provide the main contractor with copies of descriptive Schedules
5.4	Provide the main contractor with necessary further drawings or details
5.8	Send all certificates to the employer and the duplicate of any certificate to the main contractor
6.1.3	Instructions on statutory requirement to the main contractor within seven days
7	Determine levels
13.3.1	Instruct the main contractor on Provisional Sums
13.3.2	Instruct the main contractor on Provisional Sums within nominated sub-contracts
17.1	Certify Practical Completion
17.2	Compile a Schedule of Defects and instruct the main contractor to make good the defects
17.4	Certify completion of making good defects
18.1.1	Certify value of part possession within seven days of occupation
18.1.3	Certify completion of making good defects on part possession
25.3.1	Extend the contract period or not as provided for
25.3.3	Amend or confirm the date of completion within 12 weeks of completion
25.3.5	Notify all nominated sub-contractors of amendments to the contract period
26.1	Ascertain loss and expense
26.3	State the extensions made under Clause 25
26.4.2	State the extensions for sub-contract works
27.4.4	Certify employer's costs on determination of contract

30 1.1.1	Certify interim payments
30 5.2	Certify retentions (including NSC retentions)
30 6.1.2	Send Quantity Surveyor's final valuation to main contractor
30.7	Certify on interim certificates NSC's final sums
30.8	Issue Final Certificate
34.2	Instruct the main contractor on antiquities, etc
34.3.1	Ascertain the main contractor's expenses arising from 34.2
35.7	Send main contractor completed NSC/1, NSC/2 and Nomination Notice, etc
35.8	Instruct main contractor if disagreement with selected nominated sub-contractor
35.10.2	Instruct main contractor on NSC/3
35.11.2	Instruct main contractor on nomination where NSC/2 and Agreement NSC/2 not used
35.13.1.1	Instruct main contractor on amounts for nominated sub-contractors included in interim certificates
35.14.2	Operate NSC/4.4 (a) on nominated sub-contractor's request for an extension
35.15	Certify nominated sub-contractor's failure to complete on time
35.16	Certify Practical Completion of the NSC's works
35.23	Re-nominate if nomination does not proceed, or issue Architect's Instruction
35.24.4.1	Instruct main contractor concerning NSC's alleged default
35.24.4.3	Re-nominate on nominated sub-contractor's insolvency
35.24.6	Re-nominate on NSC's own determination
35.26	Direct main contractor on amounts of Interim Certificate for determined NSC
36.2	Instruct main contractor for nominated supplier
36.4.1	Approve quality of nominated supplies

Non-mandatory actions that the Architect *may* take

4.3.2.2	Confirm oral instructions prior to Final Certificate
8.3	Instruct contractor to open up work for inspection or to test materials
8.4	Instruct main contractor to remove work or materials not in accordance with the terms of the contract
8.5	Exclude employed persons from the works
13.2	Issue variations and sanction variations
22c.2.3.2	Instruct main contractor to remove debris
23.2	Postpone any work
25.3.2	Shorten contract period when work omitted after 25.3.1
27.1	Formally notify main contractor of default
32.2	Instruct main contractor on protection of the onset of hositilities
33.1.2	Instruct main contractor to remove war damage

Practical completion of the contract

It follows that when the Architect is contemplating the issue of the Practical Completion Certificate, JCT Form of Contract 1980, Clause 17.1, it is essential to realize that the contractual position is at this stage quite critical, for having once issued the certificate these matters are put in train

(1) The Defects Liability period begins,
(2) The main contractor is entitled to the release of one half of the Retention Sum retained under Clause 30.5.2,
(3) Where the main contractor has insured the works against Clause 22 perils (footnote (m) of contract page 23) the employer assumes this responsibility,
(4) Period of final measurement begins.

Before the issue of the certificate it is vital that, so far as is possible and for all practical purposes, the works are completed with none left outstanding, since the only money remaining after (2) above will be the residue of the Retention Sum to encourage the contractor to complete, including any subsequent latent defects which may arise during the Defects Liability period.

It is relevant to quote here remarks regarding practical completion which were made by Lord Dilhorne in Westminster City Council *v* J Jarvis Ltd (1970). He said that it does not mean the stage when work 'was almost but not entirely finished' but 'completion of all the construction work that has to done', subject to defects which may thereafter appear, as provided for in Clause 17.

When the Defects Liability period has ended, usually six months from the time of occupation by the employer, and within 14 days thereafter, the Architect must provide the main contractor with a Schedule of Defects which in the Architect's opinion arise from faulty workmanship or materials. Such a schedule will of course include the work of nominated sub-contractors, the materials and goods of nominated suppliers, and the work of domestic sub-contractors for whom the main contractor is responsible.

When the defects have been made good to his satisfaction, the Architect must issue a Certificate of Making Good Defects under Clause 17.4. This certificate having a direct relationship to the ultimate issue of the Final Certificate under Clause 30.8, as this is the certificate which the Architect issues on behalf of the employer, saying in effect that the Architect is satisfied with the works, including the making good of defects, generally within the terms of the contract.

The only redress the employer has after this time, being contractually bound to pay the sum certified by the Architect in full and final settlement of the completion of the works, is to sue the Architect if it is considered that the certified value of the completed works is incorrect for any reason which may be supported by law.

The building owner, whoever this may be at the time, may have redress for latent defects by reason of the Limitation Acts, the periods of six years for simple contracts and twelve years for specialty contracts in which claims for alleged latent defects could be pursued in the Courts, ran from the completion of the building up to the time of the judgement of Lord Denning in the Sparham Souter *v* T & C Developments etc and Benfleet UDC (*see* page 23). Lord Denning decided that the statutory period for claims would run from when the alleged defects were discovered.

This would seem to negate the purpose of the Limitation Acts to some degree, since presumably their function was to prevent, after a reasonable time, the bringing of actions into the courts based upon dubious evidence and absent or unreliable witnesses. To some extent the problem of defects is exacerbated by the prolific use of nominated sub-contractors and suppliers, many of whom in an uncertain economic climate go into liquidation and thus make any subsequent redress against them very difficult, if not impossible, to achieve.

8.1.4 Litigation and arbitration

The Architect may act as an Arbitrator by appointment or may assume the role by contractual or statutory authority, e.g.

(1) He may act as Third Surveyor under Part VI, Section 55, London Building Acts (Amendment) Act 1939, sub-section (m), or under Part VII, Section 63, 2(a) of the Act, in party-wall matters, or dangerous structures. In this capacity he adopts the role of an Arbitrator, and is in the former case written into the Party Wall Award by name, or (and this obtains in the latter case) he may be appointed when a dispute has arisen which cannot be resolved by the appointed Surveyors or Engineers acting for the respective building owners.

(2) When he administers a building contract he may act as a 'quasi-arbitrator' within the authority vested in him by the terms of the contract and his agency with the client. There has been doubt expressed as to whether this term is valid following the case of Sutcliffe *v* Thackrah (referred to in Chapter 2, 2.1.4) but this case dealt only with certification of money due to the contractor. Extensions of the contract period, the dismissal of workmen from the site, etc, are still within the Architect's prerogative.

(3) The Architect may be named in the building contract as Arbitrator with the agreement of the parties, or he may be named and appointed by the President or Vice-President for the time being of the RIBA on application from either of the contracting parties in the event of a dispute arising.

Obtain from RIBA Publications Ltd a copy of the book *The Architect as Arbitrator* which clearly sets down the procedure to be followed.

In (1) above, in the making of a separate Award which is binding upon the Building and Adjoining Owner's Surveyors, the Third Surveyor acts as an Arbitrator, and under Section 55, (n), (o) of the London Building Acts (Amendment) Act 1939, his Award may be challenged in the County Court on appeal (*see* Diagram 2, page 7), or to the High Court if the appellant decides to exercise the provisions laid down in the Act. See also the Third Surveyor appointment under dangerous structures procedure under the London Building Acts (Amendment) Act 1939, Part VII, Section 63(1).

In (3) above, Article 5 of the JCT Standard Form of Building Contract 1980 provides for arbitration in the event of a dispute, and either party to the contract may challenge the appointment of such an Arbitrator if they consider, within reason, that the person appointed is not appropriately qualified to deal with the difference or dispute.

In Article 5.5, the law of England is described as the 'proper law of the contract' and one should refer to the footnote in the Form of Contract regarding the law of Scotland or any other country.

The following extract from *The Law Relating to the Architect* (Rimmer) is worthy of note.

> The procedure of arbitration pre-supposes that a difference or dispute exists between two or more parties, and although an Arbitrator may be appointed by name either before or after a dispute arises, his duty as Arbitrator can begin and continue only as long as there is a difference between the parties to be determined. Thus, agreement between the parties as to either a part or the whole of their differences precludes the Arbitrator from concerning himself with questions which have been settled by agreement. Moreover, a reference to the arbitration of a named Arbitrator can be varied by agreement

between the parties, who may dispense with the services of the named Arbitrator and either appoint another or have their differences decided in another way. For this reason an Architect should hesitate before accepting nomination as an Arbitrator in a contract of long duration before a dispute has arisen. In such cases a dispute may never arise, or the parties may change their minds as to the manner in which they wish their dispute to be determined. In the meantime the Architect, who has accepted the nomination, will be precluded from advising any of the parties to the contract or accepting any duties which may involve him in questions relating to either party. Acceptance of the position of a standing Arbitrator may be equally prejudicial and, unless the parties are willing to pay an annual fee which will recompense the Architect for work he may lose in consequence of his accepting the nomination, he is advised not to accept any nomination as an Arbitrator until a dispute has arisen between the parties. Various examples of professional men who have accepted appointment as Arbitrator before any dispute has arisen, and thereby have been precluded from taking work for which they would have otherwise been engaged, have come to the attention of the Editor.

This extract refers to the JCT Form of Contract 1963, Clause 35, but is equally valid in terms of the JCT Form of Contract 1980.

There are three arbitration Acts, as follows –

(1) The Arbitration Act 1950, which may well be regarded as the Principal Act, sets down the majority of arbitration law and consolidating previous law.
(2) The Arbitration Act 1975 is concerned with arbitrations containing foreign elements (*see* Article 5.5 of the JCT Form of Contract 1980) and reference is made to Section 34 of the Act of 1950.
(3) The Arbitration Act 1979 which replaces Section 21 of the Act of 1950 (Special Cases, Remission and Setting Aside of Awards, etc) by a new appeals procedure in lieu of 'in the form of a special case for decision of the High Court'.

    By Section 5, it also provides for the High Court to empower an Arbitrator to make 'unless' orders.

To determine arbitration it must have been agreed between the parties that

(1) in the event of difference or dispute that there should be a judicial enquiry,
(2) they wished the referee to act as Judge.

Sometimes the Architect is faced with a dispute or difference in the absence of a contract, or any reference to arbitration in the event of difference or dispute arising, particularly where work has been carried out on the basis of letters of acceptance or verbal acceptance of written estimates. In such circumstances it may be possible to find a reference to arbitration in the event of dispute within the terms of the estimate. Alternatively, the Architect can suggest to the parties that another independent person be appointed to negotiate with him to achieve a settlement of the dispute which would be acceptable to both sides.

In practice such disputes usually revolve around money, directly or indirectly, and the danger in such cases is that they may result in a dutch auction situation, particularly where work carried out is based upon little documentary evidence, and much of which may be covered up and incapable of measurement or assessment, and this should be avoided at all costs.

Before embarking upon such a course of action, the Architect should commit the terms of the undertaking to writing and get agreement of both parties that the decision of himself and the independent person will be acceptable to both, and the fees of both will be based upon the RIBA Architect's Appointment, Part 4, 4.9. Do not make the error of quoting fees before the settlement of the dispute has been reached.

An arbitrator is a judge in fact and not in law, although he may be assisted at the hearing by a Solicitor or Counsel advising him on matters of law, but he must not delegate any of his judicial powers to such an adviser without consent of the parties to the arbitration.

If the parties agree to the appointment of a legal adviser, from whom the Arbitrator may hear legal statements at any time during the hearing, such advice or legal argument may be disregarded by the Arbitrator if he does not agree.

If either party to the arbitration objects to the presence of a legal advisor during the arbitration hearing, the Arbitrator should accede to their request to proceed without him, and it is very desirable to obtain agreement to such an advisor before the hearing takes place.

The date for the first hearing may be agreed by the parties or set down by the Arbitrator, and at this time the Arbitrator will presumably have read the first pleadings submitted by the parties, and any supporting documents such as letters, drawings, etc, and he may also have decided to visit the site and to see the subject matter of the dispute. In his *The Law Relating to the Architect* the author, Rimmer, suggested (on page 166) that 'the practice of parties sending to the Arbitrator correspondence and documents which are to be used in evidence at the hearing before the hearing takes place is to be very severely deprecated, and any attempt on the part of one party to do so without the fullest consent of all the parties should be resisted by the Arbitrator. Similarly, unless there is some special reason why a view of the subject matter needs to be taken before the hearing – and such need exists if an alteration is to be made in the meantime – it is generally better that the Arbitrator's view should take place during or after the hearing. The reasons are obvious; the Arbitrator should not do anything which may, in the slightest degree, prejudice his open mind before the whole case has been opened before him, the evidence taken and the submissions made on behalf of the parties'.

The procedure at the hearing should follow that generally observed in civil courts.

The question as to whether one pursues arbitration or litigation in the event of disputes as a means of achieving a decision is a matter for debate. The argument that arbitration is quicker and cheaper, and that the persons chosen as Arbitrators are more closely at the 'cutting face' of constructional matters, appears to be in some doubt. Solicitor Robert Fenwick Elliot in his book *Building Contract Litigation* states in Chapter 7 the following:

> Contrary to popular belief in the construction industry, arbitration in building contract matters is generally slower, more expensive, and less certain than High Court litigation. Many people in the industry take the view that it is essential to have their dispute heard by someone with a working knowledge of building contracts and the practices that are prevalent in the industry. They often lean towards arbitration as a means of achieving this end. They frequently fail to take account of the Official Referees Court, which is almost invariably the Court within the High Court that takes building contract matters, at any rate in London. The official referees are appointed from leading Counsel and spend a great deal of their time hearing disputes about building contracts. They have therefore come to acquire a detailed working knowledge of the construction industry in much the same way as professional Arbitrators who are almost always qualified Architects.
>
> There is a common view in the industry that Arbitrators are able to bring to bear more common sense than are High Court Judges, and are able to cut through the red tape. This is largely fallacious. Where an Arbitrator takes it into his head to cut through the red tape, his decisions will be frequently appealable in the Courts. Sometimes it will go further. For example, in the recent case of Modern Engineering (Bristol) Ltd *v* C Miskin & Son Ltd, the Arbitrator was faced with a point of law as to whether the Architect's certificate could be reviewed. The Arbitrator evidently thought he knew the answer to that point, and made an interim formal award without listening to full legal argument. That attempt to short-cut the proceedings backfired. The Arbitrator was removed for misconduct under the Arbitration Act 1950, Section 23(1), and his award was set aside under Section 23(2).

The above case decision should be read in the light of the decision in Northern Regional Hospital Board *v* Derek Crouch Construction Co Ltd (1984).

Being an Architect and not a lawyer, the present author makes no comment on the foregoing extract, but it is interesting that these beliefs are widely held in the architectural profession and the building industry as a whole. In any event it is better to try to avoid having recourse to either of the procedures if it is at all possible since it is certainly true that they are time consuming and expensive.

References

AJ Legal Handbook, A. SPEAIGHT and G. STONE (Architectural Press)

Tendering and Contractual Arrangements – Which Builder? THE AQUA GROUP (Crosby Lockwood)

Contract Practice for Quantity Surveyors, J. W. RAMUS (Heinemann)

Building Contract Litigation, R. J. FENWICK ELLIOT (Oyez Longman)

Questions and Answers on the Law of Contract, R. S. SIM (Butterworths)

The Law Relating to the Architect, RIMMER (edited GILL) (Batsford)

9

Building research

9.1.1 Codes of practice, standards, and research organizations

The British Standards Institution, 2 Park Street, London W1A 2BS, publishes British Standards and Codes of Practice which are extensively used throughout the building industry, particularly in specification writing and Bills of Quantities. They are also extensively used in building legislation, where they are not mandatory.

These publications appear in the British Standards Year Book, including abstracts and prices, a sales bulletin is issued on a subscription basis containing lists issued every two months which are cumulative, including all publications issued since the publication of the last Year Book.

A sectional list, SL16, groups Building Standards in accordance with the CI/Sfb Construction Indexing Manual 1976 revision, and information on this system is available from the RIBA.

The British Standards Handbook No 3, *Building Materials and Components for Housing*, has been a valuable aid to specification writing for many years, and a new publication, *Manual of British Standards in Building Construction and Specification* was due for publication in 1985.

9.1.2 The use of British Standard codes and specifications in practice

In a survey carried out in 1982 by the British Standards Institution to ascertain the use of Standards and Codes among Architects, Quantity Surveyors, and Engineers, the following information was deduced.

(1) The majority of firms (71) said that British Standards and Codes of Practice were very important to them.

(2) Firms buy BSI documents because they need them, and for larger firms price was not a major consideration.

(3) Some of the reasons why people do not use BSs and CPs as much as they feel they should are

 it takes too much time,
 they are not always relevant,
 copies are not always available,
 people still work by rule of thumb,
 people are sometimes ignorant of their contents,
 people feel that they can manage without them.

(4) Handbook 3 is extensively used by Architects and Quantity Surveyors because it often gives the required information, and is more convenient to use than the full texts. Most Handbook users would like fuller summaries in the Codes.

(5) Almost half the sample said that they sometimes have problems locating the appropriate BS or CP; all Quantity Surveyors experienced this.

(6) Over 80 per cent of the sample said they sometimes or often need to refer to more than one BS or CP to get the information needed to solve the problem.

(7) Around 50 per cent of the sample sometimes had difficulty in retrieving the information they needed within BSs and CPs.

It is perhaps interesting to note that comments made by Architects on why they did not use BSs or CPs as much as they should were 'they were only relevant in disputes', and 'specification writing is left to the Quantity Surveyor'; this latter remark is surely reflected in the new RIBA Architect's

Appointment booklet, Part 1 (1.6), but what happens when there is no QS? Perhaps this is why the Small Works Architect's Appointment booklet places the specification production squarely on the shoulders of the Architect?

The use of BSs and CPs in legislation merely places in the hands of the enforcement officers acceptable standards of materials and workmanship which although not mandatory may be used as a basis for discussion.

Standards, as mentioned in (3) above, are not always appropriate, e.g. door frames and linings BS 1567 would be suitable for low-cost housing, but would be entirely unsuitable for high-class joinery work.

When used in specifications and Bills of Quantities, BSs and CPs have contractual significance since the Contractor is asked to carry out work under the contract on the basis of what is written in them. It is therefore necessary on the part of the specifier to ensure that they understood and correctly quoted, e.g. Roofing Felts BS 747 (Bitumen and Fluxed Pitch) should quote not only the BS number but also the table and type number.

In site supervision it is important to ensure that the correct BS number is stamped on materials and goods, e.g. asphalt, drainpipes, etc, as there is a great difference in quality between natural and synthetic asphalts, and drainpipes which are British Standard Tested Quality or British Standard Quality, and of course difference in cost.

9.1.3 Research organizations in the building industry

The advancement in building technology since the end of the Second World War owes much to research organizations, both private and government-subsidised, although there are critics who will say that research has lacked proper finance, imagination, and innovation. Many materials and constructional methods in building are spin-offs from research in other industries, or have come about to satisfy a particular need at a particular time. For example, the emergence in the nineteen-thirties and post war of a family of some 40 plastics was not concerned primarily with building materials or methods. When Japan overran Malaya and the East Indies during World War Two, almost the entire supply of rubber to the world was cut off and the Allied nations needed a synthetic rubber quickly. In two years America was producing two million tons a year, the basic chemical being styrene, already used in Germany before the war which at the time became the most important plastics material for injection moulding. Styrene itself was first discovered in 1831 as vinyl benzene.

The need for prefabricated structural systems after the war to meet the demand for housing invoked in Europe a large research programme; in the early nineteen-fifties there were in use some 50 systems many of which originated in France. The legislative demand for better thermal and sound insulation in dwellings, and the need to save energy in domestic and commercial buildings, led to a research programme to find suitable materials for the purpose, but many of the early ones subsequently proved to be disastrous, e.g. some foams for cavity-wall insulation, asbestos-impregnated sheets and other products.

Demolition research has been necessary to cope with the demolition of buildings having pre- or post-stressed reinforced concrete structural systems posing enormous problems in the demolition process, now covered by BS 6187 1982.

The British Standards Institution works in close liaison with some of the long-established research organizations such as the Building Research Establishment, and the Fire Research Establishment, who have contributed much to British Standards and Codes of Practice used in legislation, e.g. BS 746 1953 as amended to date for fire testing of materials and elements of construction, etc.

Listed below are some of the research organizations related to the building industry:

Agrément Board (British Board of Agrément)
British Standards Institution
Building Research Establishment
Cement and Concrete Association
Department of the Environment
Fire Research Establishment
Government Development Groups
Home Office
Industry-based organizations
National Building Commodity Centres (popularly called 'Building Centres', of which there are six at the time of writing: London, Manchester, Durham, Bristol, Peterborough, Glasgow.) These centres deal with a vast number of enquiries each year, from both the general public and those involved in the building industry.
RIBA Research Steering Group
Timber Research and Development Association
Universities and Polytechnics and other educational establishments undertaking research programmes.

References

British Standards Institution Year Book 1984
BSI Sectional List of British Standards SL 16

10

The profession and the building industry

10.1.1 Current concepts of professionalism

In the pre-Second World War years when the country was in a state of deep recession with massive unemployment, and little social security or State support, there was a sharp division between the so-called 'white-collar' workers and the 'working class'. The term 'professional person' had a connotation different from that existing today. Scholarships such as the Junior County and the Trade Scholarship, academically or vocationally structured, were the usual means by which children could attain secondary education, but even if a child was successful in passing them, particularly the former, it was usually financially impossible for the majority of working-class parents to sustain their children through secondary education, and for the majority of children their formal education ceased at the age of 14 years.

Matriculation was the generally accepted level of entrance into the universities. In the profession of architecture there were very few full-time schools, mostly in universities, and the independent Architectural Association.

For many children apprenticeship was a way of learning a trade, and in the architectural profession pupilage was a way of learning the basic skills of an Architect, supported by part-time study in technical schools. A premium was normally paid to the Principal of the practice to whom the pupil was indentured, and this fact, coupled with the lack of any payment to the pupil for perhaps two or three years from the commencement of the pupilage, made it prohibitive for many parents. Pupilage continued in the profession well into the post-war years, and may even exist today, together with sponsorship schemes of one sort or another.

After the Second World War the clamour for the resettlement of the armed forces, and the vast sums of money made available by central government for this purpose, filled the further education establishments with masses of people pursuing anything from short trade courses of a few weeks duration to seven-year courses in architecture, although these were limited at the time with strict entry rules. Full-time courses were supplemented by a vigorous part-time and evening school system. Architectural education varied widely across the schools, some having part or full recognition of the RIBA, the upsurge in full recognition taking place in the early nineteen sixties, other schools had no recognition at all. The old Intermediate and the part 1 Final Examination being taken either wholly in school or partly at the RIBA, culminating in the Professional Practice Examination at the RIBA. Many readers will doubtless remember the old RIBA Testimonies of Study in design, and the Special Final Examination for those of mature age and experience in the profession.

The emergence over the following years of the educational facilities through the 11-plus examination and the GCE system in the schools, coupled with State-aided grants for children successfully completing their secondary education, has made it possible for most children to achieve entry to universities and other higher-education establishments, and thence into the professions.

Seen in the light of diminishing outlets for newly-qualified persons in the continuing recession since the nineteen-seventies and the vast number of degrees and other qualifications obtained by young people, some of which, although academically valuable, have little relevance to the harsh world of industry and commerce, it is inevitable that society's attitudes to professionalism have changed. The social changes since the Second World War with the improved educational facilities have largely obliterated the sharp division between 'working class' and 'middle class' which had existed for generations.

Although parental pressure upon children to pursue academic excellence and to 'better themselves' is just as strong as hitherto, the massive cuts in education funding and facilities in the past five years or so in the schools and colleges, coupled with continuing high unemployment, must have had a significant effect, engendering disappointment and frustration among young people unable to find outlets after long years of hard work and study.

The architectural profession is naturally dependent upon a buoyant economy to provide work; but employment for qualified and unqualified people in both the public and private sectors has been very difficult to sustain. The public sector in the early days of the recession absorbed large numbers of persons previously employed in the private sector, until the cut-back in resources began to bite.

If one considers also the 700 or so students and an equal number of diplomates each year seeking either 'year out' or more permanent employment on an already overburdened profession, it is remarkable how they get absorbed into the professional system. There are signs that the profession, and indeed industry as a whole, is coming out of the recession, although there are many factors which condition this alleged recovery, but even so it will be a long time before the boom years are seen to be returning, if indeed they return at all.

There is also a different attitude in society towards the closed-shop point of view, including 'élitist societies'. The Monopolies Commission has looked closely at the accounting, legal, and architectural professions in the light of their selective and protective memberships, controlled by their own rules of conduct, and charging self-determined fee scales. The architectural profession has had to change its fee scale from a basic rate scale below which an Architect was not permitted to work, to a negotiable fee scale based upon RIBA guide lines.

The RIBA, together with ARCUK, has changed the Codes of Conduct and widened the sphere of activities in which an Architect may become engaged. The new RIBA Code of Professional Conduct, and the re-titled ARCUK Conduct and Discipline document, now rely almost entirely upon the professional integrity of Architects in the performance of their professional duties.

As discussed in Chapter 1, the continuing appraisal and re-appraisal of the architectural profession by the RIBA, from both the educational and professional activity standpoints, continues.

Historically, it is interesting to note that in 1968 Lord Esher and Lord Llewellyn-Davies in their joint paper titled 'The Architect in 1988' (*RIBA Journal*, October 1968) commenting on the RIBA *Office Survey*, on the changing role of the Architect in society said, *inter alia*, '. . . we would suggest that the reason the *Office Survey* did not provide a complete basis for forward planning was that it almost exclusively dealt with the need to make the Architect's office more efficient, and did not consider the parts the Architect ought to be playing at other stages of the processes by which society gets its buildings. Thus it deals with diversification simply as a need to bring back certain lost skills into architecture as practised, and we would add to it the need for a more flexible attitude towards diversification in education, not simply as a prelude to the Architect's sphere of activity'.

This far-sighted prediction of the Architect's role in the 20 years since its publication was perhaps not too wide of the mark in the light of later changes in the Codes of Conduct.

To be 'professional' means offering for reward an expertise above that of the amateur or lay-person. The Architect now has the opportunity and Institute's sanction to become engaged in a wide range of activities, including executive, managerial, and directorship roles in business. However, it is one thing to have the authority to pursue such activities, it is quite another to have all the requisite skills and knowledge to pursue them with competence and confidence. The old adage 'Jack of all trades, master of none' implies a lack of overall competence in any one pursuit so that the true identity of the performer is obscured.

10.1.2 The RIBA and ARCUK

The RIBA is first and foremost a learned society. It was founded in 1834 under the style of the Institute of British Architects, receiving its Royal Charter in 1837, and is 'a Body Politic and Corporate for the general advancement of architecture, and for promoting and facilitating the acquirement of the knowledge of the various arts and sciences connected therewith'. It is also a chartered corporation having a corporate legal indentity. Broadly, it consists of a President, two Vice-Presidents, a Council, a Secretary, with several Standing Committees, and of course *ad hoc* committees, pursuing the activities of the various departments. It also has appendages such as RIBA Publications Ltd, and the National Building Specification Ltd.

Its membership, excluding overseas members, was reported in October 1982 as being 20 478, the membership being regionally represented. Probably the most important committee for members is the Professional Conduct Committee, working in close liaison with its counterpart in ARCUK, which in event of transgression of the Codes of Professional

Conduct by a member, may impose after investigation of the allegations has proved them to be substantiated, periods of suspension from both membership of the RIBA and possible removal of the Architect's name from the Register at ARCUK, which in serious cases of misconduct may be permanent. There may also ensue from the Committee inquiry action through the Public Prosecutor if the member is alleged to have been involved in activities contrary to law.

Since 1931 the title 'Architect' has been protected by law through the Architects' Registration Council of the United Kingdom, and the Registration Acts of 1931/69. The Architects' Registration Council is a statutory corporation also having its own corporate legal identity.

The RIBA is the examining body for ARCUK and a candidate having passed the qualifying examination, by whatever process, is entitled first to apply to ARCUK for registration, and if desired, subsequently to the RIBA for corporate membership.

Historically, many people did not wish to pursue the latter course, remaining as Registered Architects with the affix MInstRA. This is rarely seen today. After the Registration Act 1931, a Licentiate grade of membership was introduced for those unable to fulfil the examination requirements for corporate membership as Associates of the RIBA, and they were subsequently made Fellows RIBA, and many members who qualified by examination refrained from applying for Fellowship when entitled to do so, remaining as Associates.

The old system of membership which obtained when the Institute was founded, i.e. Probationer, Student, Associate, Fellow, was abandoned in 1971 in favour of a single class of membership.

There are many organizations existing which offer membership simply for the payment of an annual fee, and having an affix which many people use. Some organizations require additional professional qualifications and/or experience in a particular field of expertise. Some affixes indicate no more than membership of an organization without having any professional or academic standing.

The word 'chartered' has always carried with it an aura of professional standing in society, and in recent years many professional bodies have received the Royal Charter, e.g. The Royal Town Planning Institute in 1959, with a supplementary Charter in 1971; The Chartered Institution of Building in 1969; The Chartered Institution of Building Services 1976, etc.

Since the end of World War Two there has been a striving to bring about professional parity among those engaged in the building industry, and this has been reflected in many courses, some of them at degree level through the National Council for Academic Awards (NCAA); also the emergence of the polytechnics as centres for degree, diploma and other professional courses, has in the last decade contributed greatly towards this end. Perhaps this emphasis on academic excellence may in some measure have denuded Architects and others in the building professions of some of their basic skills and contributed to the demand by industry generally for more vocationally-oriented graduates, but there is opposition to this point of view.

10.1.3 Status in the architectural profession

Whether or not they are fully qualified, architectural assistants, or assistant Architects employed in practices or any other organization, are simply employees when they offer a contract of service and are paid a salary. Their employers are accountable for their actions, and the worst that can happen to employees is that they will be dismissed from their employment in the event of ordinary errors or misdemeanours in performance of their duties. They are protected under the Employment Acts 1975/80 and the Employment Protection (Consolidation) Act 1978, and have recourse to an industrial tribunal if they consider they have been unfairly dismissed from their employment. If they belong to a Trade Union they may enlist the aid of their Union in stating their case to the Tribunal. (*See* page 78).

Qualified Architects are sometimes offered 'Associate' status either in the practice in which they are employed or independently, and their names appear on the practice notepaper as 'in association with'. Several names may appear in this manner, and the RIBA has suggested that the names should appear at the bottom of the page in order to avoid confusion with the names of the Principal(s) of the practice. Such a title as 'Associate' has no foundation in law, and is merely an inducement to retain valued employees, or to make the practice appear larger than it really is. Terms such as 'Associate Partner' must be used with great care due to the legal responsibility attached in law to 'partners', as is described in the following Section. (*See* RIBA Practice Notes, September/October 1981).

10.1.4 Partnerships

A partnership is an unincorporated association of persons wishing to create a relationship between themselves the legal basis of which will be a matter of agreement between them, express or implied.

The maximum number of partners is usually 20, and for banking business 10 but these maxima may be extended in certain cases by Sections 119, 120 of the Companies Act 1967 for persons such as solicitors, accountants, members of the Stock

Exchange and others as may be prescribed by Statutory Instrument.

In England a partnership does not have an artificial legal entity as does a company or a corporation, and exists only as long as the partners wish it to, or it is determined by the death or bankruptcy of any partner, unless provision has been made otherwise. In the event of losses some of the partners may have a limited liability to the partnership but the law requires that at least one partner must remain fully responsible for the partnership debts. The term 'sleeping partner' is sometimes used for a person having some financial interest in the partnership but who is not allowed to take an active part in the management of the partnership business. (*See* RIBA Practice Note, May 1974).

In the event of default in the payment of losses, creditors have the right to distrain in law against the personal property and effects of the partners.

The function of the partnership is regulated by the Articles of Association of the partnership, and these govern the actions of the partners individually and collectively, and may be freely altered in any way by agreement of all the partners concerned. The Articles are confidential to the partners, and unlike company's accounts are not subject to public scrutiny.

A partner is entitled to take part in the management of the firm, and as such acts as an agent for the firm, but cannot transfer his share to another person outside the partnership in substitution for himself. Each partner may bind the others in the partnership in contracts which are normal to the pursuit of the firm's business.

Apart from the Registration of Business Names Act, a partnership is largely contained statutorily within the terms of the Partnership Act 1890.

There must be three basic elements for a partnership to exist, which in the event of dispute or appeal will be closely scrutinised. They are

(a) There must be a business,
(b) The business must be carried on in common, and
(c) There must be a view to profit.

This is explicit in the Partnership Act 1890, Section 1, which states 'Partnership is the relationship that subsists between persons carrying on a business in common with a view to profit'.

Section 45 of the Act states that the expression 'business' includes every trade, occupation, profession.

'Business' has been defined in law as 'a series of acts which will produce gain' (Brett, J). It seems, therefore, that a single act or transaction does not constitute a business as such, but a trade, occupation or profession pursued on a continuous basis for gain would appear to be so. (Cf continuity of business for Inland Revenue purposes, page 72).

Business 'in common' implies that the persons concerned with it are well acquainted with each other, as the inherent 'agency' of the partnership implies this. 'With a view to profit' implies the sharing of net profits (*see* comments on Associate status, page 69), but from the wording of the Act it cannot be construed that the sharing of gross profits, of itself, is *prima facie* evidence that a partnership does or does not exist. Insofar as net profits are concerned, however, the Act section 2(3), states that where profits are shared this does not, of itself, create a partnership, and examples of this are

(a) Where a person receives payment of a debt or other liquidated amount by instalment or otherwise out of the accruing profits of a business.
(b) Where a servant or agent receives by way of remuneration a share of the profits of a business in which he is employed.
(c) Where a widow or child of a deceased partner receives by way of annuity a portion of the profits made in the business in which the deceased was a partner.
(d) Where the money is lent to a person engaged or about to become engaged in business, or terms that the lender shall receive a rate of interest varying with the profits or a share of the profits arising from the carrying on of the business, provided that the contract is in writing and signed for and on behalf of all the parties thereto.
(e) Where the vendor of the goodwill of a business (*see* page 72 for 'goodwill') receives, in consideration of of a sale, a portion of the profits of a business, whether by way of annuity or otherwise.

A partnership is a form of contract made in accordance with the Law of Contract. Partnerships may be held to be illegal on account of the nature of the association or on account of its objects.

Since a partnership is an unincorporated association, the persons forming it are called a 'firm' collectively within the Act, Section 4(1), and the name in which the business is carried on is the 'firm name'. There must be nothing in the chosen 'firm name' that in any way implies that it has a limited liability, such as exists in a limited company, but affixes may be included such as Co, Company, and Son(s), or Bros, which are very common titles.

The Business Names Act 1916, the Companies Act 1948, Section 435, and the Companies Act 1981, Section 23 (c) and (d), require every firm to have its place of business and the firm's name registered in the United Kingdom, with the exception of businesses carried on in the true names of the partners without additions. The following may be added without registration:

(a) The true Christian names of the partners or the initials of the Christian names.
(b) Additions which indicate that the business is carried on in succession from a former owner, e.g. 'formerly John Smith & Son'.
(c) The addition of an 's' where two or more partners have the same surname, e.g. Truetts & Co.

The RIBA Code of Professional Conduct 1981, Rule 2.5, obtains as regards architectural practice partnerships.

In terms of indemnity insurance 'cross indemnity' may be entered into whereby partners dealing with their own jobs within a partnership practice may protect each other from possible actions in negligence.

Scottish law of partnership differs from the remainder of the United Kingdom, and the Bibliography gives a suitable reference.

Architects may now practice in the style of limited liability companies. (*See* RIBA Practice Notes).

Such incorporated associations which have an artificial legal identity separate from those who for the time being form the association, are subject to the Companies Act 1948/1981. Anyone wishing to form a limited company must follow this procedure:

(1) Select a name for the company (check it against specified word(s) under the Companies Act 1981, Section 23(c) and (d)); apply for permission where necessary under the Act. The title must not include the word 'limited' except as a last word, and have no implied governmental or local governmental connections.
(2) Draft:
    Memorandum of Association
    Articles of Association
(3) Prepare forms G1, PUC1, G41a, Form A2.
(4) Arrange a meeting of the Directors of the proposed company and the Company Secretary to sign all documents against a signature check list.
(5) Send to the Registrar of Companies all documents, i.e.
    Memorandum of Association
    Articles of Association
    Forms G1, PUC1, G41a, A2 (as appropriate) + registration fee.
(6) Decide on a Banker and open an account(s).
(7) Await the Certificate of Incorporation from the Registrar.
(8) Order firm stationery and Company Seal, buy Company Book.

This is only an outline of the procedure and it may vary according to the size and type of company to be formed. The Common Seal is the artificial legal identity of the company for use on contracts and other documents. The Memorandum of Association and Articles of Association set down the terms, aims and objectives for which the company is formed, and these are very important in later contractual matters in which the company may be involved. The Company Certificate is sent by the Registrar of Companies to the applicants for display in the company office, which may be a holding address.

The Company Book sets down the rules for limited companies, providing space for entering names of Directors with their occupations and private addresses, also the Company Secretary's details, with provisions for any changes which may take place which must be notified to the Registrar forthwith. There is no provision for the name of the Chairman of the company as any member may be appointed to the chair at meetings as provided for.

A limited company may be private or public, and in the event of failure of the company its members are liable for the amount of their personal shareholding; or, in the case of a company limited by guarantee, the amount of the individual guaranteed amount. A company may be voluntarily liquidated, either in failure or to reform the company, by personal application or by an application of creditors. A Receiver appointed to wind up the company will realise such assets as the company may have to meet creditors' claims in whole or in part; there is an order of priority for monies to be paid to claimants.

Architects may practice in various other unincorporated associations. other than partnerships, e.g. consortia, group practices, which are largely synonymous in law. The RIBA *Handbook of Architectural Practice and Management* gives guidance under 'Group Practice and Consortia'.

10.1.5 Starting an architectural practice

Starting a practice on one's own account requires basically these three essentials: working capital, an office with reasonable secretarial facilities, and a continuity of work.

The winning of an architectural competition has been the launching pad for some successful practices, but is not always of itself sufficient to sustain them, and continuity of work is the hardest to achieve.

Some older books on professional practice advised young Architects to join golf clubs and similar organizations where one came into contact with prospective clients. It has also been said that more contracts are arranged in pubs and churches than anywhere else. If this were true it would go hard for the aethiest teetotaller!

Frankly, one can 'put up one's shingle' as the Americans say, outside your newly-appointed office, but few will even be aware of your existence or beat a path to your door. A large element of luck is involved and being in the right place at the right time also plays a significant part. Work seems to engender more work, but the problem is making the initial start. Everything undertaken, no matter how small, should be done as well as possible as the old adage 'great oaks from little acorns grow' is not without truth.

If one has the good fortune to obtain a large commission, remember the anticipated fee will have to stretch over a long period of time, anticipated because you may in the end get only a part of it, or none at all. It takes a long time to accumulate working capital, and bank managers, contrary to popular slogans, are not philanthropically-minded people, and they quickly see through your well-groomed façade, asking you difficult questions about cash flow, profitability, collateral, etc, knowing only too well that money flows out of the practice every day to pay the butcher, baker and candlestick maker. As your work load increases, and your hours for leisure and sleeping diminish, you will have to employ someone to help you cope, and you will have to pay their salaries and their insurance, etc, and salaries are among the largest drains on capital which cannot be deferred.

In looking for office accommodation, it is a commonly-held view that the office address location is important to attract good clients, and a couple of rooms over a Chinese take-away may not be ideal, but many an established practice has started from humble rooms in a not too salubrious area. Sharing more expensive accommodation, with the use of a room or two, and shared secretarial facilities on a full- or part-time basis, with a telephone answering service to bridge the gaps in office manning, may suffice for a time.

Working freelance from home is not commensurate with practising on one's own account, but if one is careful with money and can build up good contacts, it is a way of accumulating some capital as a preliminary to starting a practice. Freelance work can be of the contract type through an agency, or ghosting for an established practice for an agreed fee or on a time basis, the accountability for the work remaining with the parent practice.

The Inland Revenue Acts recognize that people can work from home, and proportional allowances may be set off against the running costs of the home, e.g. heating, telephone, lighting, rates, etc and also some agreement as regards car running, travelling, and other expenses necessary to the work undertaken. Work has to be on a 'continuous' basis. (*See* page 70 for definition of 'business'), and the proportion of the home used for business purposes must first be agreed with the Inland Revenue for Schedule D assessment, e.g. 10 per cent of the gross floor area of the home, which may be the basic proportional amount of the set-off for expenses. If one contemplates working in this way, it is advisable to discuss it with the local Inland Revenue Officer in order to establish the correct working basis. You will need an accountant to prepare and audit your accounts each financial year for tax purposes. As a self-employed person you will have to pay your own National Health Insurance as required by law.

The terms of acceptance of contract or ghosting work must be very carefully considered, particularly where possible errors and claims may ensue from your work. Make some provision for your death or incapacity in your agreement, especially where you have dependents.

You should take out indemnity insurance to protect yourself against claims for alleged negligence, etc. This can be expensive, and is sometimes ignored in the hope, or worse the notion, that it will 'never happen to me', but not to do so is to live in a fool's paradise, since a claim for £20 000 (a relatively small claim today in practice) plus legal costs if the court finds against you, could ruin you and force you into bankruptcy.

The converse argument that large amounts of indemnity insurance makes one a 'target' for claims is often posed, but it is surely better to go into battle wearing expensive armour than none at all.

Buying into an established practice as a partner, or taking over an established practice from a retiring practitioner, are also ways of starting a career, but in the former case it is necessary to have a legally drawn up partnership deed clearly setting down the terms of the partnership, including the notional salary you will receive, the extent of your liability in partnership losses and, conversely, your share of profits (*see* page 90). Fees and their apportionment are always a problem where individual partners bring work into the practice, and there may be a proportional fee allocation scheme. It is also necessary to establish from the outset what will happen if the partnership is dissolved, or you leave the practice; especially what you or your beneficiaries will be entitled to from 'fees received' and also 'fees receivable'.

Where an existing practice is taken over, the goodwill of the practice will be regarded by the vendor as a saleable asset, but this does not mean that, when you take over, established clients will continue to come to the practice, and one should be careful of taking over any unfinished commissions in terms of the client/Architect relationship and contractual position, especially outstanding fees. If the premises is leasehold, you may find that the ground landlord will require different terms in granting a new lease, often much more expensive that that existing under the old lease. It would be wise to prepare a Schedule of Ingoing Condition of the premises when you occupy them, as there may be dilapidations accruing from the previous leasehold which will be the responsibility of the previous lessee, or some arrangement to set off these will have to be made.

Finally, do not forget the liability for insurances for the premises and its contents, also for the Employer's liability where there are staff, including for staff travelling and visiting building sites and premises in the course of the firm's business – and being the prime mover in all this, do not forget to insure yourself.

The following are some of the Statutes of which employers should be aware:

Employer's Compulsory Insurance Act 1975
Fire Precautions Act 1971
Health & Safety at Work etc Act 1974
Offices, Shops & Railway Premises Act 1963
Sex Discrimination Act 1975
Race Relations Act 1976
Finance Acts 1972/77
Equal Pay Act 1970
Employment Protection (Consolidation) Act 1978
Employment Act 1980

10.1.6 Office organizations and structures

The structure of Architect's offices, and chains of command, vary considerably, as do the attitudes of the Principals to the Staff, from hierarchial organizations where one rarely sees the Principals, or where each partner has a direct-line control over certain designated members of staff, are quite common. The participation in the work process for the staff can vary from being given a 'sketch design' to 'work up', to being involved with a design team and having a real contribution to make, or having a project or projects to cope with from inception to completion with very little supervision.

The terms 'Group Leader' and 'Job Architect' have become standard terms in Architect's offices, having replaced the older terms 'Senior Assistant' and 'Architect's Assistant'. When one couples this with the Architectural Technician status, we rarely hear the term 'Architectural Draughtsman' any longer, the overlapping of functions in the office, the chain of command, responsibility, and accountability can become somewhat confused.

Meetings within such groups are usually *ad hoc* but those between senior staff and partners can be more formal and held at pre-arranged times. These will cover a wide range of matters, but will deal principally with job progress both on the site and in the office, work loads within the group, and the economics of the work being done by the group in terms of the budgetary control of the office as a whole. Contact with clients is sometimes reserved to the Principals, but senior staff frequently sit in on such meetings to provide information and support. It is difficult to generalize on office structures (*see* typical office structure chart, page 74), but it is interesting to note that about 80 per cent of architectural practice still consists of the single Principal office, or the smaller office structure. Management terms such as 'decentralization' where the whole task to be performed is fragmented and requires co-ordination, are probably more applicable to large organizations. There are three types of decentralization:

(1) Specialist or functional decentralization,
(2) Whole product or federal decentralization, and
(3) Process decentralization.

The first of these types entails breaking down the task into parcels of work of a similar kind which are themselves complete and which have to be coordinated with others to achieve a balanced design solution.

The second means breaking down the task into parcels of work which are complete in themselves, e.g. a design team may handle only one kind of design project, say housing. The team is an autonomous unit although part of the whole organization, and the leader of that team has the control of all the resources and decisions concerned with it.

The third system consists of design teams, production and information teams, site supervision teams, each concerned with one aspect of the whole project. It has inherent problems, not least among which is adhering to the original design concept; e.g., in the United States there is a professional body dealing only with specification writing. Any such process involves delegation, responsibility, authority, accountability, relationships.

Responsibility may be delegated but not without authority; accountability, which is a corollary of responsibility, cannot be delegated.

10.1.7 The building industry

In his book *Building – The Evolution of an Industry*, the author P. Morton Shand writes, 'between 1275 and 1296 masons' wages had remained fixed at 5d per day in summer, 3d in winter and 4d in spring and autumn, but new regulations for what may be comprehensively described as 'builders' were promulgated in 1356. These laid down that

> every man of the trade may work in any work of the trade if he be properly skilled and knowing in the same'.

More than six centuries later the building industry still makes a clear distinction between 'tradesmen'

RIBA A A = Architect's Appointment 1982 Edition

ARCHITECT (Principal(s) accountable to the Client)

OFFICE STAFF

Accountable to the Client — Partner(s) (see Page 69); Consultant Architects (RIBA A A 2.46)

Accountable to Principal(s) — Associates (see Page 69); Architectural staff (see Page 69); Technicians (SAAT); Office Manager (large offices); Secretarial Staff; Others, e.g. Structural Engineer, etc

SITE STAFF

Site Architect - accountable to Principal(s)

Site Engineer - accountable to Consulting Engineers

Clerk of Works (see Page 104) - recommended and appointed by Architect in agreement with the Client or by Architect (see RIBA A A 3.11, 3.12) (see JCT 1980, Clause 12)

QUANTITY SURVEYOR

Preliminary estimates
Cost planning and cost control
Bills of Quantities preparation
Contract advice
Advice on Contractors
Preparation of tender documents
Checking tenders
Variations and extra works assessment
Valuations and Dayworks
Fluctuations and other claims
Preparation of Final Account, etc

SPECIALIST CONSULTANTS

Structural engineering
Mechanical engineering
Service engineering
Electrical engineering
Landscape & garden design
Civil engineering
Town planning
Furniture design
Industrial design etc

recommended by the Architect, appointment in agreement with the Client, paid by the Client (see RIBA A A 1.4 and 2.45 2.46)

Consultant services may be of the 'package deal' type where consultation, design and erection costs are included in the quotation for the total works; e.g. steelwork design and erection

MAIN CONTRACTOR

OFFICE STAFF (variable)

General secretarial
Estimating and costing
Contracts
Material buying and distribution
Labour (wages, bonuses, etc,)
Plant, site planning and organisation
etc

SITE STAFF (variable)

Agent(s) (large contracts)
Person-in-Charge (JCT 1980, Clause 10)
Trades Foremen
Surveyor/Estimator in liaison with Quantity Surveyor
Contract Manager (may be involved in several contracts)
Administrative staff e.g. Wages Clerk, Checkers, etc

Nominated Sub-Contractors (JCT 1980, Clause 35 et seq, NSC1/4a procedure) nominated by the Architect usually on Prime Cost procedure quotation. own labour force + 'attendance' by Main Contractor working within Main Contractor's site programme. — Estimates should include 2½% discount to Main Contractor for cash

Nominated Suppliers (JCT 1980, Clause 36 et seq, TNS 1/2 procedure) nominated by the Architect usually on Prime Cost procedure quotation. — Estimates should include 5% discount to Main Contractor for cash

Domestic Sub-Contractors (JCT 1980, Clause 19 et seq, DOM 1/2 procedure)

Diagram 11: Professional relationships – 2

and 'labourers' and the rates which they are paid for their work. Membership of Trades Unions also figures largely throughout the industry (*see* page 76).

The term 'builder' is a generic one, covering a wide range of people and businesses from jobbing builders, general contractors, builders and decorators, etc, many of which are one-man or small unincorporated associations. The industry has in the past decade or so attracted to itself a wide range of so-called 'specialists', e.g. double-glazing, cavity-wall insulation, damp-proof coursing, timber treatment, and others; many such undertakings are run on a 'shoe-string' basis and in recent times has absorbed a lot of unemployed people who by necessity have to try to supplement their incomes in one way or another.

In general building terms however, the 'pool' of labour has remained much the same, the operatives falling within recognizable categories:

(a) Tradesmen,
(b) Labourers,
(c) Trainees and apprentices.

These categories apply also to Nominated Subcontractors and Suppliers, and Domestic Subcontractors. Further sub-division of labour forces is brought about by the employment of direct labour forces by local authorities and other organizations to carry out works of repair, maintenance and even new buildings. 'Lump' labour is a term that dies hard in the industry; it refers to itinerant groups of workmen, in all trades, skilled and unskilled, carrying out work for a 'price', cash-in-hand.

It is asserted that the Inland Revenue has largely eliminated this form of labour by the 714/5 certificate procedure, but interestingly one reads in the local paper advertisements such as 'Bricklayers wanted, 715 preferred', the nature of building work being such that the cash-in-hand operatives will always find employment somewhere in the industry.

If we ignore the jobbing builder for the purpose of the exercise, we can say that the vast majority of work done in the industry is carried out by the small- and medium-sized builders, some of whom may be long-standing family business with their assets rooted in their plant, yard, buildings, and goodwill. Their field of operations is confined to a relatively small area, and they carry a nucleus of skilled operatives who may stay with them a very long time; but they also employ local operatives either as domestic sub-contractors or on the cash-in-hand basis. This type of organization tends to be prevalent in country districts where the quality and reliability of the work undertaken is inherent in the continuing goodwill of the firm. Some may become private limited companies or remain as unincorporated associations, e.g. J Bloggs & Sons, Harris & Co, Builders, etc.

The medium-sized contractors almost always become incorporated limited companies for their own protection, particularly as the level of failure and bankruptcy in this area is very high, especially where a builder may extend the general building business side into a specialist function, say plastering, joinery, shopfitting, electrical work, etc. Liquidity is the problem for builders; like Architects and others in the building industry, the builder takes work on trust, and in undertaking work with no professional supervision, which is quite a large proportion, he may have outstanding debts owed to him in very large amounts. A local builder told the author that he had outstanding debts amounting to £24 000, and pursuing them through the County Court would be unlikely to produce more than judgements or offers to pay on a protracted basis in a number of cases.

Builders have a continuing cash-flow problem, many being dependent upon the Architect's certificate as collateral for continued advances from the banks, and it requires only a period of severe weather to tip the balance in some cases towards over extension of resources (particularly when geared to a precarious credit facility) and failure of the business.

The internationally-structured organizations, who clearly are not in the same league as the small- and medium-sized builders, may have a wide range of interests and holdings at home and overseas covering building, structural and civil engineering, and interests in other pursuits such as site investigation, mining for minerals, quarrying, property, etc. also they have the facility to transfer capital resources to those areas of their interests as demand dictates, and to float more shares in the parent and subsidiary companies to attract more capital. The names of such companies are recognized world wide. They are really vast financial organizations. building being one facet of a multi-faceted undertaking; therefore, in building work their cash flow, profit margin and resource allocation will be quite different from that of an ordinary builder's business, some of which may be quite large but having single aims and objectives within their stated Articles of Association. The former may of course have small works departments, and one must be careful in inviting tenders that such organizations do not have an unfair advantage over the latter.

Training in the building industry has conventionally been divided between the apprenticeship path to a trade, and the executive path dealing with the clerical, administrative and supervisory sides of building. The City and Guilds Institute has long been established in the industry and it works in close liaison with the trade schools through the day-release or block-release course structures, under the auspices of the CITB (the Construction Industry Training Board). After the Second World War the

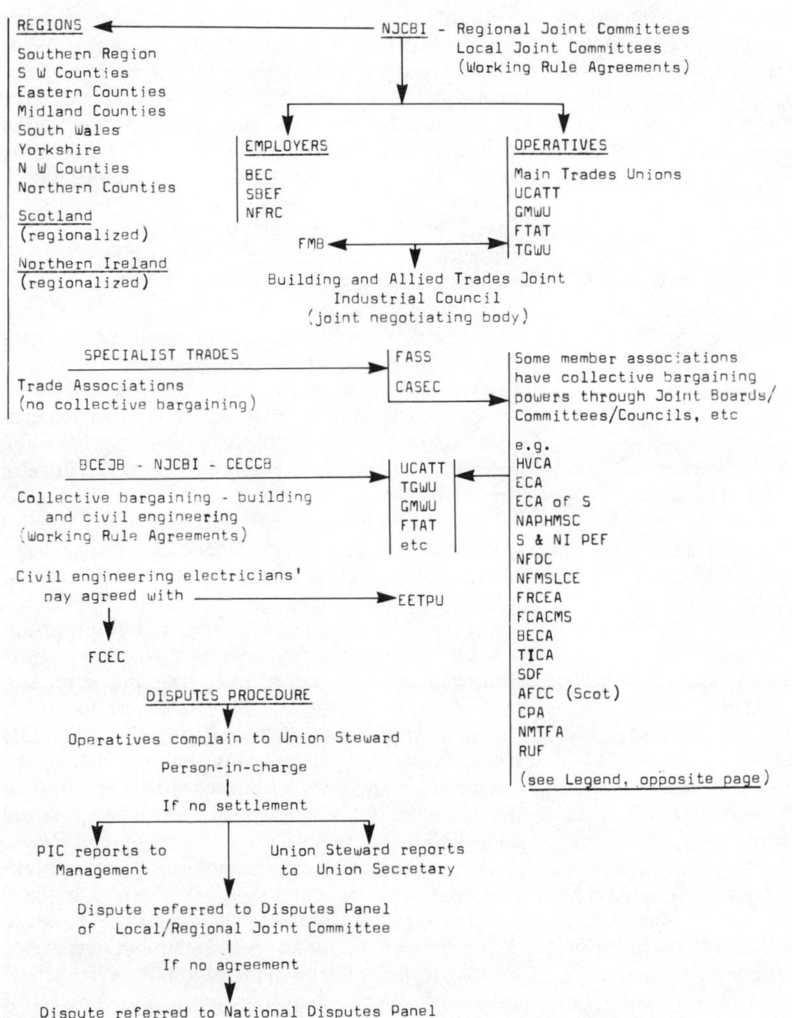

Diagram 12: The structure of the building industry in the UK

LEGEND

(Diagram 12, facing page)

Employers' Organizations – Trade Organizations – Trade Unions

ACAS	Advisory, Conciliation and Arbitration Service
AFCC	(Scotland) Association of Floor Covering Contractors
BCEJB	Building and Civil Engineering Joint Board
BEC	Building Employers' Confederation
BECA	British Exhibition Contractors' Association
CASEC	Committee of Associations of Specialist and Engineering Contractors
CECCB	Civil Engineering Construction and Conciliation Board
CPA	Contractors' Plant Association
ECA	Electrical Contractors' Association
ECA of S	Electrical Contractors' Association of Scotland
EETPU	Electrical, Electronic, Telecommunications and Plumbing Union
FASS	Federation of Associations of Specialists and Sub-contractors
FCACMS	Fencing Contractors' Association. Chestnut Fencing Management Society
FCEC	Federation of Civil Engineering Contractors
FMB	Federation of Master Builders
FRCEA	Felt Roofing Contractors' Employers Association
FTAT	Furniture, Timber and Allied Trades Union
GMWU	National Union of General and Municipal Workers
HVCA	Heating and Ventilating Contractors' Association
NAPHMSC	National Association of Plumbing, Heating, and Mechanical Services Contractors
NFDC	National Federation of Demolition Contractors
NFMSLCE	National Federation of Master Steeplejacks and Lightning Conductor Engineers
NFRC	National Federation of Roofing Contractors
NJCBI	National Joint Council for the Building Industry
NMTFA	National Master Tile Fixers' Association
RUF	Refractory Users' Association
SBEF	Scottish Builders Employers' Federation
SDF	Scottish Decorators' Federation
S&NIPEF	Scottish & Northern Ireland Plumbing Employers' Federation
TGWU	Transport and General Workers' Union
TICA	Thermal Insulation Contractors' Association
UCATT	Union of Construction, Allied Trades and Technicians

Ministry of Education became responsible for courses leading to certificates and diplomas, ordinary and higher grades, for those aspiring to the managerial and supervisory positions. These are now under the jurisdiction of the BTEC (the Business and Technician Education Council) who, from October 1983, assumed responsibility for all current courses of the Business Education Council (BEC) and the Technician Education Council (TEC). The stated objective of the BTEC says 'The Business and Technician Education Council exists to advance the quality and availability of work-related education for those in, or preparing for, employment. The fundamental aim of the Council is that students on BTEC courses develop the necessary competence in their careers in their own, employers' and national interests'. The BTEC has prepared and issued guidelines and units of study for use in the schools.

Where educational entrance qualifications are adequate, there are also degree courses in building and associated pursuits, entry to which may be achieved by 'bridge' qualifications of which the former National Diplomas and Certificates, and the TEC Diplomas and Certificates, together with the new BTEC Diplomas and Certificates, provide suitable vehicles for advancement into higher educational courses, and entrance to the wide range of professional organizations associated with the building industry.

The advent of the so-called 'higher technology' in the building industry since World War Two has greatly increased the number of specialist sub-contractors covering a wide range of products, components, and services. In Chapter 13, 13.1.2, it was said that the inclusion of too many of these firms has the effect of 'process decentralization' in which the control of the various 'parts' may jeopardize the completion of the 'whole', since the main contractor's control over the provision of labour and materials and the method of construction is diminished, except for minimal contribution under 'attendance', and he acts merely as a co-ordinator within his own overall programme. Although it could be argued that the provisions of the contract provide protection both for the main contractor and the employer, it would seem that the use of Nominated Sub-contractors and Suppliers extends today far beyond the 'uniqueness' of a product or a service which the main contractor was unable to provide from his own resources, which, in the author's opinion, was the original intention of the nomination procedure.

In normal times it is said the industry as a whole employs over 1 000 000 people, and provides one eighth of the gross national product, but in the present economic climate this is very difficult to assess, for as Disraeli said, 'there are lies, damned lies, and statistics'.

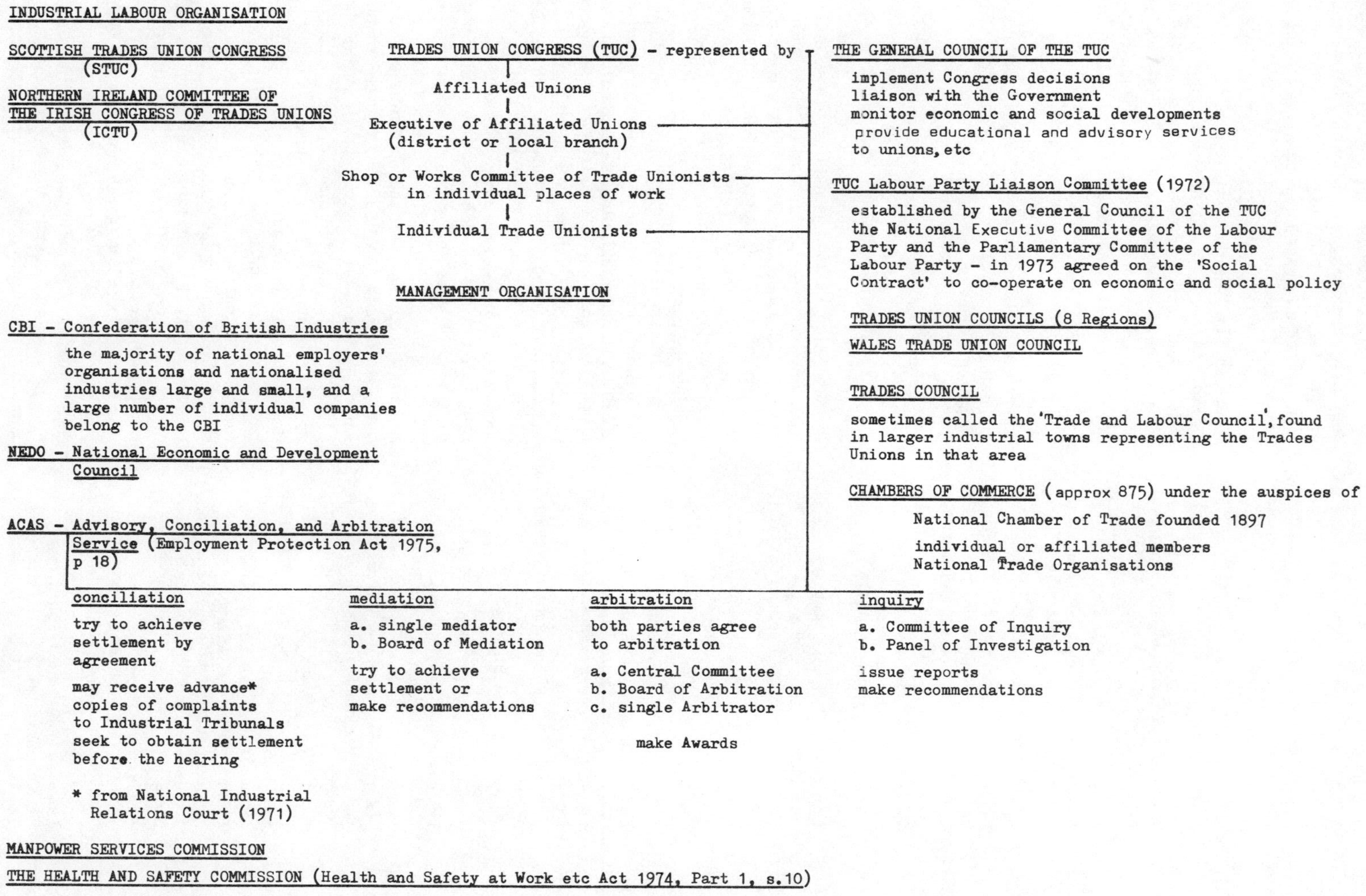

INDUSTRIAL LABOUR ORGANISATION

SCOTTISH TRADES UNION CONGRESS (STUC)

NORTHERN IRELAND COMMITTEE OF THE IRISH CONGRESS OF TRADES UNIONS (ICTU)

TRADES UNION CONGRESS (TUC) - represented by

Affiliated Unions

Executive of Affiliated Unions (district or local branch)

Shop or Works Committee of Trade Unionists in individual places of work

Individual Trade Unionists

THE GENERAL COUNCIL OF THE TUC

implement Congress decisions
liaison with the Government
monitor economic and social developments
provide educational and advisory services to unions, etc

TUC Labour Party Liaison Committee (1972)

established by the General Council of the TUC the National Executive Committee of the Labour Party and the Parliamentary Committee of the Labour Party - in 1973 agreed on the 'Social Contract' to co-operate on economic and social policy

TRADES UNION COUNCILS (8 Regions)

WALES TRADE UNION COUNCIL

TRADES COUNCIL

sometimes called the 'Trade and Labour Council', found in larger industrial towns representing the Trades Unions in that area

CHAMBERS OF COMMERCE (approx 875) under the auspices of

National Chamber of Trade founded 1897

individual or affiliated members
National Trade Organisations

MANAGEMENT ORGANISATION

CBI - Confederation of British Industries

the majority of national employers' organisations and nationalised industries large and small, and a large number of individual companies belong to the CBI

NEDO - National Economic and Development Council

ACAS - Advisory, Conciliation, and Arbitration Service (Employment Protection Act 1975, p 18)

conciliation	mediation	arbitration	inquiry
try to achieve settlement by agreement	a. single mediator b. Board of Mediation	both parties agree to arbitration	a. Committee of Inquiry b. Panel of Investigation
may receive advance* copies of complaints to Industrial Tribunals seek to obtain settlement before the hearing	try to achieve settlement or make recommendations	a. Central Committee b. Board of Arbitration c. single Arbitrator make Awards	issue reports make recommendations

* from National Industrial Relations Court (1971)

MANPOWER SERVICES COMMISSION

THE HEALTH AND SAFETY COMMISSION (Health and Safety at Work etc Act 1974, Part 1, s.10)

Diagram 13: Industrial labour organization

The two sides of the industry are represented, on the one side, by the Building Employers' Confederation, and on the other by UCATT, TGWU and FCAT, etc, which represent the building trade operatives with representation on the National Joint Council for the Building Industry. Contractors are represented by the Federation of Master Builders and the Federation of Associations of Specialists and Sub-contractors, among others. There are ten Regional Joint Committees including Scotland (regionalized) and Northern Ireland (regionalized). (*See* Diagram 13, page 78).

The National Joint Consultative Committee for Building (NJCC) representing the

Royal Institute of British Architects (RIBA)
Royal Institute of Chartered Surveyors (RICS)
Association of Consulting Engineers
*Building Employers' Confederation (BEC) (formerly National Federation of Building Trades Employers)

and

Federation of Associations of Specialists and Sub-contractors
Committee of Associations of Specialist Engineering Contractors

is an independent committee between the National Joint Council for the Building Industry, the Regional Joint Committees, and the employers, operatives and contractors, and is of course responsible for the issue of Procedure Notes and Practice Notes including the JCT Standard Forms of Building Contract. A set of these excellent notes, which contain advice on many matters affecting building procedures, can be obtained on application to the Secretary**. They are constantly up-dated and being on the mailing list should be an essential undertaking for any practice. They also offer assistance and advice on contract matters should the need arise.

10.1.8 Safety on site

The Health & Safety at Work etc Act 1974 governs the health, welfare, and safety of persons working on building sites, and with other legislation, protects the public in the course of these works, and controls the use of dangerous substances.

The Health & Safety Commission under the Act is responsible for the policy-making and amendments to the Act, and instigated the Health & Safety Executive and the Inspectorate, embodying Factory Inspectors and others, into a comprehensive system of control covering all persons at work.

The following regulations made under the Factories Act 1961 set out the requirements which relate to all building operations and works of engineering construction

Construction (General Provisions) Regulations 1961: SI 1961:1580
Construction (Lifting Operations) Regulations 1966: SI 1961:1581
Construction (Working Places) Regulations 1966: SI 1966:94
Construction (Health & Welfare) Regulations 1966: SI 1966:95
Construction (Health & Welfare) Amendment Regulations 1974: SI 1974:209

Supplementary guidance and advice is given in the *Construction Regulations Handbook* published by the Royal Society for the Prevention of Accidents (ROSPA).

The Building Advisory Service (a division of the Building Employers' Confederation) publishes *Construction Safety*, a handbook of practice recommended by the Construction Industry Board as interpreting and explaining the Construction Regulations. This is a loose-leaf binder which is up-dated from time to time.

Other aids, e.g. BS 6187 concerned with demolition processes are also, among other things, guides to safety procedures.

*Catalogues are obtainable from BEC Publications, Federation House, 2309 Coventry Road, Sheldon, Birmingham B26 3PL.
**NJCC, 18 Mansfield Street, London W1M 9FQ.

References

RIBA Handbook of Architectural Practice and Management, (RIBA Publications)
The Evolution of an Industry, P. MORTON SHAND (Token Construction Co Ltd)
Partnership Law, J. WESTWOOD (revised by) (Donnington Press)

11

Management and administration

The concepts and theories of management have been developing from the turn of this century, and many books have been written which refer to and expand on theories of the early pioneers of management including Taylor of America, Fayol of France, Urwick of Britain among others. Examples of the application of these theories have been frequently reiterated, including the Sears Roebuck and General Electric business stories. Later developments have been classified under numerous titles, among which the following are common:

(1) Accountable management.
(2) Behavioural science.
(3) Management by objectives.
(4) Participative management.
(5) Systems analysis.

To what degree any or all of these concepts and theories can be applied to project management is not clear; what *is* clear is that the processes of programming and progressing are indeed relevant to the design and construction of buildings from inception to completion.

The diagram opposite, in various guises attributed originally to Fayol, also appears in the RIBA *Handbook of Architectural Practice and Management*. It illustrates the cycle of processes operating at each stage of a project from inception to completion. The two sides of the diagram have been described in several ways, e.g.

ACTIVE	*PASSIVE*
dynamics	mechanics
doing	arranging
people	things
productive	non-productive
progressing	programming

Each of these tries to describe both 'active' and 'passive' sides of the management process, which are complementary and must be followed sequentially through the management process for the completion of the cycle and the success of the undertaking. It also follows that on the 'passive' side the extent to which the 'tools' of management are used and the degree of sophistication these attain will be related to the kind of project involved.

Many attempts to define 'management' have been made, but the short and succinct 'making a success of an undertaking using to the best advantage all available resources' seems adequate.

The processes shown on the diagram are concerned on the 'passive' side with matters which may have to be dealt with by the manager alone, or in collaboration with others. The 'active' side will be more labour-intensive and more concerned with human relationships, co-ordination, and leadership. The whole cycle is held together by good communication within the aims and objectives of the undertaking, which can be termed the 'framework' or 'target' of the project.

The active side is monitored and assessed as to its effectiveness against anticipatory processes of the passive side, making such adjustments as necessary to bring all the separate functions into a coordinated whole.

In managing construction projects the six areas of active and passive activity may briefly be described as follows:

Forecasting
Policy
Objectives

The client, being the prime mover, makes the initial decision to build after thorough investigation of all the alternatives.

For the Architect commissioned to provide a new building, or to extend or adapt existing premises, his function is to provide the right building, at the right time, at the right cost. Since all projects in his office have these aims and objectives his office team and organization must be effective and efficient.

Planning and Programming — This section involves the breaking down of the total task into manageable pieces, resolving the order of priorities, assessing and allocating target dates, durations, and resources for all the activities involved.

Organizing — Whatever the task it is necessary to organize temporary or permanent groupings of people into a team or teams, and to determine the functions of the groups and of the individuals of which they are composed, defining the roles and responsibilities, and the lines of communication between them.

Selecting Motivating Directing — This is directly related to the structure of the team; the larger the team the more diffuse the inter-relationships become, making the task of co-ordinating their efforts and achieving unity of effort more difficult and calling for good team leadership.

Controlling Progressing — This area assesses the actual progress made against the programme forecast, and the time for making adjustments to the performance to bring disparities into line with the target is of major importance.

During the stages described above it will be seen that the progressing and programming stages' functions will operate at each level and stage of a project, and can be described as

Strategic level — Where the whole project is planned and broad strategies are determined – this may extend over a long period.

Tactical level — Main activities are planned at each stage in the shorter term.

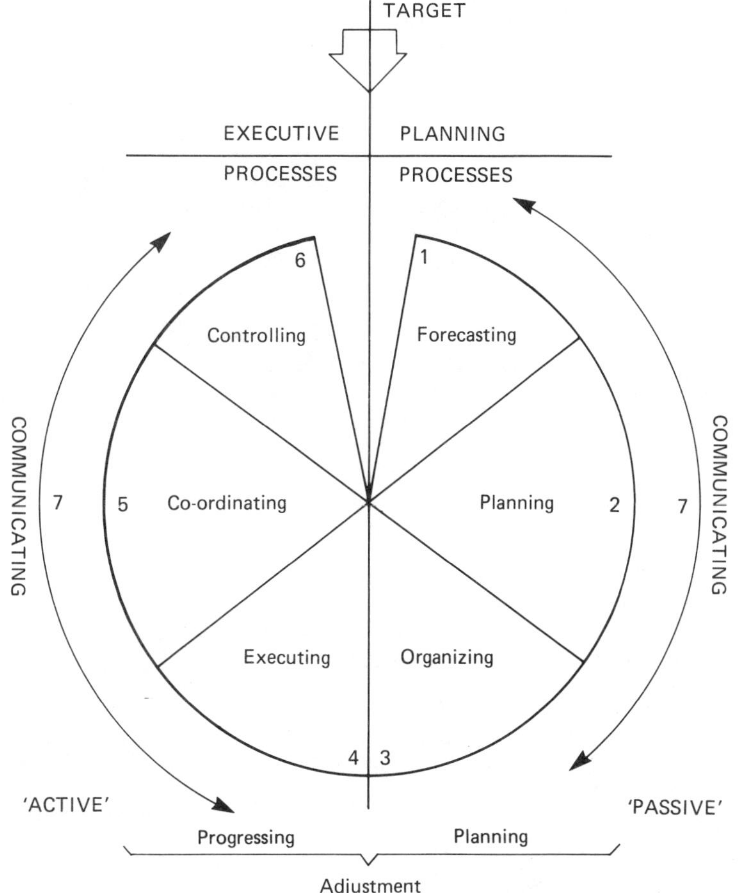

Operational	Where individual activities are planned at each stage in the short term.

The overall aim of such programmes is to plan and control resources in terms of money, manpower and materials, against time.

Applying management theories to the construction industry compared to general industry is quite different, the latter producing commodities in large numbers for the consumer public. Obviously some components used in the building industry such as standardized components, equipment, etc, can be directly compared. In general terms, however, there is little direct comparison, building projects having unknowns unique to each project, e.g. the site, sub-strata, weather, etc, projects ranging from small house conversions and extensions to multi-million pound projects involving civil, structural, service engineering, etc of great complexity. Each project has different resource allocation, different duration of the activities involved, the programming and processing system being adapted to suit individual needs.

Most Architects' offices deal with a range of projects, usually a number of small jobs and a few large jobs, each demanding its own resource allocation in funding, manpower, and communication, with supportive consultancy, level of office control, etc. The larger jobs will by their nature account for a larger share of office resources.

There is a long-standing theory, one might say assertion, in management, that 20 per cent of the work force produces 80 per cent of the profits, but like most generalizations this one is suspect. It is interesting, however, to remember that in 1974 during the three-day week period in industry, productivity actually rose. Overmanning in industries, particularly in the public sector, has long been a bone of contention between right-wing government and the Trades Unions. There has also been a long-standing criticism of the use of direct labour forces in the building industry where the competitive factor coupled with the disincentive to complete work has been the subject of much debate and argument.

In the Introduction to this book the term 'conscious management' was used as opposed to 'intuitive management', implying that the former is based upon some concept or theory of management as opposed to a 'hit-or-miss' approach. For many years in architectural practice it could be said that the latter was the norm, and even today there are many 'creative' people to whom the word 'management' is like a red rag to a bull, who see management as an inhibiting, restrictive process shackling their creative ability.

Be that as it may, in the author's opinion, designing is a managerial process since it is concerned with decision-making employing the collection, synthesis, and application of information towards the solution of a problem within the framework of a 'target', which in architectural terms is called a 'brief'. The decision-making process, which involves acceptance, rejection, or compromise of facts and information, is conditioned by the imaginative and creative ability of the designer in arriving at a solution, which elevates the design process to an art form. Where designers are employed in commercial undertakings, however, their creations are subject to all the market forces which prevail.

The manifestation of a building from inception to completion is concerned with a large number of people working with a common purpose towards a common aim, the completion of the building. Each may not be wholly conscious of the concerted efforts of others, but having a part to play in the completion of the task to be performed, and this is inherent in all management processes.

Primarily, management is not concerned with computers, word or data processors, critical path analyses, charts, graphs, etc – these are the tools of management. Management is about people and their behaviour in the group situation, which is as old as group activity itself.

It is said that we are all three persons, 'what we think we are, what others think we are, and what we really are', playing roles, adopting postures, attitudes, as the occasion demands.

The prediction of any one person's reaction to a given situation is very risky indeed, being concerned with creatures whose physiological/psychological make-up is so complex as to achieve the highest and the lowest forms of behaviour towards each other, according to the time, place, motivation, and circumstances prevailing. When we move away from the basic creature comforts, extending the needs of human beings into the realms of self-esteem, pride, social position, recognition, ego, etc, and couple these with the underlying traits of love, hate, greed, avarice, jealousy, deception, cruelty, etc, mixing them over any random sample of the human race we get some very complicated creatures indeed.

In any group situation a leader emerges, or is appointed; someone who for one reason or another inspires in the followers feelings of security and confidence, and upon whom their very survival may depend. Whether they like the person or not is not too important, as long as the leader is considered to be the right person for the task ahead. The reasons for the choice may be obscure, individuals being swayed by mass opinion, emotional pressures, coercion, etc, but whatever the choice and the means of choosing, the fervent hope is that the choice will be the right one in the end.

There was once an accepted theory that managers were born and not made. In order to 'manage' one had to have a complete understanding of the design, processing, manufacturing, advertising and marketing of a product from shop floor to board room level. This theory no longer obtains; two world wars have shown that men and women can accept command and leadership, organize groups large and small, and achieve targets successfully without years of preparatory training and the need to understand every discrete detail; indeed the concept of the 'think tank' was based on this theory of uncluttered minds bringing fresh thought and ideas to bear upon a problem and achieve solutions.

The human being is able, and willing, to adapt to new skills and to learn quickly. A squad of raw recruits with two left feet could in a few short weeks be welded by threats, insults, cajoling, wheedling, bullying, swearing, praise, not to mention sweat and tears, into a proud, self-reliant, well-drilled unit, which on the passing out parade was going to be the best squad on the parade ground. This is called *esprit de corps*. The NCO responsible for this miracle of endeavour, who was always born out of wedlock, became 'not a bad bloke really', when it was all over, and consumed numerous pints of beer paid for by the 'lads' who hitherto had hated his guts; such are the vagaries of human nature.

One of the most important traits of leadership defined by Officer's Training Units and similar organizations is 'character', this being quite different from 'personality'. A pleasant, charming personality may exhibit unacceptable qualities under duress or stress such as deceit, cowardice, dishonesty, etc, or attempt to avoid responsibility for actions taken.

Character-building is a complex process, family upbringing, schooling, religious instruction, genetic traits, etc, forging innate attitudes and principles which are adhered to and defended.

In adversity the leader is expected to remain calm, think clearly, and take decisions, having due regard for others in the process. The poem 'If' by Rudyard Kipling says it all – 'If you can keep your head when all about you are losing theirs and blaming it on you.........etc.'

Trust is probably one of the most fragile of human feelings which, once destroyed by the discovery of deception and lies – those two most insidious of human traits – is probably lost for ever; so honesty plays a very important part in the forming of character. Thus, we see the leader emerging as a person who can be relied upon and is respected and trusted. In the armed forces it was said that 'good disciplinarians were never liked but always respected'; be that as it may, respect has to be earned, and a spoonful of humility, and a modicum of good manners in anyone's make-up do not come amiss either.

Leaders have to delegate responsibility to others; the 'if-you-want-a-job-done-properly-do-it-yourself' manager is useless. The person who delegates must be sure that the person accepting the delegation is capable of doing the work without doubt, and is willing to accept it, for having delegated the leader should leave the person concerned to get on with the task, unless help is requested, so that initiative, self-discipline and self-control can develop.

The manager is always accountable for the work of his subordinates, just as Principal in practice are accountable for all the work done in the office and must accept the mistakes of their staff as their own. This does not imply constantly looking over the shoulder of the assistants, but building up mutual trust and respect. A leader must never be afraid to admonish, but equally never fail to give praise where it is due, and avoid the temptation to accept the kudos for the work of others.

Team-building is a difficult process not quickly achieved, and 'hire-and-fire' policies do not make for good relationships or effective organizations. A good team is built upon knowing the strengths and weaknesses of each team member, and giving mutual support, help, and encouragment. The leader's task is to foster this corporate spirit and channel it towards successful achievement of the aims of the team.

As the leader of the team, whatever its size, one should be on the lookout for future leaders, who may not always be the oldest or the most experienced of the group; on the contrary, too much importance is attached to experience as if it were a panacea for all ills. Flair and ability, tempered with a realization of one's shortcomings, energy, drive, and enthusiasm, are also valuable assests to be encouraged. In considering promotions, the older, more experienced person may feel that he has a right to be promoted before other, younger colleagues, but in fact he may be quite the wrong person for the promotion; a person who may perform very well for many years within a group from whom he derives support and some protection, in the leader role may be quite out of his depth.

Work of itself is quite useless without management and all the machinery of marketing; every product needs resources to make it and methods by which it can be marketed. In recent years motorcycles and sewing machines have been seen to pile up in co-operatives as useless stocks with no outlet to sell them or to pay for their production.

The Marxist theory that profit is unethical as it is the workers who produce the wealth, is a somewhat simplistic theory. Management is comprised of productive and non-productive elements, each being complementary to the other in the pursuance of successful business ventures.

11.1.1 Communication

The skeletal structure upon which the flesh of management is supported is communication, and often the lessons have still to be learned; the 'mushroom syndrome' (i.e. 'kept in the dark and fed on manure') is still prevalent in industry today, manifested in workers being told without prior warning that their jobs are to be lost due to a board-room decision to 'streamline production' or some other excuse.

The level of communication is difficult to determine, as it is relative to the situation in which it is used, be it oral or written.

The person responsible for the communication has to decide upon the best form of the communication and what is intended to be conveyed to the recipient. The First World War story of the field telephone message 'am going to advance send reinforcements' which eventually became 'am going to a dance send three and fourpence' may seem a little far-fetched, and the last-war Admiralty signal 'Wren's clothing will be held up until the requirements of the Fleet are satisfied' may in their own ways be illustrative of faulty communications for different reasons. Rudyard Kipling wrote a little jingle, 'I kept six honest henchmen they taught me all I knew, their names were What and Why and When and How and Where and Who', which is worth bearing in mind when communicating anything to anyone.

'Brevity', it is said, is the best form of wit, but it may also be taken too literally. There is a story that when visiting a girl's school the author W Somerset Maugham was asked what he considered to be the essentials of successful short-story writing. He replied, 'religion, persons of noble birth, surprise, mystery, but above all brevity'. Later, on being asked to embody these literary 'gems' into a short story, one girl quickly wrote 'My God, said the Duchess, I'm pregnant, I wonder who did it?' – hardly a literary gem, but illustrating the point.

Spelling and syntax play an important part in good communication, and are taken into consideration in the Final Examination, Part 3, both in the written examination and the Case Study.

The use of the right word in context may have legal significance, e.g. though 'job' and 'contract' are often regarded and used as interchangeable, a court would apply very definite separate interpretations.

Jargon plays an important part in language, as does idiom, but both can be used to the extent that they become unintelligible to all but the initiated.

One should be careful in quoting what are purported to be 'facts' unless one is absolutely sure that they are and can be substantiated. Also, avoid heresay remarks, especially concerning people, which may be derogatory; the law of libel can be an expensive way of learning not to do it!

Letters

Never write a letter in anger, no matter how incensed you may be by the contents of the letter under reply; better to sleep on it for at least 24 hours and then avoid abuse in the reply. 'The silver tongue turneth away the wrath' can also apply to the written word.

In dictating letters it is a good plan beforehand to make a list of salient points to be made in reply, carefully checking and verifying any facts or figures to be quoted. Try to be brief without losing the gist of what you want to say, avoiding rhetoric and flowery language. For 'the management would be grateful if patrons would avoid walking on the carefully tended lawns' read 'keep off the grass'.

Most offices have a well-designed letterheading on expensive paper, this being a form of advertising the practice, but the effect is ruined if the contents of the letter are badly set out on the page and unrelated to it. A good typeface devoid of typing errors is important; references, if given, should be quoted and any enclosures should be listed.

Signatures are also important, and the relationship of the writer to the practice, using p.p. (*per pro* = for and on behalf of), should be shown. Males present no problem in signing letters as mostly they are addressed as Mr; females can pose problems to recipients, e.g. Jane Smith, Personnel Manager, can be Mrs, Miss or Ms.

When writing in the capacity of agent on behalf of the client it is very important to disclose this agency, as discussed in Chapter 2, 2.1.1; phrases such as 'on behalf of my client', 'as Architect for', etc, are clearly understood.

Drawings

The time-honoured principal communicative method adopted by Architects is through drawings, and as such we tend to assume that the drawing is of itself sufficient for the purpose. We tend to forget that not all people understand drawings, and that drawings are sometimes related to other communicative documents such as Specifications, Bills of Quantities, Schedules, etc, which may be equally unintelligible to others. In producing drawings for any purpose, it is wise to remember the jingle by Rudyard Kipling.

For many years Architects have initially produced small-scale drawings which, like Topsy, tend to grow through a series of larger-scale drawings up to half- or even full-size details, each purporting to achieve a better understanding of what the original small-scale drawing intended to convey.

Drawing is an expensive process which devours a great deal of the office working capital, as discussed in Chapter 12, page 88 *et seq*, and is demanding of staff time. The increased use of aids to draughtsmanship, especially applied transfer lettering, cars, people, trees, etc, has not only increased the time spent on drawings, but seems to have resulted in a loss of personal drafting skill and individuality, and to have become an aesthetic pursuit in itself, perhaps in the process losing sight of the original intention which was to communicate information.

Building sites are often wet, windy, and dirty places, and the issue of drawings frequently lacks consideration of this fact. Very large drawings which often are rolled up, and also smaller drawings, which are on non-durable material for use on site, maybe in rain and wind and in precarious positions on scaffolding, etc, are not good for communicating intricate information.

We also tend to forget that many people working on building sites (without whom we could build nothing) may not have had the educational advantages, thus necessitating the breakdown of initial information into intelligible form by the Agent, Foreman, or Trades Foremen, which manifests itself on site as scribbled notes on newly-plastered walls, etc. The man either clearing the site with a bulldozer or digging the foundation trenches, or the crane driver, is just as much interested as anyone else in what he is helping to build, so a copy of the drawings, or a line perspective if there is one, and certainly copies of the progress photographs, should be put up for all to see. They may, of course, bring forth hoots of derision, but will achieve a sense of 'belonging' to the site team.

Pre-printing drawing sheets with the firm name, etc, is a well-established practice which makes much easier the standardization of sizes, posting and filing. The use of microfilm for recording drawings and other project information for permanent storage and retrieval on finished jobs is now quite common.

Telephone

The telephone should be our servant not our master, as it is also one of the largest drains on capital resources, and should be used only when it is absolutely necessary.

If information or instructions affecting in any way the professional or contractual position in terms of the works are given or received by telephone, record them in the Job Book together with the time and the date, and confirm in writing as soon as possible with copies to all interested parties. For some years now such information in Job Books and Diaries has been acceptable as evidence in court in the event of arbitration or litigation arising from disputes.

Filing systems

These vary from office to office, most of which develop their own system, but the aim should be clarity of information and ease of retrieval. Hours spent in searching through bulky files containing every letter, memo, instruction, variation, consent, etc, concerned with the job, to ascertain the absence or presence of some piece of information, is a time-wasting and frustrating procedure. Filing divided into separate sections of communication, e.g. building controls, client, contractor, QS, etc, with a coloured-copy system related to each, is a simple way of avoiding confusion, and a chart in the front of the building-controls file will assist in avoiding those embarrassing times when one realises that a consent has not been applied for or an amendment to a consent not notified to the authorities. Sophisticated techniques of computer storage, data processors, etc, are becoming widely used in practice, but when starting a practice, and even in established smaller practices, the older methods still obtain.

Memos

A word about memos; they are fine as long as they do not reach the 'bombardment' stage when the recipients despair and simply drop them in the waste-paper basket.

Models

In the light of what was said earlier about drawings, it is sometimes helpful to make or have made a model of the scheme to be presented for appraisal and approval, especially where lay persons are concerned. Models also have a degree of advertisement value for the practice, as do good perspective drawings, and one should consider whether or not the cost of producing either is justified in the circumstances.

11.1.2 Meetings, generally

Meetings have a unique function in the daily process of business. They vary from *ad hoc* meetings of two or more persons to pre-arranged, carefully-organized meetings which may involve hundreds of people. Whatever the nature or size of the meeting, its function is to enter into discussion and to arrive at decisions, or to make recommendations to enable others to reach decisions.

Meetings may be variously titled, the most common being committees and sub-committees, board meetings of various kinds, working groups, study groups, project teams, etc. The group function of the members of the meeting is important; are they static, or do they change periodically both individually or collectively? Is the group motivation corporate, individual, competitive, etc? How are decisions reached, by majority vote, general consensus, etc?

The control of the meeting may be on a continuous basis under an elected Chairman, or the Chair may be taken at each meeting by agreement (*see* (d) below).

Meetings may be public or private. The Defamation Act 1952 defines a public meeting as *bona fide* and lawfully held for a lawful purpose and for the furtherance or discussion of any matter of public concern, whether admission thereto be general or restricted'.

A private meeting is one to which admission of the public is restricted.

In the matter of public and private companies the Law of Meetings obtains, and certain points must be rigidly observed, e.g.

(a) The meeting must be properly convened.
(b) The meeting must be properly held in accordance with any relevant rules.
(c) The Chairman must be appointed in accordance with the Articles of the company, and all relevant provisions must be complied with.
(d) Where no such provision obtains, the Chairman of the Board of Directors may preside at every general meeting. If there is no such Chairman, or he is not present 15 minutes after the appointed time of the meeting, or is unwilling to act, the Directors present shall appoint one of their number to act as Chairman.

The Chairman's basic duty is to preside over the meeting, to preserve order, and to conduct the meeting in a proper manner using the Agenda items as set down as the order of procedure, the 'Any other business' item making provision for members to discuss matters which are not itemised. The Chairman should steer the group through discussion to arrive at a conclusion or a decision as effectively as possible, moving the discussion forward with tact and skill, having due regard for individual opinions, but not letting the discussion get out of hand and lapse into uncontrolled argument. The Chairman must not bully, harangue, cajole, wheedle, or lapse into argument, but must try to interpret and clarify discussion where possible and impart a sense of urgency into the proceedings to bring discussion to an effective conclusion. When voting he must use his casting vote of the Chair with fairness and honesty. Pursuasiveness should be the Chairman's aim, not constantly banging the table and calling for order.

Minutes of meetings are very important. Whatever form these are to take, and this should be decided at the outset, they must follow the order of the items on the Agenda for the meeting, the following items being the basic essentials:

The venue of the meeting, and its date and time.
Names of all present, including the name of the person taking the chair; apologies for absence.
All Agenda items and attendant points discussed, and all decisions reached should be recorded. If action was agreed on, the name(s) of the person(s) responsible for ensuing action is to be noted.
The main points of discussion leading to decisions. Some Minutes may record names of those members contributing points, arguments, motions, etc, but it is suggested that it is better to omit names.
The place, date and time of the next meeting.
The time at which the meeting closed.

A record should be kept of the distribution of Minutes.

In limited companies the Minutes of the meetings are filed in the Company Book by the Secretary, and any changes in the Board of Directors or Company Secretary are also entered; since the Chairman may be appointed at each meeting, and may be a different person each time, his or her name is not entered in the Company Book.

Notice of the meeting and a copy of the Agenda should be sent to all those who are to attend well in advance of the meeting, usually fourteen days. The Agenda is important and time should be spent in making sure that the procedural order of the meeting deals with matters arising from the Minutes of the previous meeting first; when the previous Minutes have been approved they are signed by the Chairman and passed to the Secretary for filing. The Any-other-business item should be the penultimate item on the Agenda, followed by the date of the next meeting. 'Any other business' may vary from no business at all to very protracted discussion; the latter situation will exercise the Chairman's skill and patience since it can tend to become a platform for members' pet subjects, or to pursue personal vendettas against members. In such cases the Chairman must be tactful but firm.

The date of the next meeting is important, and should not be hastily decided, as the on-going group function depends upon the solidarity of the membership. If it is a 'standing committee' the meetings will take place at pre-determined times during the period of its function, e.g. the first Monday in each month at 2 p.m.

Site meetings

One should allow the main contractor to organize his own domestic sub-contractor meetings. There may also be some altercation as to who should take the Chair at site meetings, but traditionally it has been the prerogative of the Architect as leader of the building team, but not everyone agrees with this. It has been suggested that such meetings should be kept to a minimum, and the notification, Agenda, and recording of proceedings should follow that as discussed above.

The number of meetings will depend upon the length of the contract period, but once a month would, in the absence of emergencies, seem to be about right. The number of persons attending the meeting should be kept to a minimum, ten being suggested as a maximum and preferably less. Those attending should be primarily concerned with the progress of the works in terms of the agreed programmes, dealing with such immediate matters as may affect the future progress of the works.

Requests for information from the Architect are normally channelled through the Clerk of Works, if one is employed, having regard to the provisions of the contract (the JCT Standard Form of Contract 1980, Clause 26.2), otherwise in direct discussion with the Person-in-Charge; confirmation of such requests in writing from the main contractor's head office is important in terms of the possibility of claims by the contractor under Clause 26.

By their nature these meetings tend to beome forums for apportioning blame for delays or non-performance, or recriminations of one kind or another, and may degenerate into personal arguments which must be avoided at all costs. The Architect must avoid taking sides in such disputes, unless directly involved, and even then avoiding invective or personal abuse regardless of provocation, as one's professional status may be irrevocably damaged in the process.

If as Architect you have made a mistake in the drawings or any other documents, or have not fulfilled a course of action expected of you, admit it, apologize, and remedy the position as quickly as possible. We all make mistakes, and it is not a good policy to lay down a smoke screen to cover one's inadequacies, although these may lie with staff members. All problems are eventually resolved, but people's memories of how they were resolved remain for a long time afterwards, and you may have to meet them again on future jobs.

It is sometimes necessary to complain about work on site, or about an individual, and this should be done through the Agent or Person-in-Charge, never directly to the operative concerned or the Trades Foreman; there is a site protocol to be observed.

Do not forget to offer a word of thanks or a word of praise for a job well done; and on completion of a contract, if it is merited, write to the contractor's head office expressing your thanks generally to the company and specifically to any personnel you wish to mention, such as the Agent or Person-in-Charge; this will be appreciated. Observe also the traditional ceremonies such as 'topping-out.'

References

RIBA Handbook of Architectural Practice and Management, (RIBA Publications)

Management Applied to Architectural Practice, BRUNTON, BADEN-HELLARD and BOOBYER (George Godwin)

Imaginative Management Control, R. OGDEN (Routledge & Kegan Paul)

Video Arts Publications, VARIOUS AUTHORS Video Arts Ltd

Note: Films on many aspects of management are available from Video Arts Ltd 68 Oxford Street, London, as an adjunct to their various booklets.

Questions and Answers on the Law of Meetings, R. S. SIM (Butterworth)

12

Programming, budgetary control, accounting

12.1.1 Capital resources and cash flow

Whether one starts a small one-man business or a multi-million-pound business venture, both will have two things in common:

(1) An initial source of capital, and
(2) A decision as to how that capital is to be invested in the business.

Initially the source of capital may be from one's own resources alone, or from long-term borrowing (i.e. five years or more), or a combination of these which, in management terms, is called 'gearing', i.e. the ratio between one's own and borrowed capital.

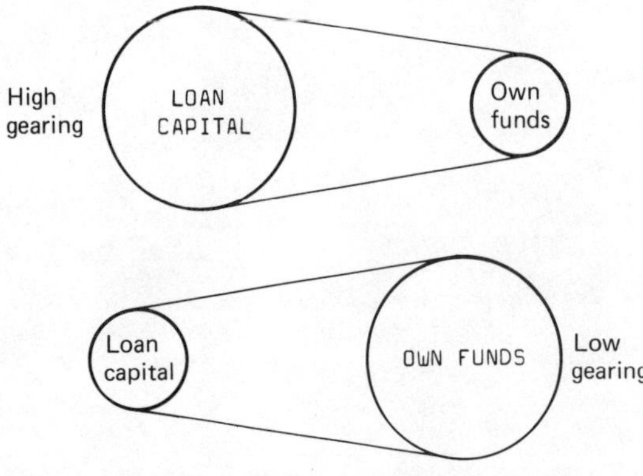

It follows that high gearing, compared to low gearing, is much more risky, since loan capital has to be serviced from the working capital, and if not secured on a fixed interest basis for a fixed term, the interest charges may increase to a level which is disastrous for the business by turning profits into losses.

In any business, management has to decide how capital is to be allocated to the various areas of the business, and it matters not whether the business is a manufacturing one or a servicing one, the apportionment of the capital has to be decided according to the needs of the business. This can be shown within the framework of Diagram 14 opposite, from which it will be seen that there is a source of income and an allocation of working capital from this income spread across the various areas of the business, constantly moving and circulating as the business demands. Initially each proportion allocated may be a fixed sum, e.g. it may be decided to allocate 30 per cent to 'cash-in-hand' from the total working capital. The diagram shows that there are two areas of assets, fixed and unfixed – the former it is intended to keep, e.g. freehold land, buildings, office equipment, etc, the latter it is intended to dispose of in the process of the business, e.g. raw materials, finished or partly finished goods, etc.

The aim of the manager is to spread the investment risk so that the products of the business are effectively produced for the minimal capital outlay, and the initial capital is turned over as many times as possible in producing the end product for profit. This may be achieved by extending credit limits to the maximum, obtaining good trade and other discounts, maximizing on labour output for the wage rates and salaries paid to the work force, etc. In manufacturing businesses the output has to be carefully monitored, firms employing rate fixers and progress chasers on the shop floor to ensure that agreed rates are adhered to or adjusted as required. In manufacturing business it has been said that the line manager's dream is the marketing manager's nightmare. The cost of production must be carefully related to sales, as in the event of over production and the build-up of large stocks, the business could face disaster in the event of market outlets drying up, and goods appearing as sales in quick-turnover market outlets to cut absolute losses and selling at prices at or below cost.

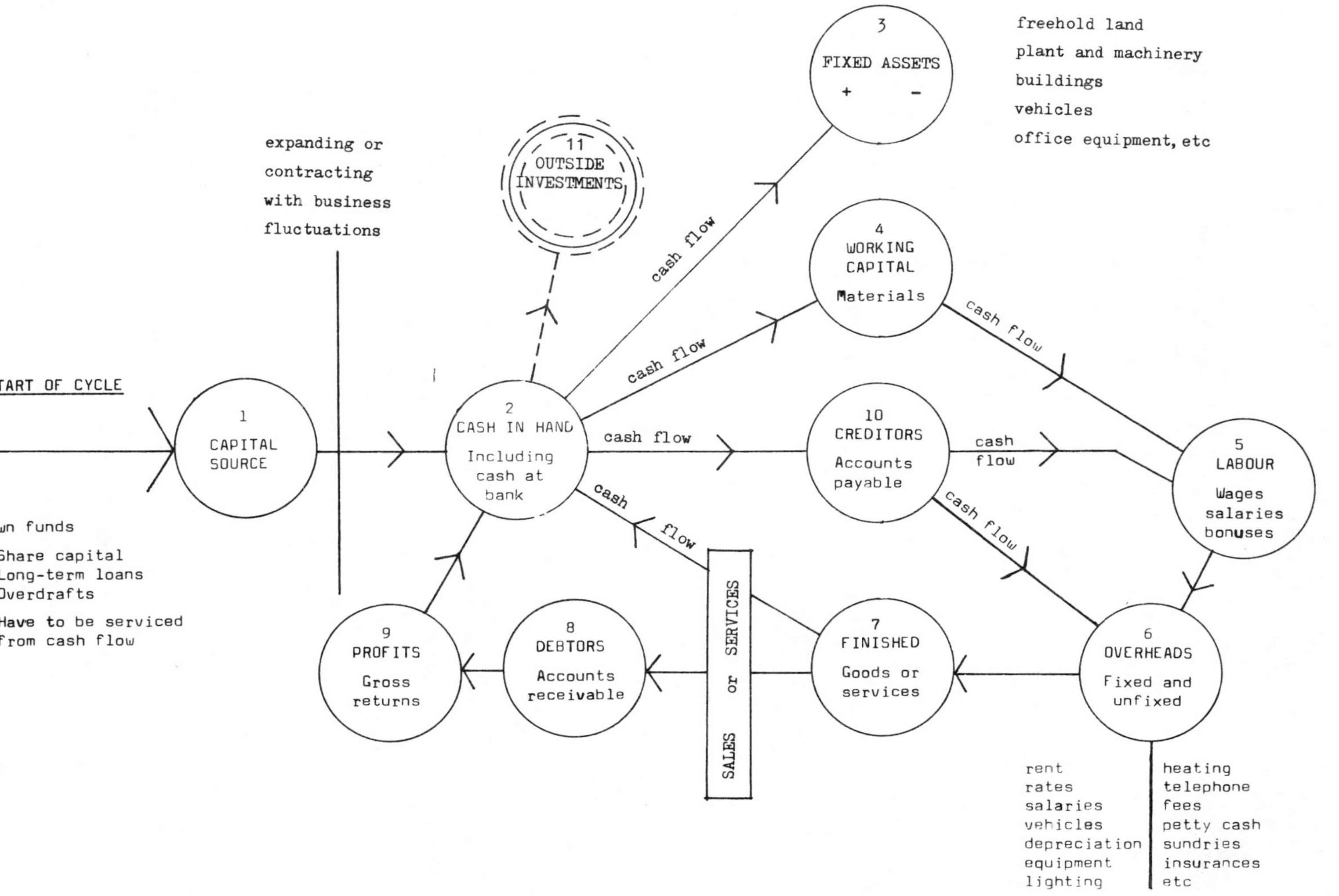
START OF CYCLE
1
CAPITAL SOURCE
Own funds
Share capital
*Long-term loans
*Overdrafts
*Have to be serviced from cash flow
expanding or
contracting
with business
fluctuations
2
CASH IN HAND
Including cash at bank
11
OUTSIDE INVESTMENTS
cash flow
3
FIXED ASSETS
+ -
freehold land
plant and machinery
buildings
vehicles
office equipment, etc
cash flow
4
WORKING CAPITAL
Materials
cash flow
cash flow
10
CREDITORS
Accounts payable
cash flow
cash flow
5
LABOUR
Wages
salaries
bonuses
6
OVERHEADS
Fixed and unfixed
rent
rates
salaries
vehicles
depreciation
equipment
lighting
heating
telephone
fees
petty cash
sundries
insurances
etc
7
FINISHED
Goods or services
SALES or SERVICES
cash flow
8
DEBTORS
Accounts receivable
9
PROFITS
Gross returns

Diagram 14

In any business there is a break-even point in the process of the manufacturing of goods or the provision of a service, where production costs equal the invested capital outlay, and when one passes through that point and investment costs are lower than the return on output one is making a profit, which is conditioned by market forces.

The job of the manager is to monitor cash flow, making such changes and adjustments in good time as may be necessary to meet demands and to keep the business solvent. The two areas of cash flow which are continually under review are debtors and creditors. In order to reap the advantage of trade and cash discounts it is necessary to be able to pay invoices promptly and, conversely, to be paid promptly for the goods or services one is selling. It may be necessary on occasion to increase working capital by either converting fixed assets into cash or drawing upon reserves.

If the business is succeeding in its aim to be profitable and moves into a position of surplus capital, provision can be made for outside investments which may be directly related to the business and of use in providing support for the main business, e.g. a firm may invest in providing one or more of its own raw material sources, or invest in its own method of transport. As these will expand or contract as occasion demands, they are shown as broken lines on circle 11 of Diagram 14.

The term 'profitability' means more than just making profit – it is a measure of the effectiveness of the business in relation to its productive output, and can be expressed as a percentage:

$$\frac{^{*}\text{nett profit}}{\text{turnover}} \times \frac{\text{turnover}}{\text{capital employed}}$$

$= \%$ return on capital employed

The ROCE, 'return on capital employed percentage', is the ultimate measure of the success of the business financially. The greater the turnover secured for the same capital investment, the more successful the use made of capital resources.

*There are variations as to how this profit figure can be calculated. Three small businesses may present figures as follows:

	A	B	C
Annual turnover	£500 000	£250 000	£100 000
Nett profit	£50 000	£25 000	£10 000
Nett profit as % of turnover	10%	10%	10%

At face value each business appears equally profitable, but related to capital employed:

Capital employed	£100 000	£37 500	£10 000
ROCE	50%	66⅔%	100%

These figures show that business C is the most profitable.

12.1.2 Budgetary control

Architectural practice, like most businesses, is subject to peaks and troughs in its cash flow; commissions do not come in a steady stream, sometimes they do not come in at all, and a 'write off' of bad debts must always be allowed for in the budget of any practice.

The dreary trail of polite and not-so-polite letters to debtors, the Solicitor's letter to follow, and perhaps ensuing court proceedings, may not in the end bring in any money, but will certainly cost money to pursue.

A budget is a programme of anticipated income and expenditure, related to a period of time, usually one year ahead. Budgetary control is comparing anticipated income with actual income and taking corrective action and making such amendments as are necessary to the budget forecast. The important factor being the time element. It follows that if income is steady and outgoings commensurate with forecast it will not be necessary to make frequent checks, but they should be done regularly.

The manner in which additional income can be obtained in the event of anticipated shortfall in the budget forecast is a matter for the individual business or practice, e.g. turning fixed assets into cash, obtaining more orders or commissions, obtaining or extending a bank overdraft, obtaining a loan, drawing on reserves, etc, but remember that overdrafts and loans have to be serviced, and realization of assets and reserves affect the inherent stability of the business.

One must also remember that depreciation of assets must be adequately provided for. They should not be undervalued; many an ailing business has been bought out cheaply and the undervalued assets stripped and sold at a good profit to the benefit of the purchaser of the business.

12.1.3 Staffing costs

In any business wages and salaries account for a large proportion of the working capital which cannot be deferred, and increases in wages and salaries must be allowed for and may have to be met from reserves. In a working day not all time is productive; non-productive time will include such items as holidays, sickness, training, office administration, etc. The earning rate per hour of the staff must reflect this and a percentage be added to the nett hourly productive rate. It follows that distinction between technical and administration staff will have to be considered according to the type of office structure and the nature of the business.

In Architects' offices the term 'notional salaries' has been used to enable cost calculations to include partners earnings, these being commensurate with

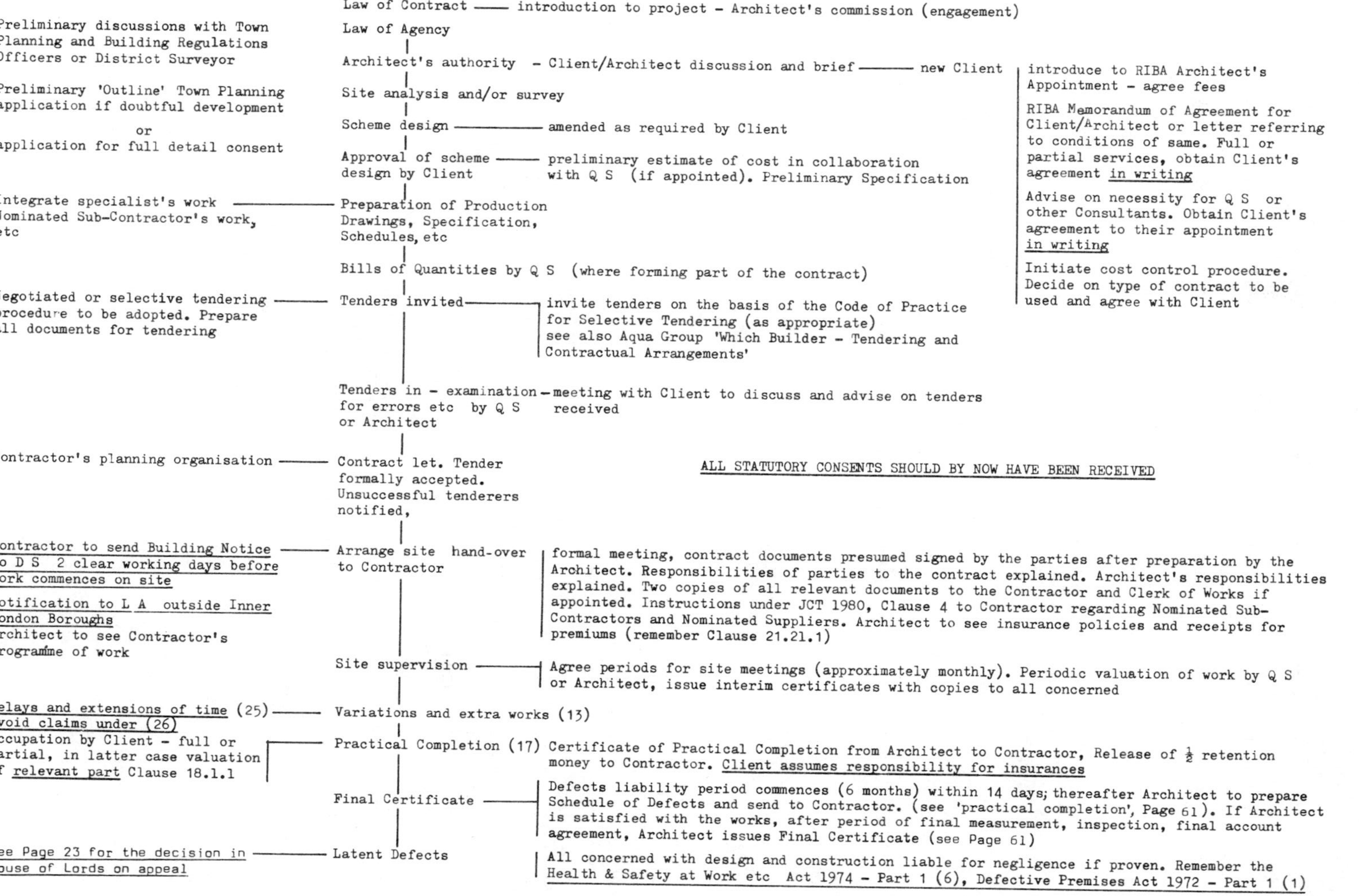

Diagram 15: Typical job progress chart

what a partner might have earned on a salaried basis elsewhere. They may vary from one partner to another, according to gross annual turnover.

If it has been decided that 50 per cent of total fee income is to be allocated to professional and technical salaries we can determine, at least in theory, what it will cost the practice to employ a person at a salary of £10 000 per annum, e.g.

$$\frac{100}{50} \times £10\,000 = £20\,000$$

Assuming that the productive time expended on actual projects is 200 days per year, the office cost of an effective day is, therefore,

$$\frac{£20\,000}{200} = £100$$

This is the basis for calculating how much time in man-days an office can afford to spend on a project in terms of budgeted costs. For example, a building estimated to cost £1 000 000 in Class 1 New Works would attract a fee of say 5 per cent, i.e. £50 000. If the average salary of the architectural staff is, say, £10 000 (office cost per day £100), then the number of man-days that the office can afford to spend on the project is

$$\frac{£50\,000}{100} = 500 \text{ man-days}$$

These man-days can then be allocated to the project stages, e.g. as shown in the RIBA Plan of Work, from inception to completion. Since offices employ staff at differing levels of salary and responsibility it is obvious that staff may not be continuously employed on the same project, and there will be both intensive periods of activity and slack periods. For example, where a scheme is going through town planning or building control appraisal, a 'flow chart' system may be adopted so that 'float' times can be utilized to best advantage, and allowance made for unexpected absence of staff at any time. Team leaders and individuals given a project to run should keep a careful check on the man-days allocated to it, particularly at the design stage. Also, they should record why decisions in the development of the scheme solution were taken, so that in the event of the scheme being taken over by another team or person they can follow the thought process of the designer up to that point. Masses of paper covered in indecipherable scribbles may be intelligible to the person who made them, but not to a successor trying to discover what stage a design scheme has reached.

If drawing is a large drain on capital resources, site visits during the construction stage are equally time-consuming *pro rata* to the allocation of fees for this stage of the project. Supervision must be viewed in the light of necessity, not just as an opportunity to get out of the office for a few hours. Local site visits can be made early in the morning on the way to the office so that the rest of the day can be planned without interruption. Visits which are not local must also be planned with care and a list made of things to be observed and recorded, progress photographs to be arranged, discussions to hold with the Clerk of Works, Person-in-Charge, and visits made to the local authority if required. Do not forget to advise people in advance that you are coming so as to afford them an opportunity to list things they want from you. Transport has to be considered according to whether one or more sites has to be visited, and if the visit is to be prolonged what accommodation is to be allowed for. (*See* Architect's Appointment, Part 4, 4.32).

12.1.4 Accounting

Forecasting and budgeting are means of assessing probable trends in cash flow, while accounting gives an accurate picture of the finances of the business showing whether it is making a profit or a loss. This is normally deduced annually from a balance sheet at the time when it is drawn up, and is a comparison of totals of money spent and money earned, or liabilities and assets, which must end up as equal totals when profit or loss are included.

Since management needs are geared to making adjustments as business progresses through each year, intermediate checks are necessary to achieve this; these are called 'trial balances', which may be drawn monthly or quarterly as the need arises (since the profit and loss figures are vital), and a'profit and loss' account is produced to show how the figures in the balance sheet are arrived at.

The services of an Accountant will be necessary to prepare the annual accounts, which will be audited, for Inland Revenue purposes. The ramifications of taxes are beyond the scope of this book, and an authoritative guide, such as the current edition of the *Hambro Tax Guide*, should be referred to.

References

Understanding Business Finance, Charterhouse CMC/ HUGO Management Courses (*see* Acknowledgements)

13

Project management

13.1.1 Resource allocation and control

We have already discussed the 'risk element' in investment of any kind, and equally there is the same risk involved in undertaking a building project for a client, from small extension or conversion work to large complex developments. From the outset the client will almost always want to know 'how much is it going to cost', and we are immediately involved in 'guesstimating' of one sort or another. For whatever techniques are used, and some are very sophisticated, they are all in the category of 'crystal-ball gazing', from 'off the top of the head' guesses through to 'cost yardsticks', 'cubic method', 'superficial-area method', 'storey-enclosure method', 'elemental cost analysis', etc, each in its own way having advantages and disadvantages, its own built-in 'unknowns'.

When we relate these methods to the design process, the site, its locality, sub-strata, topography, environs, orientation, access, to say nothing of the exigencies of town planning and building regulation requirements, it is obvious that forecasting building costs is a daunting task since the information which is usually available at the time on which to base an approximate estimate is usually very flimsy indeed. When one relates approximate estimates to the tendering procedure which later ensues, as discussed in 13.1.3, it is clear that certain unknowns in the first estimate procedure cannot be resolved at that stage, if indeed they can ever be resolved at all.

There are some matters which are entirely in the hands of the designer from the beginning of the project, e.g.:

(1) The topography of the site and its relationship to the mass of the building(s) and the disposition of the elements of the plan or the complex, bearing in mind also the drainage and other service relationships.

(2) Access to the site and the disposition of any roads to be built, and their relationship also to the site topography and services. Ensuring always that maximum use of the road is made to service any elements of the design complex.

(3) That sloping sites are considered in the design in terms of cut-and-fill ratios and stepped foundations.

(4) That the massing of the building(s) is carefully considered in terms of sub-strata conditions and the loads to be carried, and early investigations are undertaken to ensure, as far as possible, that any unforeseen areas of made-up ground, old foundations, services, etc, do not suddenly appear in the course of building without due warning.

(5) That problems arising from adjoining land or buildings are considered before design work progresses, thus avoiding costly alterations and delays later on in the building process.

(6) The plan form, considering carefully such matters as perimeter-wall factor (*see* Figure, page 95), lifts and staircases and their economic use in relation to circulation and height of the building, particularly means of escape in case of fire.

(7) The methods and types of construction to be used in relation to the function and the size of the elements, with particular reference to (4) above.

The basic cost index of each element of construction relative to the apportioned cost from the total cost target.

(8) The specification level, e.g. Fletton bricks or good quality facing bricks, concrete or hand-made sand-faced clay tiles. Such decisions will not manifest themselves on the

design drawings, but they should be borne in mind by the designer and contained within the cost target.

(9) Costs in use, and long- and short-term maintenance; this may be very important in developers' design schemes (*see* page 104), where the highest capital return on investment may preclude consideration of long-term maintenance since they will not be long-term occupants or 'consumers' of the building(s).

(10) Additions to the basic construction, such as thermal and sound insulation requirements.

Orientation of the building plays a large part in this (*see* Figure, page 97), and is related to the decisions in (5), (6), (7), (8) and (9) above.

(11) Services, such as drainage, sewerage, water, gas, electricity, telephone.

The availability or adaptibility, or otherwise, of such services is an important cost factor which is frequently overlooked in the early stages of design schemes.

In addition the 'extra over normal' services which may not have been properly considered in the first estimate of cost, particularly where one is using 'break-down' unit costs from an existing building as a comparison.

(12) Landscaping and external works. These usually appear on design drawings as transfer trees, shrubs, etc. without any real thought of the final cost of the landscape works. The requirements of the planning authority may be considerably in excess of what was originally envisaged. A fee spent on landscape consultancy in the early stages of the scheme may pay dividends in the long term.

(13) Tendering procedure to be adopted (*see* page 100).

At first sight these points may seem very obvious to some Architects, but in reading many Case Studies over the years, the author, and probably other examiners, are frequently presented with long discourses on problems arising on jobs which with some foresight could have been avoided, and which were embarrassing to the Architect and costly for the client.

As any book on cost planning and cost control will tell you, the latter is any method which permits allocated costs to be monitored and adjusted within a cost control system as the work proceeds. The Architect has a duty within the RIBA Architect's Appointment to undertake both the first estimates of cost (Part 1, 1.8, 1.9, 1.10) and develop these estimates through quality design considerations and subsequent cost checking, usually with the Quantity Surveyor's assistance, through to completion. (Part 1, 1.13, 1.14, 1.23, 1.24, or SW 1.4, 1.7, 1.12, 1.13).

Whichever method is adopted, the critical factor is 'adjustment'; this will have to consider all the relative factors according to the nature of the change and its size and complexity, as they may affect other elements in the cost plan. Also the change may be of such a critical nature as to affect the contractual structure. Remember that, in considering variations, the JCT Standard Form of Building Contract 1980 states 'No variation required by the Architect or subsequently sanctioned by him shall vitiate this contract' (Clause 13.3). In lay terms this means no change in the works described under the terms of the contract shall be of such a nature that the original intent of the contract is transformed to an unacceptable extent. For example, if the contractor has contracted to build 20 houses, and halfway through the client decided to change the contract to ten houses and a block of maisonettes, it is suggested that this would vitiate the original contract and therefore a new agreement would be necessary. Curtailment of a contract as tendered for will involve the contractor in a loss of profit to which he is contractually entitled.

Most books on cost planning describe in detail the various methods of obtaining preliminary estimates as previously mentioned, and space does not permit these to be reiterated *in toto*, but it is worthwhile mentioning some of the points which should be borne in mind when using them.

The RIBA *Cube Measurement for Buildings* gives the rules for measuring a building so that a 'cube' unit price can be applied. The Figure opposite shows that vertical dimensions are taken from the top of the concrete footings, or the underside of the hardcore, as appropriate, and the comments in (1), (3), (4), (5), (6) and (7) above obtain. This method has very limited use since it considers the total cube of the building, omitting the floors, and could be difficult to apply in complicated floor plans. The danger in using it is the large cumulative error that can accrue in the choice of the 'cube unit price', since this deals with very large numbers of units, and a small error in the basic unit price could grow to a very large error in multiplication of the total cube content. The measurement of the additional appendages can also be difficult to achieve.

Superficial measurement of buildings is less risky since cumulative errors in multiplication of units is reduced, but careful measurement is essential, especially in multi-storey buildings; forgetting to measure areas overall or missing out one or more floors could be a disaster. There is also the problem of the 'weighting factor' for work above and below ground. The comments in (1), (3), (4), (6) and (7) above also obtain in this method.

The cube method and the superficial area method both rely upon a 'basic unit price' or a 'single-price

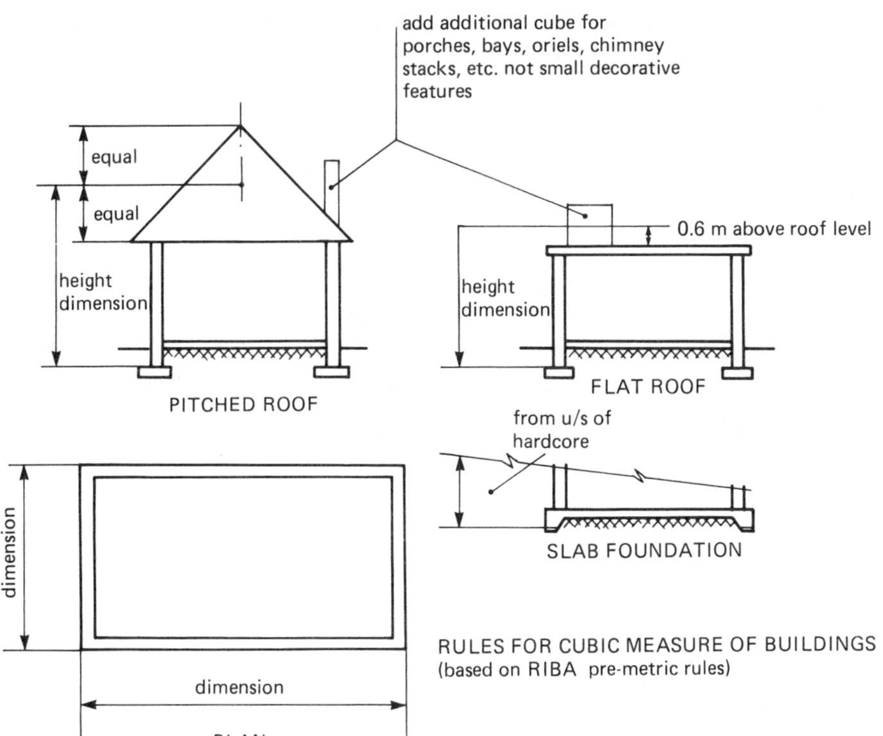

RULES FOR CUBIC MEASURE OF BUILDINGS
(based on RIBA pre-metric rules)

rate', or SPR as it may be called, and the way in which this is achieved is of paramount importance in its successful application. The Quantity Surveyor may keep cubic and superficial rates based upon current or passed work, which can be updated by the use of 'indices' published by the Building Cost Information Service or from some other source which predicts future cost trends in labour and materials, etc.

Unit costs may be taken from comparison 'break-downs' of existing buildings of the same type and size as the proposed project, where cost elements are shown as a break-down of the overall cost of the existing buildings as completed. The number of elements may vary according to how detailed the break-down is.

The specification level must be comparable in both the existing and the proposed buildings, with due regard given to additional services, extra-over-normal foundations, circulation space, lifts and staircases, landscaping, etc, as previously discussed.

The example on page 102 shows how such an estimate may look, and it is essential that the client understands the true nature of such estimates in relation to the tenders which will be obtained at a much later stage.

In the provision of educational, entertainment, welfare buildings, etc, they may be priced initially on a cost-yardstick basis, e.g.

Schools and colleges	cost per pupil or student place
Hospitals	cost per bed
Theatres	cost per seat
Hostels	cost per residential place
Car parks	cost per car space.

Such methods are very 'rough cut' guides and unreliable, but they may be used perhaps in preparing a feasibility study provided that the client understands the position.

Cost control

Perimeter wall factor – effect of plan shape on cost

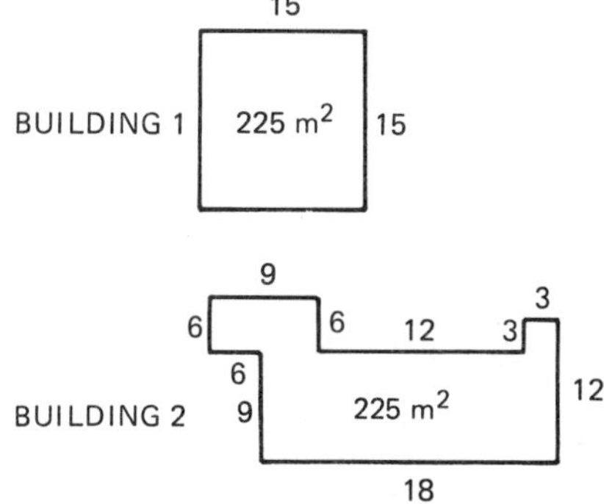

Relating the plan shape to the enclosing wall element, i.e. composite element of external walls, windows, external doors, it is clear that these elements are directly affected by the perimeter wall factor.

Ratio of enclosing walls per square metre to floor area if the height is constant in both buildings, say 3 m.

BUILDING 1 (page 95)

$$R = \frac{EWa}{Fa} = \frac{60 \times 3}{225} = 0.8$$

BUILDING 2 (page 95)

$$R = \frac{EWa}{Fa} = \frac{84 \times 3}{225} = 1.12$$

Thus, expressed as a comparable percentage the enclosing wall in Building 2 is

$$\begin{array}{r} 1.12 \\ .8 \\ \hline .32 \end{array} \qquad \frac{.32 \times 100}{.8}$$

= 40% more expensive than Building 1 for the same area enclosure in the terms of the enclosing wall element.

Could produce identical results from building where

$\frac{P}{A}$ were quite different

where P = perimeter, A = area.

Costing in building

Definitions (after James Nisbet, FRICS)

Cost and price: 'Cost' is the amount paid by the purchaser and the 'price' is that received by the vendor. Consequently, a tender is at one and the same time both the cost incurred by the client and the price offered by the builder. Since the professionals are acting for the client they are concerned with his 'costs'.

Cost analysis: Cost analysis is a systematic breakdown of cost data according to 'elements' which account for cost so as to facilitate examination.

Cost plan: A cost plan is a statement of how much it is intended to spend on each 'element' of the proposed building within a total sum in relation to a defined standard of quality. The allowances set against each element are 'cost targets'.

Cost planning: Cost planning is a method of controlling the cost of a project within a predetermined sum, during the design process, and includes the preparation of the cost plan as well as subsequent stages of cost checking.

Cost checking: Cost checking is the process of checking the estimated cost of each element against the target set for it in the cost plan.

Approximate estimating: Approximate estimating is the process of determining what the cost of a building should be. It occurs before the preparation of the cost plan and should be based upon the client's fundamental requirements.

Element: An element is a major component of a building, which, irrespective of construction or specification tends to perform the same function or functions.

Use requirement: Use requirements are the areas of accommodation, the activities for which the building is required, and the quality standards it should achieve, as stated by the client.

Cost control: Cost control is a generic term embracing all methods of controlling the cost of a building throughout its various stages from inception to completion.

Cost study: Cost study embraces all methods of investigating building costs, including capital, maintenance, and running costs. Cost research is a synonymous term.

13.1.2 The Quantity Surveyor

In the nineteenth century and before, the costing of buildings was done by a system of 'measure and value'; the Architect, or some other person, measured and valued the works in accordance with agreed rates or cost experience when the works were completed. Such a system was fraught with problems, and was gradually superseded by single or competitive systems based upon rough quantities. By the middle of the nineteenth century the term 'Bill of Quantities' had become established, and contracting procedures with builders widely used.

The demand for tenders by clients before work was started, coupled with the builder's requirement for a competitive tendering system which was equable, and upon which a contract sum could be based, began to emerge.

There was a gradual refinement of methods of measuring building costs over the latter half of the nineteenth and the first half of the twentieth centuries, and in 1909 the form of contract 'with quantities' was introduced in the RIBA Form of Contract. In 1922 when the first Standard Method of Building Measurement was generally adopted, the title 'Quantity Surveyor' became familiar.

During the period between the wars, from 1920 to 1939, cost-control methods were little used, prices being stable within 12 per cent or so of a norm, and having almost identical 'cost index' levels. Most buildings were traditional in design, construction,

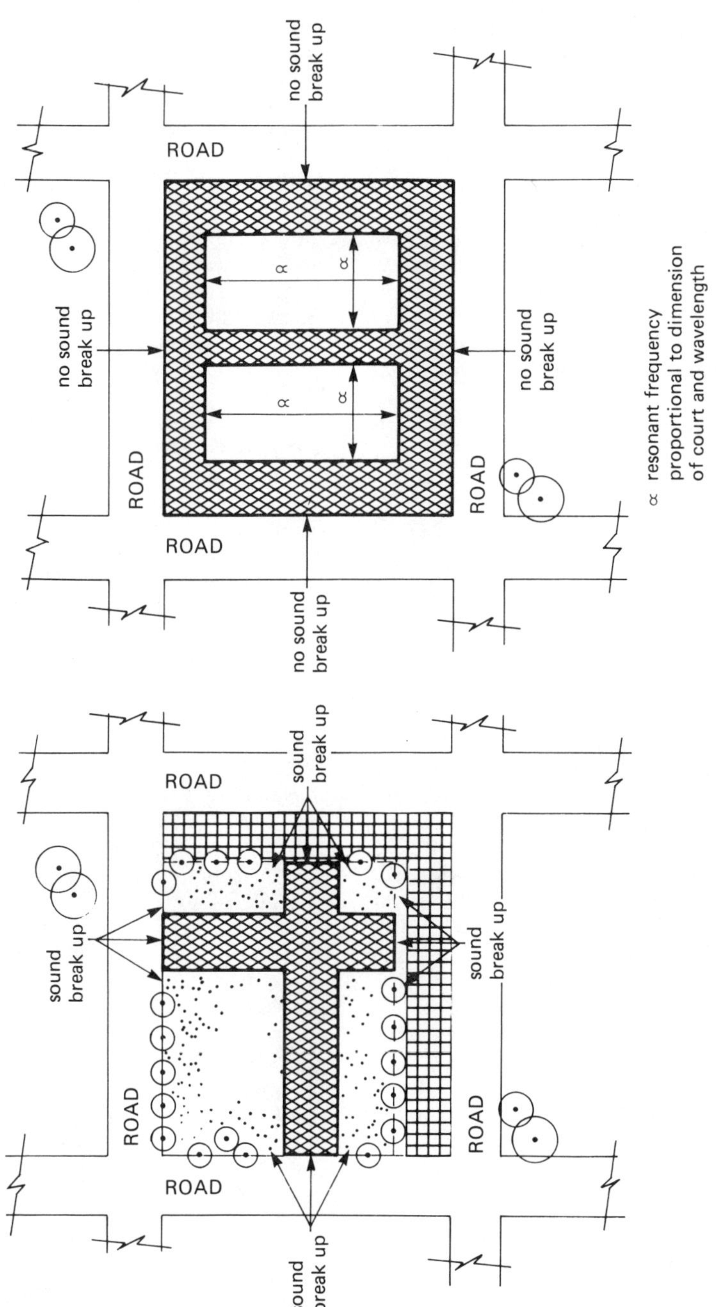
no sound
break up
ROAD
no sound
break up
no sound
break up
∝
∝
∝
∝
ROAD
ROAD
ROAD
no sound
break up
∝ resonant frequency
proportional to dimension
of court and wavelength
sound
break up
ROAD
sound
break up
sound
break up
ROAD
ROAD
ROAD
sound
break up

materials, and the 'cubing', 'superficial area', and 'approximate quantities' methods of pre-tender estimating were generally in use.

The post-war building boom brought the need for more cost control and cost planning development in the light of a large-scale building programme, particularly in the public sector, in the provision of depleted housing stocks, schools, hospitals, etc.

The Town & Country Planning Act 1947, the Principal Act, had its effect upon development, and the provision of open space around dwellings, coupled with the demand by local authorities for high-density developments, gave birth to the tower blocks and the use of system building techniques; in the early nineteen fifties many systems were in use, some imported from Europe. They also had the advantage that, with approximate estimating for external works, and the use of the newly introduced 'one-pipe' and 'single-stack' plumbing system, they were relatively easy to price.

It is clear that as demand for more accurate pre-tender pricing systems emerged, more sophisticated methods were developed, including the storey-enclosure method, and this, together with the cubic and superficial area methods, have been gradually replaced by elemental cost analysis and planning.

In 1961 the progressive book *Estimating and Cost Control* was written by James Nisbet, FRICS, which introduced the concept of elemental cost analysis which, in later publications, has been developed by other authors. A number of technical journals produced elemental cost break-downs of various buildings over the years, including, *inter alia*, the *Architects' Journal, Specification* and *The Builder*.

The demand for quantity surveying services, particularly to assist in the production of pre-tender estimates, has grown with the years, and the RICS and IQS are the principal sources of expertise in this field. The extension of the Bill of Quantities, providing not only tender and valuation information, but also the pre-tender cost information, has made the preparation of investment budgets for building design work possible. This is one of the most important roles of the Quantity Surveyor.

With the exception of Operational Bills of Quantities, there is still a deficit of information on the costing of building methods, although their implication in arriving at tender rates has been discussed in many books published in recent years.

Measurement and valuation, cost advice

The process of producing the Bill of Quantities begins, or should do so, with a good set of construction drawings and details, and a specification of workmanship and materials (*see* Chapter 13, 13.1.4, Quality control).

There are of course deviations from this ideal in practice for many reasons, but one must always be conscious of the dangers in undertaking building work with documents which do not adequately describe the work, and which may be subject to expensive re-measurement on site as work proceeds, where the client should be apprised of the cost control problems of such work, and its relationship to provisional estimates which may have been given at feasibility stage.

The Bill of Quantities is based upon the Standard Method of Measurement of Building Works in current use. The Bill of Quantities providing for labour, materials, services, including Provisional and Prime Cost Sums, Preambles to Trades and Preliminaries. The contractor inserts against the items in the Bill of Quantities his unit rates carrying them to a page summary and thence to a final total.

Much of the work in the Bills of Quantities over the years is seen as 'provisional', i.e. subject to re-measurement on site when the work is done. The client paying an extra over fee for the work as re-measured by the Quantity Surveyor.

The increased use by Architects of Prime Cost Sums, i.e. Nominated Sub-contractors and Suppliers, with the Main Contractor co-ordinating the Sub-contractor's work within the overall programme, and having to cope with the problems ensuing therefrom, and being tied to selected material suppliers, has resulted in decentralisation of the contractor's function, placing him in the position of an entrepreneur between the Architect and the Nominated Sub-contractors and Suppliers. This has a direct effect upon the Bill of Quantities, and one has only to turn to the Summary of Prime Cost and Provisional Sums in Bills of Quantities to see the percentage of overall building cost that these cost factors represent.

The Bill of Quantities is 'measured' from the drawings on dimension paper according to the Standard Method of Building Measurement, i.e. as superficial area, cube, linear, number, etc, the description of the items being related to the drawings and specification read together, or to questionnaires passed between the Quantity Surveyor and Architect. The dimensions are then abstracted and billed under the trades, with Preliminaries, Summaries and Schedules at the front and back of the Bill respectively; the printing and binding, and sometimes the invitation to tender, is undertaken by the Quantity Surveyor as part of his overall services.

Frequently in practice today the Quantity Surveyor is asked to abstract the specification from the information used in the preparation of the Bill of Quantities. The RIBA Architect's Appointment, Work Stages F and G, Production Information 1.16, seems now to concur in this practice.

Advice on type and form of contract

The types of contract in use today are described in Chapter 8, 8.1.1. The Quantity Surveyor may give advice on the appropriate type of contract suitable for the work to be done, and which contract document would best suit these conditions. He may also advise on any optional clauses within the form of contract to be used to be deleted, amended. or retained.

Advice on suitable contractors

The Quantity Surveyor has close contact with contractors, both main and sub-contractors, of all kinds in the course of his daily duties, and is able to suggest names of firms who may be suitable for a particular development.

Preparation and despatch of tendering documents

It is usually convenient for the Quantity Surveyor to assemble and despatch the invitation to tender documentation, this being in close consultation with the Architect in terms of drawings, schedules, details, specification, forms of tender, etc, and the time for tendering.

Checking tenders received

When tenders are received the Quantity Surveyor will check the prices in intimate detail, each discrete item being perused for arithmetic errors, rates for pricing, etc. It is assumed that the Quantity Surveyor will use the NJCC Code of Procedure for Selective Tendering (C/33b 1977 Single-stage) or Tendering Procedure for Industrialized Building Projects (C/33a 1984), for this stage of the work. After checking, the Architect will be advised of the outcome, and possible courses of action to be taken in recommending acceptance or rejection of any or all of the tenders.

A comparison will be made with the original cost plan, and the Quantity Surveyor will have to account for differences which may arise.

Variations and extra works

The Quantity Surveyor may be called upon to prepare 'addition' and 'omission' Bills; these may occur before the contract is 'let' in the light of differences between the tender accepted and the cost plan.

Interim valuations

In the course of the contract the contractor receives interim payments, usually monthly, based upon work completed, unfixed materials on site, or as provided for in the contract, less a sum for 'retention', usually 5 per cent of the total valuation, and such valuations are made by the Quantity Surveyor, usually with an Estimator from the main contractor present on site.

The Architect is not duty bound to accept this valuation (R B Burden Ltd *v* Swansea Corporation), but having accepted it, and certified accordingly, the client is bound to pay it within the prescribed time stated in the contract.

Daywork accounts

These works are such as are incapable of measurement either at the tender rates, or at an agreed rate.

There is a document called *Definition of Prime Cost of Daywork Carried Out Under a Building Contract (1975)* (Jobbing and Maintenance Works edition 1980) which can be used, or other rates agreed between the parties concerned.

It is important for the Architect to ensure that the use of daywork is carefully controlled, and provision in the specification for such work to be carried out on his written authority only is very advisable. The Quantity Surveyor will check daywork sheets and adjust them for their proper evaluation.

Fluctuation claims and payments

Where the contract contains a 'fluctuations clause' (*see* pages 58 and 100), the Quantity Surveyor must agree such accounts and the amount payable. It is very rare that such amounts are decreased costs, but they should be mentioned.

Claims under the contract

Claims by the main contractor for 'loss and expense' arising from matters outside his control, are checked and agreed with the Quantity Surveyor and forwarded to the Architect for payment and adjustment to the contract sum.

Preparation of the final account

When the contract has been completed, and within the time stipulated in the form of contract, the main contractor will furnish such information as is required for the preparation of the final account of the total cost of the contract works, and this will be negotiated and agreed for presentation to the Architect for issue of the Final Certificate. (*See* Chapter 8, page 62).

Cost analysis and cost checking

When the contract works have been completed it is possible to analyse these costs in terms of cost data for use on future jobs where preliminary estimating may be undertaken (*see* page 101). The following services may also be included in the Quantity Surveyor's appointment.

Specification writing
Negotiating contracts
Land and building surveys
Schedules of dilapidation (*see* Chapter 7, 7.1.5)
Schedules of fire damage (*see* Chapter 6, page 41)
Expert witness in Courts of law

The following duties are some of those carried out by the Quantity Surveyor under the JCT Standard Form of Building Contract 1980.

Clause

13.4	To value valuations and expenditure of Provisional Sums in accordance with the rules under Clause 13.5 (including deemed variations under Clause 2, 2.2.2)
13.6	To afford the contractor the opportunity to attend site for purposes of measurement
26.1	If instructed by the Architect to ascertain loss and/or expense by the main contractor
30	
5.2.1	If instructed by the Architect make statements of Main Contractor's and Nominated Sub-contractor's retention in each interim certificate
30	
6.1.2	To prepare final valuations under Clause 13
39	
39.5.3	The Quantity Surveyor may agree fluctuations
40.5	May agree to modification of Formula Rules for fluctuations.

Other than under Clauses 38.4.3 and 39.5.3 the Quantity Surveyor is not obliged to agree valuations or other sums and prices with the main contractor, as this is a matter for his own professional judgment, but it is normal for him to negotiate and consult with the main contractor.

The main contractor's remedy if he disagrees with the Quantity Surveyor's decisions, in the absence of any support from the Architect, is to go to arbitration.

13.1.3 Tendering procedures

In 1966 the then Research and Development Directorate of the Building Management of the Ministry of Public Building and Works published a definition of tendering procedures as follows:

> The purpose of any tendering procedure is to select a suitable Contractor at a time appropriate to the circumstances and to obtain from him at the proper time an acceptable tender or offer upon which a contract may be let.

This statement, rather than definition, may at first sight seem obvious, but if we look at some of the key words and phrases used we get a more complex understanding of the position.

First, 'select a suitable contractor'. In the Housing and Construction Statistics 1982 approximately 80 per cent of all building contracts were below the £150 000 total cost size, and a substantial proportion of them were of traditional construction. Small and medium contractors may be one-man businesses, or an unincorporated association of more than one person, or an incorporated association operating as a limited company. This latter structure may operate in its own name but be within the framework of a parent company, or operate as the 'small works' department of a large company.

It is suggested that the Code of Procedure for Selective Tendering be followed as a good basis for the selective tendering process. The Aqua Group suggest the following five bases for the selection of the contractor (*Which Builder – Tendering and Contractual Agreements*).

(1) The economic use of building resources,
(2) The assessment of the Contractor's contribution in relation to the design,
(3) The incentives to make production cost savings and their control,
(4) Continuity of work in all aspects, and
(5) Risk and the assessment of who should take it.

In the author's experience, the selection is usually made from a list of builders who have been known to do satisfactory work for the practice before, or whose work has been inspected, and confirmed by other Architects and perhaps the local authority as being satisfactory, and who are willing to tender within the time required.

In central government contracts and local authority contracts it is usual to see these offered to contractors by public invitation in the press and trade journals, and the number of tenderers may be very large indeed, and a 'performance bond' may be required as a condition of contract for the successful tenderer. This is a sum of money, perhaps 10 per cent of the total estimated contract costs, which the successful Contractor must guarantee as an indemnity against his performance in completing the work included in the contract.

Having made the selection of contractors to tender from a list that is not too large, it is essential that they all tender on the same basis, i.e. tender documents and time for tendering. Any extension of this time granted to one contractor must be granted to all.

Tenders should be delivered to the Architect's office at the same time as stated in the tender invitation form, clearly marked 'Tender for ....'; late tenders should be rejected as 'out of time'. All tenders should be opened at the same time in the presence of the QS, if one is appointed. Some clients insist on being represented or attending personally, but this is not essential as the Architect is acting as the client's agent and the checking of tenders has yet to be carried out, and it is better to advise the client of the outcome after this has been done.

When the Architect or the QS has checked the tenders, errors should be dealt with in accordance with the Code of Procedure for Single-stage Selective Tendering. When a tender has been selected and notified to the client for acceptance, the unsuccessful tenderers should be notified of the results, listing the tenders in numerical order highest to lowest but without names. It is important to do this, not merely from the courtesy point of view, but it is the only feed-back that the contractor has of his estimating performance.

The contents of priced Bills of Quantities are confidential.

It may well be that a 'first estimate of cost' or 'pre-tender estimate' has been given to the client in accordance with the Architect's Appointment, Part 1, Work Stage C, 1.9, or Small Works SW1.4, and the problem is to reconcile this first cost with the tenders received, as discussed in this chapter.

In selective tendering procedure the first sight the contractor and his estimator have of the intended works is the receipt of the tender documents, and they therefore can bring little influence to bear on the involvement in the design in terms of plant use, site organisation, and methods of construction. He is obliged to price on what the tender documents ask him to do. These documents may also be liberally laced with Prime Cost Sums for nominated sub-contractors and suppliers, against which the estimator merely puts a profit and attendance figure.

Profit is also an unknown factor to anyone but the contractor, each of whom will have his own cash flow and capital resource problems. The only clue may be reflected in the rates for the various sections

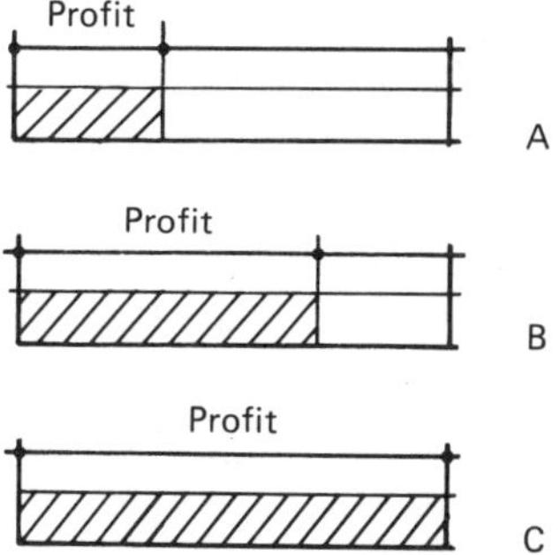

of the work tendered for. Such rates may reflect what is termed 'front-end loading', e.g. taking three contractors, their profit may be spread over the contract period as shown in the Figure above.

From this it will be seen that the front-end loaded tender could cause problems of incentive to complete the works when the profit has been taken. This would be deduced from the rates by the Quantity Surveyor when tenders where checked.

There are other unknowns in tendering which do not get mentioned in what are otherwise excellent books dealing with the costing of building works, but which may have a profound effect upon the tender, e.g.

(1) The contractor's opinion of the tender documents, which may become for him the contract documents, in terms of advantage or disadvantage.
(2) The contractor's opinion of the site; for example, if it is a rather 'lush' site for a house, the contractor may well feel that the client is not short of money and will price accordingly.
(3) The Architect, Quantity Surveyor, employer, may be known from previous experience of the contractor to be 'difficult'.
(4) In certain areas there may be 'price rings' existing between contractors and builders' merchants and other sources of supply.
(5) The ratio of successful to unsuccessful tenders which a particular contractor is experiencing, since the former have to bear the cost of the latter, and may influence the 'contractual risk' the contractor is prepared to take to secure a contract.
(6) The ratio of own labour force to hired labour, and own plant to hired plant.
(7) Some contractors may not want the job, but wish to remain on tender list for future jobs, subsequently submitting a high tender, called 'taking a cover'.

There may be other unknowns in the selective tendering process, but the real danger is in anticipating that they will come into close proximity with the original pre-tender 'guesstimate', frequently they do not, and the Architect is faced with reconciling the difference with the client, who frequently does not remember the conditions under which such estimates are given, and is discontented with the 'paring down' of the project to bring the tender price within the cost target. This makes for frustration, loss of time, and loss of confidence in the Architect, albeit unfairly in most cases. The two methods of arriving at a total cost of works are, after all, different in their basic methods, and both contain different unknowns and risks.

It must always be borne in mind that even when the tender price has been reduced to a level acceptable to the client, and a start on the works has been made, in the absence of a fixed-price contract there is always the uncertainty, during the progress of the works, of extras arising in the form of variations and extra works, or fluctuations, seen and unforeseen. In the latter case the Contingency Sum may soon be expended. The view held by some Architects that the client always pays in the end may not be realized, and the remarks at the end of the Introduction, page XI, may well obtain.

In relation to selective tendering procedure, negotiated tenders are uncommon; they do happen, particularly on large jobs where there are circumstances which warrant such a procedure. Usually they fall under one of two headings:

(1) On the basis of competitive rates for similar work under similar conditions in another contract.
(2) An agreed estimate of the prime cost of the works plus an agreed percentage for the contractor's overheads and profit.

It is generally held that negotiated tenders are more expensive than selective tender contracts. There seems to be no real reason why this should be so as they may be used for various reasons which are at the time advantageous to the client; e.g. a client may use a particular contractor because it is advantageous to his business to do so. It may entail the continuation, repetition, or extension of an existing building contract where the client's confidence in the contractor may outweigh any other consideration. The client may wish to make a quick start on his works to take advantage of a particular trading period, say the holiday season or Christmas, and the contract may well be of the prime cost + fee type.

There are inherent dangers in using the same contractor for all jobs, however, and these should be obvious.

First estimate of costs (p.94)

PROPOSED LABORATORY AND OFFICE BUILDING, LANDSDOWNE WAY, LONDON SE 16

Clients: Daneslaw Chemicals Ltd
16 Western Avenue, Middlesex

PRELIMINARY ESTIMATE OF BUILDING COSTS (excluding land costs and charges)

Single Price Rate source:
Similar building for Daneslaw Chemicals (Insecticides) Ltd at Pullman Road, London N1.
completed October 1981, final cost £375.00 m²

Projected cost index increases from 1981 to September 1985 (starting date for new building) 17.5%†

Revised SPR for proposed building £440.00 m²
Total gross floor area of new building 1260²

Projected cost per m² = 1260 × 440 =		£554 400.00
ADD		
(a) Extra over normal foundations	£12 450*	
(b) Extra over for additional drainage to laboratory	£3 400*	
(c) Extra over for landscaping	£2 400*	
(d) Extra over for specialized laboratory equipment	11 280**	
	£29 530	£ 29 530.00
		£583 930.00
ADD		
(e) Preliminaries @ 8%		46 712.00
(f) Contingencies @ 2%		11 678.00
Preliminary building cost		£642 320.00
ADD		
Preliminary estimate for professional fees		
Architects @ 5%, say	£31 610	
Quantity Surveyor @ 2%, say	£12 846	
Structural Engineer @ 3%, say	£19 270	
	£63 726	£ 63 726.00
Preliminary total cost		£706 046.00

* Quantity Surveyor's estimates
** Preliminary quotation specialist supplier
† Fictitious

13.1.4 Quality control

In his book *Principles of Design* (Design Council 1979), W H Mayall wrote 'Quality is defined in a glossary produced by the European Organization for Quality Control as "the totality of features and characteristics of a product or service that bears upon its ability to satisfy a given need"'. '"Reliability" is the ability of an item to perform a required function under stated conditions for a given period of time'.

Mr Mayall qualifies the latter statement by drawing attention to the deviation from the norm which most products undergo to a more or less degree in the process of their manufacture, resulting in components failing at a time exasperating to the user. Also, that 'performance specifications' are related to 'function cost analysis' which examines the various functions and characteristics of a product or component in terms of its performance, taking into consideration the cost of achieving these functions within a stated overall cost target for the product. The reliability of the product or component having a direct relationship to correct maintenance throughout its effective life.

A building is a product composed of a large number of components, some of which, particularly in the mechanical services area, fall within the factory product remarks, including such terms as 'built-in obsolescence', 'total component replacement' which are common today.

In building work, 'quality' is much more difficult to define since the building as built breaks down into a number of elements which, in the broadest terms, consist of

(a) The sub-structure (work below ground)
(b) The super-structure (work above ground)

which can be further sub-divided into

(c) Carcassing,
(d) Cladding (including fenestration),
(e) Services (drainage, plumbing, electrical, mechanical),
(f) Finishes,
(g) Fixtures and fittings, and
(h) External works, e.g. landscaping.

There is an overlapping of 'factory product' and 'building work' in many of these elements of construction; e.g. lifts, sanitary fittings, air-conditioning equipment, etc.

Quality in buildings may be judged simply in aesthetic terms, and there have been many cases of buildings, many by famous Architects, which having been praised in architectural terms, subsequently manifested failures of one sort or another, e.g. condensation, water penetration, etc.

The client expects value for money, and it is the Architect's duty to see that this is achieved. In law it has been said that 'one cannot expect a Rolls Royce for a Morris Cowley price', and the best person to judge whether he gets it is the Architect. There are many today who would regard this statement with scepticism, but the clue to it is in comparison of cars, since that time building has progressed and developed to a level of sophistication which may add weight to the alternative viewpoint.

Quality of workmanship and materials is often regarded as being 'geared' to the price paid, although omnibus clauses in specification which are intended to regulate these matters frequently are ignored, e.g. 'work shall be in accordance with acceptable building practice' is subject to the interpretation of 'acceptable', and it turns on what the builder thinks he can get away with. It is, therefore, understandable that many young Architects have never seen really good quality work, as depressed standards have tended to become the norm. Sometimes the nature of material rejected as below specified standard is such that replacement may be as bad or even worse. Timber is a good example of this, where the contractor has little control over the quality delivered, even when covered by a British Standard. It is inherent in the nature of the supply, conversion, and seasoning of the material, young growth softwood, kiln-dried, mass-machined.

Architect's design drawings, from quite small schemes to large complexes, look very much alike; they delineate the enclosure of space in terms of the 'massing' of the building, expressing in plans, sections and elevations how this space is organized as usable space, vertical and horizontal circulation, related to the site in terms of access, topography, aspect and prospect, orientation, etc. The drawings are expressing the 'broad brush' concept of the designer's solution to the problem within the dictates of the brief.

The drawings do not at this stage, except in aesthetic terms, express 'quality'; the scheme as a completed building manifesting the built structure, the carcass, the cladding, services, fixtures and fittings, will be grafted on as the project proceeds through detail design, and production information stages, and of course cost planning and cost control procedure. The degree to which the designer has control over these stages of the project, i.e. carrying the design thought process through to the completion of the building, will influence in no small measure the final statement that the building makes as a piece of architecture, as opposed to mere building, where all the parts come together as a whole, which may be admired or detested according to taste. An American Architect some years ago described a vast down-town development as 'the greatest sea of Travertine marble for over 3000 miles'! If one looks at the work of Architects such as Ralf Erskine, Werner Küenzi, Georg Wellhausen, among others, where simple materials are used with skill and imagination, even in severe climatic conditions, one learns that the use of costly materials in pursuit of quality is not necessarily the right path to take. On the other hand, the choice of say, a sandfaced Fletton brick today to limit costs, may in 20 years or so prove to be the wrong choice when prevailing weather reduces the sand facing to nothing more than patchy Fletton brickwork.

Clearly, the material quality of the building should be in the mind of the designer from the outset, and a basic level of specification determined which can be developed through the stages of design to completion. It is a question of apportioning the money available for the scheme across the elements of the building so that each element has the correct 'weight' in relation to the whole. It is obvious that adjustments will have to be made within the cost plan, but not to the extent that the marble-lined walls end up as render and set and two coats of emulsion paint.

The use of British Standard Codes and Specifications in specifications carried through into Bills of Quantity does not guarantee that any particular Code or Specification will do any more than provide a point of departure, a norm as previously discussed. For example, natural and synthetic asphalts, hand-made sand-faced tiles and concrete tiles, are covered by British Standards, but there is a world of difference between their intrinsic qualities and costs.

Cost control and quality control are for the Architect many-faceted problems beginning with the inception of the scheme and progressing through all the work stages in the RIBA Plan of Work, and requiring constant appraisal and adjustment where necessary so that on completion the client receives value for money in terms of capital expenditure, hoping that the building will satisfy the need, be pleasant both to look at and to be in, leaning perhaps towards those old canons of good architecture – firmness, commodity, and delight.

The 'costs-in-use' of the building will vary with the nature of the building and its use, and in the case of developer's budgets may be regarded quite differently from consumer's budgets where the building owner may be in residence or have the maintenance costs to contend with over a long period of time. The life of a building may be determined by its ability to be adapted for other purposes over its useful life.

13.1.5 Supervision of works

This aspect of the Architect's services is covered in Architect's Appointment, Part 2, 2.37, Part 3, 3.11, 3.12, SW1.12, SW3.5.

Constant supervision does not form a part of the Architect's services, and where this is required a Site Architect or a Clerk of the Works must be employed for this purpose, otherwise the degree of supervision should be considered in terms of what is reasonable in the circumstances, particular attention being paid to those areas of work which eventually will be covered up, e.g. drains, foundations, etc (*see* Chapter 2, 2.1.3).

The function of supervision is to ensure as far as possible that the terms of the contract are generally being complied with, and it will cover materials and components delivered to the site, or in the off-site workshops, which ultimately will be used in the construction and furbishment of the completed building.

Where British Standards are quoted in the contract documents, materials and components to which they refer should be checked to ensure the BSI kite mark and/or BS number is stamped on the goods.

One has to exercise some discretion on material such as timber which, no matter how well specified, has inherent defects such as sapwood, knots, resin, etc, which are outside the control of the contractor, being in the nature of softwoods grown and converted for construction use. If it is 'rank bad', to use a legal term, it must be rejected, but the replacement delivery may exhibit similar faults. It is a question of degree.

In cases in the courts which have been concerned with supervision, or the lack of it, the plaintiff may assert that the supervision was so poor as to be valueless, and the court has to decide this in terms of what a reasonable and competent Architect would have been expected to do in similar circumstances; they may decide that the fee for supervision should be either reduced *pro rata* or negated *in toto*, and in addition award costs to the plaintiff in similar ratio.

In the absence of a Quantity Surveyor, the Architect may have to make valuations of the work completed for certification purposes, and this is one of the danger areas where things can go drastically wrong; a careful record of how the valuation was arrived at should be kept, avoiding at all costs the temptation to have a quick glance round and assess the cost 'off the top of the head'. The main contractor, and his nominated sub-contractors and suppliers, have a contractual right to proper payment for the work done, and for unfixed materials and components as provided for in the contract.

A Site Architect is a relatively new position in the profession, but a Clerk of Works has been an established post since the formation of The Institute of Clerks of Works in Great Britain Incorporated in 1882. Amendments to the JCT Form of Contract, however, have reduced the function of the Clerk of Works to that of an Inspector, requiring within two working days written confirmation from the Architect to the Contractor of any instruction given by the Clerk of Works. Members of the Institute qualify by examination, and there are two corporate grades of membership, Member and Fellow. Prior to this there are three non-corporate grades, Probationer, Student, Licentiate. Honorary Members and Associates are admitted to the Institute, including qualified persons no longer engaged as Clerks of Works in the Industry. The provision of accommodation for the Clerk of Works on site is covered in the Bill of Quantities, and must be within statutory limits depending upon the number of

Clerks of Works employed and the size of the job. The Institute lays down minimum salary scales for Clerks of Works and Assistants.

Their final examination is in three parts, Intermediate, Final Parts, 1 and 2, and exemptions from the whole of any part, or subjects thereof, is possible through other recognized examinations.

The Clerk of Works is recommended by the Architect, and the appointment may be made through advertisement and interview of a number of candidates for the post. The client is responsible for payment of the Clerks salary.

The Clerk of Works has a number of duties on site where he is liaison between the contractor and Architect, and a copy of his duties and other matters affecting his appointment can be obtained from the Institute in addition to any advice or information on the appointment. His information regarding weather and labour, etc, on site can be valuable to the Architect in considering claims for extensions of the contract period by the contractor.

Site Architects are employees of the Architect, unless separate arrangements are agreed with the client for a direct appointment; this would be unusual but may occur in management contracts.

The provisions of the Health & Safety at Work etc Act 1974 should be observed, also in terms of the Clerk of Works, and any insurances which may be necessary to protect the interests of all concerned with the appointments.

References

Building Cost Control Techniques and Economics, E. BATHURST and D. A. BUTLER (Heinemann)

The Principles of Design, W. A. MAYALL (Design Council)

Contract Practice for Quantity Surveyors, J. W. RAMUS (Heinemann)

14

Surveys and Reports

In the course of general practice the Architect is at some time concerned with providing information in the form of reports following upon surveys of land and property. The RIBA Architect's Appointment, Part 2, 2.1, 2.2, 2.4, 2.6, 2.10, 2.12 and SW2.1, 2.2, 2.3, refer.

Litigation which has ensued from such services provided by Architects and Surveyors clearly indicates the heavy responsibility which rests upon the instigators of such reports. The circumstances which obtain in individual cases varies considerably, and it would be wrong to attempt to lay down standards and rules upon which cases could be judged, as this is entirely a matter for the courts. One can say, however, that a person commissioning an Architect or Surveyor to make a survey and report his findings is entitled to expect competence on the part of the person producing the report, 'competence' having that degree of professional skill ascribed to it in Chapter 2, 2.1.3. If certain aspects of the survey are outside the skill, knowledge, and competence of the Architect or Surveyor they should say so from the outset, or at least advise the client to appoint a competent person, e.g. a Structural Engineer or Valuation Surveyor, to provide the information required.

If the Architect or Surveyor elects to adopt these roles, or any others, then it would appear that the client has the legal right to expect such advice and information given by them to be commensurate with that of the Structural Engineer or Valuation Surveyor or any other expert, as this is what the client is paying for.

In the absence of dilapidations, as previously discussed, the purpose of the reports upon land and property fall within the following broad divisions:

(1) Survey and report for a prospective purchaser.
(2) Survey and report for a prospective purchaser with a view to alteration, extension, conversion, of the property following purchase.
(3) A measured survey of land or buildings with or without levels being taken.

The first essential, therefore, is to have a clear understanding from the beginning of exactly what the client requires, and to confirm this in writing, or at least to make it clear in submitting the report what the extent of the survey and report is.

The survey of the premises should have due regard for the age and the type of construction of the property, and observation of similar premises in the locality may show defects common to them all, e.g. spalling of soft red bricks, similar crack patterns, etc. Do not be misled by a good standard of decoration which may hide a number of minor, and sometimes major, faults. For example, some older methods of construction employed 'flitch beams' formed of timber beams and metal plates bolted together, all concealed in sound, well varnished beam casings, which on further investigation may reveal severe deterioration of the timber beams. Thick walls may be no more than brick skins infilled with rubble bound together with lime slurry, and may contain timber 'bonders' to spread the load in the wall. The old adage 'its the wallpaper holding it up' may in some cases not be far from the truth.

In making surveys for purchase of properties, one should consider the premises in terms of the locality as a whole, not just the immediate environs. A drive around the locality may reveal a number of undesirable aspects, e.g. the 'bijou' end of terrace property seen in the quiet of the morning may not be so quiet when the pub on the corner turns out at night, or plays its 110-decibel music. Local football club supporters and their opposition can be a source of nuisance to property owners and occupiers. Noxious smells, noise from traffic, factories, school playgrounds, etc, may all make the purchase of the property by the client undesirable.

Services should always be carefully considered before any purchase is made, especially where conversion or extension may be subsequently undertaken, and money spent on checks by statutory undertakers and service undertakers on gas, water, electricity, drainage, telephone, is money well invested.

When measured surveys are made, and levels may also be taken, it follows that accuracy is essential, particularly where the survey may be used as a basis for setting out the building by the Contractor, for whom the Architect must provide accurate drawings and levels to enable him to set the building out at ground level (JCT Form of Contract 1980, Clause 7).

Surveys and other drawings provided by persons other than the Architect should always be used with discretion, as the responsibility for the proper completion of the works rests with the Architect. The degree to which every discrete drawing provided by others should be checked by the Architect, and this includes calculations, is a difficult point to ascertain, and would appear to turn on what would be considered reasonable in the circumstances; unfortunately, the interpretation of 'reasonable' or 'unreasonable' (words which occur 45 times in the JCT Form of Contract 1980) may have to be decided in the Courts in the event of dispute.

The extent to which a survey of premises should or should not include information is conditioned by commonsense, but should cover matters which a prudent and competent person would be expected to raise.

Probably the most common faults of omission occur in surveys of premises partially or fully occupied where floor coverings, room furnishings and junk and bric-a-brac in the attic make access difficult. In the case of Kerr *v* John H Allan & Sons, Lord Birnam said, *inter alia*, '. . . the house was furnished and occupied, and the time at the disposal of the defenders was extremely short. Even so, the evidence is, and I accept it, that the possibility of dry rot is a thing that ought always to be present in the mind of a Surveyor, and he should be on the look-out for any evidence that might to his skilled mind be suggestive of dry rot; but I am unable to accept the view that in such circumstances his duty requires him, in the absence of suspicious circumstances, to cause linoleum, or carpets, to be lifted, to go underneath floors and make a detailed examination of every hidden corner of the building'.

The important phrase here is 'in the absence of suspicious circumstances' and whether these may have been present at the time when the survey was made. For example, dry rot spreads rapidly in favourable conditions, and it may manifest itself even after a relatively short passage of time after the survey. In such circumstances it may well be that the court would be favourably inclined towards the Surveyor.

In most survey reports, indemnity insurers require a standard clause inserted which may read something like the following:

> At the time of my survey the premises was occupied, fully furnished, and the floors covered, and I was unable to come to any conclusion as to the presence or absence of dry rot, wet rot, woodworm, or beetle infestation. Where surfaces indicated such may exist, this is stated in the report, and further investigation is recommended.

There has been some argument as to whether such clauses are a defence in the event of litigation ensuing from surveys, but again it turns on the circumstances prevailing, and the court's view of the evidence in any particular case.

In the course of making a survey, timber diseases are encountered which do not fall into recognizable categories, and indeed exhibit 'symbiotic' relationships between one form of timber disease or infestation and another. If in doubt seek expert advice. The Timber Research and Development Association offers expert help and advice on timber problems for reasonable fees. Many firms who carry out treatment of timber diseases and infestations also offer specialist advice prior to treatment, and although some firms may use outside specialists to investigate on their behalf, many of them employ lay-persons possessing a rudimentary knowledge of such problems to make inspections and prepare reports. Alternatively, one can send a sample of the diseased timber to TRADA for examination. The obvious advice is not to guess about timber problems as they figure high on the list of faults in surveys and reports which have come before the courts.

Bulges and cracks in brickwork are very common problems in surveys, particularly in older buildings, and some of these defects may be of very long standing, manifesting signs of earlier settlement and differential movement of one sort or another. With age the mechanical bond strength of brickwork also weakens and lime mortars degrade, and these processes coupled with poor foundations give rise to movement in the brickwork.

Changes can also occur in the sub-strata due to lowering of the water table for any reason, particularly where associated with long, dry summers. If a building has stood for many years without undue movement, and then suddenly starts to show signs of new movement, it should be obvious that the cause is acute and not chronic. It is necessary to understand the nature of the cracks which have appeared in the brickwork, and in the event of bulging, to have plumb readings taken, since parallax errors occur in observation. Before having the brickwork taken down and rebuilt, possibly at considerable cost, it is wise to have glass 'tell-tales' fixed in mortar dabs over the cracks along their length, and to observe them over a reasonable period of time, since they may be innocuous and need nothing more that 'stitching-up' and repointing. In removing old brickwork to enlarge openings, etc, it is important, particularly in the region of chimney breasts, not to use mechanical tools and to keep hammering to a minimum, as vibration can cause collapse, especially of the withes between flues in old chimney breasts.

Drains are also very important in surveys. Generally one cannot resort to carrying out an immediate test on drainage systems, but it is possible by observation to make intelligent guesses as to the efficiency of a system; lift the manhole covers, run the taps and flush the toilets and watch the results through the system (observing the cleanliness or otherwise of manholes). These actions will usually indicate whether or not the system is functioning correctly. Breakage in the drain runs, roots which have penetrated the system, and settlement, will usually be followed by blockages and 'backing-up' of the effluent, which will call for investigation to determine the cause. Temporary blockages occur for many reasons; it is quite astounding what is forced down waste pipes and flushed down toilets. patches of lush grass along drain runs can be indicative of leaks in the system, and similar characteristics can occur over areas of surface-water soakaways.

If the premises to be surveyed is very old, water-testing of drains may aggravate problems and do more harm than good, but smoke testing is satisfactory and worth while. Do not forget to look behind pipes – waste, soil, and rainwater – to ensure that there are no leaks, and examine the junctions of gutters with fascia boards.

Ineffective damp-proof courses (not 'damp courses', please), or even the lack of them, are a source of continual damage to property. Rising damp, the growth of mould and fungi on the internal and external wall surfaces, with attendant problems of wet- and dry-rot in timbers, particularly wall plates and joists in suspended ground floors, are common faults. There are many ways of treating this problem using specialist contractors, but be wary of guarantees, they are effective only for as long as the particular firm giving them remains in business. Check that the problem is not caused by the earth in flower beds being banked up over damp-proof courses causing 'bridging' and consequent damp penetration, and ensure that all air ventilators are free from obstruction and functioning properly.

Pointing is expensive to renew, and if it must be done, do not use strong cement mortars; use a gauged lime mortar that is weaker than and more compatible with the density of the bricks, thereby avoiding excessive shrinking of the mortar and subsequent frost damage.

Inspect the roof space, even if access is difficult; before you switch on your torch look for any obvious daylight showing through the roof covering, making careful note of any subsequent water ingress damage to timbers, etc. Failure of valley gutters or flashings at abutments will easily be seen from inside the roof space. Check the water storage tanks(s) for corrosion, leaks, deposits, or stagnation where two or more tanks may be connected in tandem. and one or more has ceased to work. Make a note of insulation of pipes and roof space, or the lack of it.

On suspended timber floors a gentle 'bounce' in the middle of span to test the deflection is essential to ensure that the deflection is not excessive.

Do not take heating systems, water services, etc, at face value; make sure that they are seen to be working, or recommend a test before purchase.

Appendices

District Surveyors' Offices

London Borough	District	Address	Telephone
City of Westminster	Westminster	1-17 Shaftesbury Avenue W1 V7RL	01-437 2972
	Paddington	9 Monmouth Road, W2 4UT	01-229 6661
	St Marylebone	4 Luxborough Street, W1M 3LG	01-935 0858
Camden	St Pancras	Walkden House, 10 Melton Street, NW1 2EB	01-388 0476
	Holborn	Crown Buildings, 3-9 Southampton Row, WC1B 5HA	01-405 5211
	Hampstead	Mullion Court, 112/114 Finchley Road, NW3 5JJ	01-435 4867 and 7860
Islington	Islington	Club Union House, 251 Upper Street, N1 1RY	01-226 8379
	Finsbury	58 Myddelton Square, EC1R 1XX	01-837 9349
Hackney	Hackney and Stoke Newington	Ockway House, 41 Stamford Hill, N16 5SR	01-802 0081
	Shoreditch	179 Shoreditch High Street, E1 6HU	01-739 4572
Tower Hamlets	Stepney	132 Eric Street, E3 4SN	01-981 1146
	Poplar and Bethnal Green	132 Eric Street, E3 4SN	01-981 1146
Greenwich	Woolwich	Thames House, Wellington Street, SE18 6PB	01-855 6304
	Greenwich	11 King William Walk, SE10 9JH	01-858 1157
Lewisham	Lewisham	1 Myron Place, SE13 5AT	01-852 3253
	Deptford	487 New Cross Road, SE14 6TQ	01-692 2370
Southwark	Southwark	City House, 65 Southwark Street, SE1 0HT	01-261 9511
	Camberwell	186/188 Peckham High Street, SE15 5EU	01-639 5277
	Bermondsey	City House, 65 Southwark Street, SE1 0HT	01-261 9511
Lambeth	Lambeth	365 Brixton Road, SW9 7DB	01-274 9531
Wandsworth	Wandsworth	79 Wandsworth High Street, SW18 4TB	01-870 7611
	Battersea	79 Wandsworth High Street, SW18 4TB	01-870 7611
Hammersmith & Fulham	Hammersmith	179 King Street, W6 9JT	01-748 7926
	Fulham	25 Jerdan Place, SW6 1BE	01-385 8513
Royal Borough of Kensington & Chelsea	Kensington	Fenelon Place, Warwick Road, W14 8PZ	01-373 7702
	Chelsea	1 Dovehouse Street, SW3 6JX	01-352 9574
City of London	City of London	38 Cannon Street, EC4N 6LT	01-248 0361

Swan Press 6814

DS.36

Serial No. ....

Date. ....

Greater London Council

London Building Acts 1930 – 1978

STATEMENT OF COST

To Mr. *District Surveyor for*

I/WE HEREBY STATE that the cost of the work executed by and for me/us at

pursuant to the Building Notice dated

was £

(See Note 2 overleaf)

Signature

Address

Date

NOTE — This form should be completed and returned to the district surveyor within 14 days, as required by Section 84 (3) of Act. (See Note 1 overleaf)

625 SwP

P.T.O.

DS 1

Building Notice

LONDON BUILDING ACTS, 1930 to 1978 AND BY-LAWS

MADE IN PURSUANCE THEREOF

Building Notice

To:

____

____

Note: Builders should complete sections 1 to 4 of this Notice (block capitals please) and return it to the District Surveyor's office *at least two clear days* before work commences. Personal visits in connection with this Notice should be made between 9.30 and 10.30 am. Telephone inquiries should be confined to the same hours or between 4.00 and 5.00 pm.

AS THE BUILDER (see Note 1 overleaf) I hereby give you notice that after two clear days from the service on you of this Notice the work described below will commence on site.

1. THE BUILDING(S) OR STRUCTURE(S)

Number of building in street (if any) .... Street Name ....

City of/London Borough of ....

If the site is vacant, description of its location ....

....

Number of building(s) or structure(s) ....

Proposed use of the building or structure (or of each if there is more than one) ....

....

....

....

2. THE WORK

Type of proposed work (whether new buildings or structures, alterations, additions or other work)

....

....

....

(NB: See note 2 overleaf regarding submission of plans or calculations)

Estimated cost of the work (see notes 3 and 4 overleaf) £ ....

DATE WHEN THE WORK WILL COMMENCE ....

3. THE OWNER/OCCUPIER

Name of owner instructing the builder ....

Address ....

....

.... Telephone No: ....

Name of occupier (if different from owner) ....

PLEASE TURN OVER

DS 2

Notice of objection by District Surveyor

London Building Acts, 1930 to 1978, and By-laws made in pursuance thereof

DISTRICT SURVEYOR'S OFFICE

NOTICE OF OBJECTION

To: M

of

BUILDER OR OWNER or other person causing or directing the work under the building notice hereinafter referred to.

With reference to the building notice served on me on the day of , 19 , relating to proposed work to be carried out at the undermentioned building or structure, I hereby give you notice of objection to such work, which will not be in conformity with the above Acts and/or by-laws in the following particulars:

Description and locality of Building or Structure referred to:

London Borough of

Description

Situated at

Particulars of Work that will be in contravention of the Acts (By-laws), or work that is required by the Acts (By-laws) but which it is proposed to omit:

Dated this day of 19

DISTRICT SURVEYOR

HPC 7204

[P.T.O.]

DS 3

Notice of Irregularity to Builder.

London Building Acts, 1930 to 1978, and By-laws made in pursuance thereof

NOTICE OF IRREGULARITY

DISTRICT SURVEYOR'S OFFICE

To M

of

THE BUILDER engaged in erecting the undermentioned building or structure or doing work to, in or upon the said building or structure.

I HEREBY GIVE YOU NOTICE that the work that you have done at the undermentioned building or structure is not or may not be in conformity with the above Acts and/or By-laws, and I hereby require you, WITHIN FORTY-EIGHT HOURS FROM THE DATE HEREOF, to carry out work in accordance with the particulars hereunder stated.

Description and locality of Building or Structure referred to:

London Borough of

Description

Situate at

Particulars of Work done in contravention of the Acts (By-laws) or required by the Acts (By-laws) to be done but omitted:

Particulars of work required by this Notice to be done:

Particulars of Work to be cut into, laid open or demolished, to ascertain whether anything has been done in contravention of the provisions of the Acts or By-laws or whether anything required by the Acts and By-laws to be done has been omitted to be done.

Dated this day of **19**

See overleaf.

DISTRICT SURVEYOR

2m (SwP 31473) 7/79

DS 4

Notice of Irregularity to Owner or Occupier, &c.

London Building Acts, 1930 to 1978, and By-laws made in pursuance thereof

NOTICE OF IRREGULARITY

DISTRICT SURVEYOR'S OFFICE

To M

of

THE OWNER OR OCCUPIER of the building or structure undermentioned, or other person causing or directing or who has caused or directed the work to be done at the said building or structure.

I HEREBY GIVE YOU NOTICE that the work at the undermentioned building or structure (which building or structure has ceased to be in charge of or under the control of the Builder) *or* (the owner of which building or structure does not allow the Builder to comply with the requisitions of a Notice of Irregularity, which has been duly served on such Builder) is not or may not be in conformity with the said Acts and/or By-laws in the particulars hereunder stated, and I hereby require you, within forty-eight hours from the date hereof, to carry out work in accordance with the particulars hereunder stated.

Description and locality of Building or Structure referred to:

London Borough of

Description

Situate at

Particulars of Work done in contravention of the Acts (By-laws) or required by the Acts (By-laws) to be done but omitted:

Particulars of work required by this Notice to be done:

Particulars of Work to be cut into, laid open or demolished, to ascertain whether anything has been done in contravention of the provisions of the Acts or By-laws or whether anything required by the Acts and By-laws to be done has been omitted to be done.

Dated this day of 19

DISTRICT SURVEYOR

423 AR

DS 5

Notice of Irregularity to Owner or Occupier where Building Notice has not been served

London Building Acts, 1930 to 1978, and By-laws made in pursuance thereof

NOTICE OF IRREGULARITY

DISTRICT SURVEYOR'S OFFICE

To M

of

THE OWNER OR OCCUPIER of the building or structure undermentioned or other person who has caused or directed the work to be done at the said building or structure.

I HEREBY GIVE YOU NOTICE that the work at the undermentioned building or structure in respect of which a Notice has not been given to the District Surveyor as required by the London Building Acts (or By-laws made in pursuance of the London Building Acts) is not or may not be in conformity with the said Acts and/or By-laws in the particulars hereunder stated, and I hereby require you within forty-eight hours from the date hereof to carry out work in accordance with the particulars hereunder stated.

Description and locality of Building or Structure referred to:

London Borough of

Description

Situate at

Particulars of Work done in contravention of the Acts (By-laws) or required by the Acts (By-laws) to be done but omitted:

Particulars of work required by this Notice to be done:

Particulars of Work to be cut into, laid open or demolished, to ascertain whether anything has been done in contravention of the provisions of the Acts or By-laws or whether anything required by the Acts and By-laws to be done has been omitted to be done.

Dated this **day of** **19**

2365 S & S

DISTRICT SURVEYOR

DS 6

Certificate for Public Building.

London Building Acts (Amendment) Act, 1939

DISTRICT SURVEYOR'S OFFICE

Serial No...

....19

In pursuance of Section 26(4) of the above-mentioned Act, I HEREBY CERTIFY that the public building known as

erected by

between the dates of and

accords with Sub-section (1) of Section 26 of the said Act.

DISTRICT SURVEYOR

To M

of

and all whom it may concern.

HPC 7203

DS 7

Cutting away Chimneys, etc.

London Building Acts (Amendment) Act, 1939

DISTRICT SURVEYOR'S OFFICE

....

Serial No...

....**19**

In pursuance of Section 17 (2) of the above-mentioned Act, I HEREBY CERTIFY that the chimney, chimney breast, chimney shaft built with or in the party wall of the building situate and being

DISTRICT SURVEYOR

To

(HS 35668)

The London Building Acts (Amendment) Act, 1939. **Form A**
2 and 3 Geo. VI, c. xcvii, Part vi, Section 46.

Party Structures

For definitions and notes see back

To ____
of____
and to all whom it may concern.
As Building Owner(s) of the Premises known as ________________________

____

and with reference to the Party Structure separating the said Premises from the adjoining Premises on the________________side thereof known as

____

____

I/We hereby give you notice that after the expiration of two months from the date of service hereof I/we intend to exercise the rights given to me/us by the London Building Acts (Amendment) Act, 1939, Section 46, Subsection________________by executing the works undermentioned, viz:—

____

____

____

____

____

____

____

____

and I/we propose to commence the work on or about________________________

____

I/We hereby appoint
Mr. ____
of____
to act as my/our Surveyor.
*Signature:*________________________________*Building Owner*
Address: ____
Dated this________________day of________________________19______

If the adjoining Owner does not within 14 days after the service of this notice express his consent thereto, he will be considered to have dissented therefrom (see Section 49), and in such case the Act requires him to appoint a Surveyor—Section 55.

The London Building Acts (Amendment) Act, 1939. **Form B**
2 and 3 Geo. VI, c. xcvii, Part vi, Section 46.

Party Fence Walls

For definitions and notes see back

To
of
and to all whom it may concern.
As Building Owner(s) of the land and premises known as

and with reference to the Party Fence Wall separating the said land from the adjoining land on the side thereof known as

I/we hereby give you notice that after the expiration of one month from the date of service hereof I/we intend to exercise the rights given to me/us by the London Building Acts (Amendment) Act, 1939, Section 46, Subsection by executing the works under-mentioned, viz.:

and I/we propose to commence the work on or about
I/We hereby appoint
Mr.
of
to act as my/our Surveyor.
Signature *Building Owner*
Address
Dated this day of 19

If the adjoining owner does not within 14 days after the service of this notice express his consent thereto, he will be considered to have dissented therefrom (see Section 49), and in such cases the Act requires him to appoint a Surveyor—Section 55.

The London Building Acts (Amendment) Act, 1939. **Form C**

2 and 3 Geo. VI, c. xcvii, Part vi, Section 50 (1) (a).

Intention to Build Within Ten Feet and at a Lower Level than the Bottom of the Foundations of Adjoining Owner's Building

---

For definitions and notes see back

To ....

of ....

and to all whom it may concern.

As Building Owner of the Premises known as ....

....

I/we hereby give you notice that after the expiration of one month from the date of the service hereof I/we intend to erect within ten feet of the building belonging to you on the .... side of my/our own premises, and situate and being ....

....

....

a building or structure independent of your building some part of which within the said ten feet and as shown on the plans and sections annexed hereto will extend to a lower level than the bottom of the foundations of your building, and to exercise the rights given to me/us by the London Building Acts (Amendment) Act, 1939, by executing the works undermentioned, viz: ....

....

....

....

....

....

....

....

....

and I/we propose to commence the work on or about the .... day of .... 19 ....

I/we hereby appoint

Mr. ....

of ....

to act as my/our Surveyor.

Signature: .... *Building Owner*

Address: ....

....

Dated this .... day of .... 19 ....

If the adjoining Owner shall within fourteen days after being served with the above notice give a counter notice in writing that he disputes the necessity of or requires such underpinning or strengthening or safeguarding, a difference shall be deemed to have arisen—Section 50 (2) (c)—and in such case the Act requires him to appoint a Surveyor—Section 55.

The London Building Acts (Amendment) Act, 1939. **Form D**

2 and 3 Geo. VI, c. xcvii, Part vi. Section 50 (1) (b)

Intention to Build Within Twenty Feet of Adjoining Owner's Independent Building and to a Depth as Defined in Section (50) (1) (b)

For definitions and notes see back

To ____________________

of ____________________

and to all whom it may concern.

As Building Owner of the premises known as ____________________

____

____

I/We hereby give you notice that after the expiration of one month from the date of service hereof I/we intend to erect within twenty feet of the independent building belonging to you on the __________ side of my/our own premises, and situate and being ____________________

____

____

a building or structure some part of which within the said twenty feet and as shown on the plans and sections annexed hereto will extend to the depth defined in Section 50 (1) (b). and to exercise the rights given to __________ by the London Building Acts (Amendment) Act, 1939, by executing the works undermentioned, viz:—

____

____

____

____

____

____

and I/we propose to commence the work on or about the ____________________

I/we hereby appoint

Mr. ____________________

of ____________________

to act as my/our Surveyor.

Signature: ____________________ *Building Owner*

Address: ____________________

Dated this __________ day of __________ 19____

If the adjoining owner shall within fourteen days after being served with the above notice give a counter notice in writing that he disputes the necessity of or requires such underpinning or strengthening or safeguarding, a difference shall be deemed to have arisen. Section 50 (2) (c), and in such case the Act requires him to appoint a Surveyor—Section 55.

The London Building Acts (Amendment) Act, 1939. **Form E**

2 and 3 Geo. VI, c. xcvii, Part vi, Section 45 (1) (a) (i) (ii).

Party Walls and Party Fence Walls on Line of Junction of Adjoining Lands

For definitions and notes see back

To

of

and to all whom it may concern.

As building owner(s) of the land and premises known as

I/We hereby give you notice that I/we desire to build a party wall and/or party fence wall partly on my/our own land adjoining your vacant land situate and being

and to the of my/our own said land.

The said party wall and/or party fence wall is desired to be of the following description:—

I/We shall be obliged by your consent in writing.

I/We hereby appoint Mr.

of

to act as my/our Surveyor.

Signature: *Building Owner*

Address:

Dated this day of 19

The London Building Acts (Amendment) Act, 1939. **Form F**
2 and 3 Geo. VI, c. xcvii, Part vi, Section 45 (i) (c).

Walls or Fence Walls on Building Owner's Land with Footings and Foundation Projecting into Adjoining Owner's Land

---

For definitions and notes, see back

To ______________________________

of ______________________________

and to all whom it may concern.

As Building Owner(s) of the land and premises known as ______________________________

____

____

I/we hereby give you notice that after the expiration of one month from the date of service hereof I/we intend to erect a wall and/or fence wall on my/our own land adjoining your land situate and being

____

____

on the ______________ side of the said land and premises and to exercise the right given to me/us by the London Building Acts (Amendment) Act, 1939, by erecting a wall of the following description:

____

____

____

____

____

____

____

____

and by placing the projecting footings and foundation of said wall and/or fence wall on your land.

I/We hereby appoint

Mr. ______________________________

of ______________________________

to act as my/our Surveyor.

Signature ______________________________ *Building Owner*

Address ______________________________

Dated this ______________ day of ______________ 19____

The London Building Acts (Amendment) Act, 1939. **Form G**

2 and 3 Geo. VI, c. xcvii, Part vi, Section 55.

Selection of Third Surveyor

We, the undersigned Surveyors, duly appointed to act respectively on behalf of

M..........

of..........

....

the Building Owner of Premises known as..........

....

....

and for M..........

of..........

....

the adjoining Owner of Premises known as..........

....

....

both of the said premises being referred to in the notice served by the said Building Owner on the said adjoining Owner.......... on the..........day of..........19..........

hereby select

Mr...........

of..........

as Third Surveyor.

Surveyor to the Building Owner { *Signature*.......... *Address*..........

Surveyor to the Adjoining Owner { *Signature*.......... *Address*..........

Dated this..........day of..........19..........

Reference No. 3

Certificate of Survey of Structure

To the Westminster City Council

London Building Acts (Amendment) Act, 1939: Part VII
London County Council (General Powers) Act, 1955: Part II
London County Council (General Powers) Act, 1958: Part III

DANGEROUS STRUCTURES

Having made a Survey of the Structure known as

in the City of Westminster, as required by the Westminster City Council, I hereby certify my opinion that the said Structure is in a dangerous state: and that the Owner should be required forthwith to take down repair or otherwise secure

Owner's Name and Address

Area of Structure: greater/less than 4 squares.†

Number of Storeys

**Length of time which may be reasonably allowed for the execution of Works*

days.

The premises are occupied/not occupied†

Dated this day of 19

District Surveyor

NOTES—**Please state whether the Council's contractors have been instructed**

(i) under Section 61(4) of the 1939 Act, to remove immediate danger	**Yes/No**†
(ii) under Section 62(2) of the 1939 Act, to erect shoring	**Yes/No**†
(iii) under Section 62(2) of the 1939 Act, to board in the structure.	**Yes/No**†

*This time should, except for removal of immediate danger, be not less than seven days, to allow the time for the receipt from the owner of notice requiring arbitration to elapse before a summons is issued.

Sec. 63, of the 1939 Act.

†Please delete words not applicable.

1188

Court cases quoted in text

Anns and Others *v* London Borough of Merton (1977) 2 *All ER* 492
Arenson *v* Casson Beckman Rutley & Co (1975) 3 *All ER* 901
Attorney General *v* PYA Quarries Ltd (1957) 2 QB 171
Bagot *v* Stevens Scanlon & Co (1966) 3 *All ER* 579
Bolam *v* Friern Hospital Management Committee (1957) 2 *All ER* 118
Beigtheil and Young *v* Stewart (1900) 16 TLR 177
Clay *v* A J Crump & Son Ltd (1963) 3 *All ER* 687
Coleshill & District Investment Co Ltd *v* Minister of Housing and Local Government (1969) 2 *All ER* 525, 1 WLR
Dutton *v* Bognor Regis UDC (1972) 1 *All ER* at 474, 1 QB 373
Esso *v* Marden (1976) 2 *All ER* 5
Gray *v* Minister of Housing and Local Government (1969) LGR 169
Guildford RDC *v* Fortescue; Same *v* Penny (1959) 2 *All ER* 111, 2 QB 112
Hedley Byrne & Co Ltd *v* Heller & Partners Ltd (1964) 2 *All ER* 575, AC 465
Hoenig *v* Isaacs (1952) 2 *All ER* 176
Independent Broadcasting Authority *v* EMI Electronics Ltd (1981) 14 BLR 1
Kerr *v* John H Allan & Sons (1949) SLT 20
Lakeman *v* Mountstephen (1874) LR 7 HL 17
Meikle *v* Maufe (1941) 3 *All ER* 144
Modern Engineering (Bristol) Ltd *v* C Miskin & Son Ltd (1981) Lloyds 2 135
Molloy *v* Liebe (1910) 102 LT 616
Northern Regional Hospital Board *v* Derek Crouch Construction Co Ltd (1984) 2 WLR 676 CA
R *v* Architects' Registration Tribunal, *Ex parte* Jaggar (1945) 2 *All ER* 151
R B Burden Ltd *v* Swansea Corporation (1957) 3 *All ER* 243
Rylands *v* Fletcher (1868) LR 3 HL 330
Scrivener *v* Pask (1866) LR 1 CP 715
Sharpe *v* San Paulo Railway (1873) LR 8 CH APP 597
Sparham Souter and Others *v* Town & Country Developments (Essex) Ltd and Benfleet RDC (1976) 2 *All ER* 65
Sturgess *v* Bridgeman (1879) 41 TLR 219
Sutcliffe *v* Thackrah (1974) 1 *All ER* 859, AC 727
Townsend (Builders) Ltd *v* Cinema News and Property Management Ltd (1959) 1 WLR 119
Westminster City Council *v* J Jarvis & Sons Ltd and Another (1970) 1 *All ER* 943 at 948
Williams *v* Fitzmaurice (1858) 32 LT (OS) 149

Acknowledgements

This book is based upon the author's lecture notes and other sources of information collected over 25 years, the origins of which, in some cases, have been lost in time. It is not intended to benefit from the work of others without due acknowledgement, and where possible this has been done below, or the source listed in the Bibliography. Where it has not been possible I request indulgence, in the hope that it will be accepted that all books and other sources of reference used in the pursuit of knowledge lean upon others. I hope that for many years to come students, and teachers, will continue to benefit from the wealth of information and knowledge available as I have been privileged so to do for more than 40 years.

I am indebted to the following persons and organizations for their help and advice:

E R H Jamieson, Dip Arch, ARIBA, Senior Lecturer, Faculty of the Built Environment, Department of Architecture, Polytechnic of the South Bank, to whom I am especially indebted as a colleague and friend over many years.

A J Lomnicki, Dr Iur, LLM, Member of the Polish Bar, Senior Lecturer, Faculty of the Built Environment, Department of Estate Management, Polytechnic of the South Bank, for advice and material in the housing law chapter of the book.

L W Blake, LLM, AKC, Barrister, Senior Lecturer, Faculty of the Built Environment, Department of Estate Management, Polytechnic of the South Bank, for his advice and material on Architects in the law sections of the book.

Ernest Jones, Managing Director, Mobile Training & Exhibitions Ltd, for permission to use and adapt material from his course Understanding Business Finance.

B Langford, Head of Applications and Service Section, Building Research Establishment, for permission to quote from *Aspects of Fire Precautions in Buildings* by R R G Read and W A Morris.

The British Standards Institution, for permission to quote from documents 82/10795/6.

R J Fenwick Elliott, Solicitor, for permission to quote from his book *Building Contract Litigation*.

The Greater London Council, Department of Architecture and Civic Design, for permission to reproduce District Surveyor Forms, and for providing copies.

The several staff members in the planning, highways and law departments of the Broadland District Council, Norfolk, for their help and advice.

K Turner, Librarian, Faculty of the Built Environment, Polytechnic of the South Bank, for his unfailing help and kindness over many years.

F D Entwisle, FRICS, C Eng, FI Struct E, PPIAAS for permission through his publishers to reproduce material from his book *Building Regulation – Practice and Procedure*.

Bibliography

Law

AJ Legal Handbook, A SPEAIGHT and G STONE Architectural Press

Alteration and Conversion of Houses, J F GARNER Oyez Publishing

Building Contract Litigation, R J FENWICK ELLIOTT Oyez Longman

Building Law for Students, K MANSON Cassell

O-Level English Law, D M M SCOTT Butterworths

Partnership Law, J WESTWOOD (revised by) Donnington Press

Party Structure Rights in London, W A LEACH *Estates Gazette*

Questions and Answers on A-Level Law, V POWELL-SMITH Butterworths

Questions and Answers on the Law of Contract, R S SIM Butterworths

Questions and Answers on the Law of Meetings, R S SIM Butterworths

The Law of Dilapidations, W A WEST *Estate Gazette*

The Law Relating to the Architect, RIMMER (edited Gill) Batsford

Building Control Legislation and Procedure

The London Building Acts 1930/78 GLC

The London Building (Constructional) Amending Bye-laws 1979 GLC

The Building Regulations 1976 HMSO

The Defective Premises Act 1972 HMSO

The Factories Act 1961 HMSO

The Fire Precautions Act 1971 HMSO

The Health & Safety at Work etc Act 1974 HMSO

The Highways Acts 1959/80 HMSO

The Housing Acts 1957/80 HMSO

The Offices, Shops and Railway Premises Act 1963 HMSO

The Public Health Acts 1936/61 HMSO

The Public Health (London) Act 1936 HMSO

The Town & Country Planning Acts 1947/72 HMSO

The Town & Country Planning General Development Order 1977 HMSO

Note: This list is not comprehensive and the list given in the RIBA Guidance Notes for the Final Examination in Architecture, Part 3, should be referred to.

Building Regulation Practice and Procedure, F D ENTWISLE *Estates Gazette*

Housing, Tenancy, and Planning Law made Simple, A J LOMNICKI Heinemann

Planning Law and Procedure, A E TELLING Butterworths

Note: The RIBA Final Examination in Architecture Reading List should be referred to for further reading.

Fire and Buildings

Aspects of Fire Precautions, R E G READ and W A MORRIS Building Research Establishment

Fire and the Architect, RIBA WORKING PARTY Fire Protection Association and RIBA

Tendering and contractual arrangements

Which Builder?, THE AQUA GROUP Crosby, Lockwood, Staples

Contract Practice for Quantity Surveyors, J W RAMUS Heinemann

Management and Administration

Imaginative Management Control, R OGDEN Routledge & Kegan Paul

Management Applied to Architectural Practice, BRUNTON, BADEN HELLARD and BOOBYER George Godwin

Video Arts Publications VARIOUS AUTHORS Video Arts Ltd

Note: The *RIBA Handbook of Architectural Practice and Management*, the *RIBA Job Book*, etc are sources of information.
Films on the many aspects of management are available from Video Arts Ltd, 68 Oxford Street, London, as an adjunct to their numerous booklets.

Miscellaneous

Computer Appreciation – 3rd ed, T F FRY Butterworths

Principles of Construction Management, R PILCHER McGraw-Hill

An Outline of Planning Law – 8th ed, SIR DESMOND HEAP Sweet & Maxwell

The Principles of Design, W A MAYALL Design Council

Index